# INTERVIEWING
# CHILDREN

WILEY SERIES

in

# CHILD CARE AND PROTECTION

*Series Editors*

**Kevin D. Browne**
*School of Psychology*
*The University of Birmingham, UK*

**Margaret A. Lynch**
*Newcomen Centre*
*Guy's Hospital, London, UK*

---

The Child Care and Protection Series aims to further the understanding of health, psychosocial and cultural factors that influence the development of the child, early interactions and the formation of relationships in and outside the family. This international series will cover the psychological as well as the physical welfare of the child and will consider protection from all forms of maltreatment.

The series is intended to become essential reading for all professionals concerned with the welfare and protection of children and their families. All books in the series will have a practice orientation with referenced information from theory and research.

**Published**

| | |
|---|---|
| Michelle Aldridge & Joanne Wood | Interviewing Children: A Guide for Child Care and Forensic Practitioners |
| Ann Buchanan | Cycles of Child Maltreatment: Facts, Fallacies and Interventions |
| Dorota Iwaniec | The Emotionally Abused and Neglected Child: Identification, Assessment and Intervention |
| David Quinton et al | Joining New Families: A Study of Adoption and Fostering in Middle Childhood |
| Jacqui Saradjian | Women who Sexually Abuse Children: From Research to Clinical Practice |

**Forthcoming**

| | |
|---|---|
| Leonard Dalgleish | Risk and Decision in Child Protection |
| David Middleton & Jayne Allam | Child Sexual Abuse: Working with Offenders |
| Janet Stanley & Christopher Goddard | In the Firing Line: Relationships, Power and Violence in Child Protection Work |

Potential authors are invited to submit ideas and proposals for publications for the series to either of the series editors above.

# INTERVIEWING CHILDREN

## A Guide for Child Care and Forensic Practitioners

Michelle Aldridge and Joanne Wood

JOHN WILEY & SONS

Chichester · New York · Weinheim · Brisbane · Singapore · Toronto

*Other Wiley Editorial Offices*

John Wiley & Sons, Inc., 605 Third Avenue,
New York, NY 10158-0012, USA

WILEY-VCH Verlag GmbH, Pappelallee 3,
D-69469 Weinheim, Germany

Jacaranda Wiley Ltd, 33 Park Road, Milton,
Queensland 4064, Australia

John Wiley & Sons (Asia) Pte Ltd, 2 Clementi Loop #02-01,
Jin Xing Distripark, Singapore 129809

John Wiley & Sons (Canada) Ltd, 22 Worcester Road,
Rexdale, Ontario M9W 1L1, Canada

*Library of Congress Cataloging-in-Publication Data*

Aldridge, Michelle.
    Interviewing children : a guide for child care and forensic
practitioners / Michelle Aldridge and Joanne Wood.
        p.  cm. — (Wiley series in child care and protection)
    Includes bibliographical references and index.
    ISBN 0-471-97052-2 (alk. paper). — ISBN 0-471-98207-5 (pbk.)
    1. Child abuse—Investigation.  2. Interviewing in child abuse.
3. Communicative competence in children.  4. Behavioral assessment
of children.  I. Wood, Joanne.  II. Title.  III. Series.
HV 8079.C48A54  1998
363.25'95554—dc21                                                    98–28995
                                                                        CIP

*British Library Cataloguing in Publication Data*

A catalogue record for this book is available from the British Library

ISBN 0-471-97052-2 (hb) 0-471-98207-5 (pb)

Typeset in 10/12pt Palatino by Mayhew Typesetting, Rhayader, Powys
Printed and bound in Great Britain by Bookcraft (Bath) Ltd, Midsomer Norton, Somerset
This book is printed on acid-free paper responsibly manufactured from sustainable
forestation, in which at least two trees are planted for each one used for paper production.

# CONTENTS

Series Preface.................................................. vii

Introduction................................................... ix

Acknowledgements ............................................. xvii

Dedication .................................................... xviii

1  Talking and Listening to Children.......................... 1

Events leading up to the introduction of the Memorandum—The aims of the
Memorandum—Problems associated with the Memorandum—Operational
problems associated with the Memorandum—Language problems associated
with interviewing children—An evaluation of information concerning
children's language development—Training—Summary

2  Establishing Rapport...................................... 25

Timing the interview—Location of the interview—Who should be present at
an interview?—Getting the interview under way—The rapport phase—Self-
assessment sheet

3  Free Narrative Phase: Listening to Children ............... 70

The importance of the free narrative phase—How to proceed—Children's lack
of familiarity—Children's reticence—The quantity problem—The quality
problem—Children's memory skills—The influence of language skills—Over-
hasty entry into a specific questioning phase—Providing adequate free
narrative opportunities—Helping to support children's narratives—Self-
assessment sheet

4  Asking Questions......................................... 107

Difficulties with questioning children—The purpose of the questioning
phase—Types of question—Published research: Children's understanding of
questions—Children's linguistic ability in the evidentiary setting—Published
research: Advice for professionals—Current practice: Our transcript data—
Interviewer's use of published advice—Guidelines—Self-assessment sheet

5  Interviewing Observed: Child Language and Development... 146

Using a word the child doesn't know or understand—Same word: different
meanings—Knowing the right word—Legal terms—Body part and sexual

*terminology—Emotion descriptive vocabulary—Pronouns—Prepositions—Summary—Self-assessment sheet*

6  Interviewing Children with Special Needs                    188

*Section 1: Disabled children—Section 2: Bilingual children and minority language speakers—Contact details*

Bibliography . . . . . . . . . . . . . . . . . . . . . . . . . . . . . . . . . . . . . . . . . . . . . . . . .  218

Index . . . . . . . . . . . . . . . . . . . . . . . . . . . . . . . . . . . . . . . . . . . . . . . . . . .  226

# SERIES PREFACE

The **Wiley Series in Child Care and Protection** is a series of books primarily written for all professionals in policy making, research and practice concerned with the care, welfare and protection of children and their families.

The aim of the series is to publish books on child care and protection covering both the psychological and physical welfare of the child including legal and social policy aspects. The series was prompted by the need to view child protection within the wider concepts of child care and social welfare. After three decades of remarkable growth in child protection work, which has led to widespread public awareness and professional understanding of child maltreatment, it has become increasingly recognized that child protection is enhanced by the improvements in the welfare of families and the promotion of positive parenting and child care. Indeed, child care, family welfare and effective child protection are inter-linked and cannot be separated.

Books in the series are from a wide range of disciplines and authors are encouraged to link research and practice to inform, in an easily accessible way, professionals, policy makers and the public in general. Consequently, it is hoped to further the knowledge and understanding of health, psychosocial and cultural factors that influence the development of the child, early interactions and the formation of relationships in and outside the family.

*Interviewing Children a Guide for Child Care and Forensic Practitioners* is the fifth book in the series. The authors, Michelle Aldridge and Joanne Wood, provide information on the linguistic ability of children from varying backgrounds and at different ages of development in relation to video interviews that have been conducted in North Wales since the introduction of the *Memorandum of Good Practice*.

The book is based on 100 English transcripts of video-recorded interviews with children aged between three and twelve years, with male and female gender equally represented. Most of the cases involve a victim of alleged sexual abuse with little evidence of corroboration. The descriptions of interviews with 'child witnesses' are supported by survey information collected from Police Officers involved in Child Protection within Wales.

The content of the book is presented in a logical sequence from talking and listening to children to establishing rapport and free narrative, asking questions, observing language and development in an investigative interview and interviewing children with special needs.

Overall, the book provides an excellent addition to the literature on children as witnesses, an area that would benefit from further knowledge and research to inform evidence-based practice.

# INTRODUCTION

## THE AUTHORS

This book is written jointly by Michelle Aldridge and Joanne Wood, both of whom have been involved in all stages of its production. Both are academics. Michelle Aldridge is a senior lecturer in the Linguistics Department at the University of Wales, Bangor and specializes in child language acquisition and language disorders. Joanne Wood is a Research Assistant in the same department and is working towards a PhD, under Michelle Aldridge's supervision, on child language acquisition. She has previously been Michelle Aldridge's Senior Research Assistant on a number of funded research projects from the British Academy, the Economic and Social Research Council (ESRC) and the Leverhulme Trust.

These projects have enabled the authors to carry out the necessary research to write this book. They, therefore, have a great deal of expertise in child language acquisition and it is from this perspective that the book is written. The authors have no police nor social worker training and have never carried out any investigative interviews with children. Their experience comes from empirical research in interviewing presumed non-abused children in a whole variety of language games and exercises over the years and from their knowledge and understanding of the international academic and practitioners' literature. Practitioners in this area have been consulted fully and the book stems from their need for information and their specific questions concerning interviewing young children.

## BACKGROUND TO THE BOOK

This book, then, stems from collaborative work with the North Wales Police, Interagency Unit (now known as the Community Protection

Department) which dates back to 1990. The early years were taken up with a variety of meetings with all the North Wales social worker teams, with numerous meetings with police-officers working in child protection and with meetings with senior managers in the police force. A great deal of discussion took place to establish the training needs of those involved in interviewing young children. It became apparent that one of the main needs of professionals working in this field was for further detailed information on children's language development and thus the authors were invited to work with the interagency team in North Wales to establish the strengths and weaknesses, from a linguistic perspective, of current practice in interviewing young children in North Wales. The aim was to provide information on what linguistic abilities professionals can expect from children of varying ages and backgrounds.

A variety of ethical concerns also had to be addressed before research into such a sensitive matter could proceed. For example, it was decided early on in the research programme that it would not be appropriate for the authors to watch the interview live. The difficulties envisaged were varied but fell into two main categories: ethical and practical. First, consider the ethics of the situation. It was unanimously agreed that it would not be possible, at the time of the interview, when all involved are naturally stressed and focusing on the needs of obtaining a reliable account, to stop the procedure and seek the consent of the relevant people for academics to watch the interview. As far as the current case was concerned, this observation would have no purpose but to obtain information which might help future interviews. Second, there was a great deal of concern about the status of any notes the authors might make during the interview. It was felt that these would need to be submitted along with the statement (these decisions were being made before the introduction of the *Memorandum of Good Practice* (Home Office and Department of Health 1992)) and since the authors had no training on note-taking for criminal investigations, it was agreed that their notes would not, necessarily, be helpful for the case.

There were also a variety of practical concerns. The initial interviews were often called at short notice and thus it would not be helpful to expect the person organizing the interview to take time out to call the authors to the interview as well as the witness(es) and those involved in conducting the interview. Also, there was the problem of physical space. Clearly, the witness and the interviewer should not see the authors during the interview but would need to know they were there. In the early days of the research, some of the places where the interviews were conducted were simply not big enough to accommodate the witness, the interviewer, the child's supporter and the researchers (located behind a screen). It was therefore agreed that mechanisms would be set up enabling the interview data to be seen after the event.

From the beginning of the research the work was done within a number of conditions. For example, both authors have signed the Official Secrets Act and it was agreed that any report of the findings would be available to the professionals and also to any family whose data had been used. It was also agreed that although actual examples from the transcript data could be used, it would not be possible to identify any of the witnesses, any of their family or friends, any of the accused, any of their family and friends, or any of the interviewers. Therefore, as far as possible all names have been eliminated and where this is not possible the names have been changed. The only facts available within the transcript data are the age and gender of the witness. In the transcript excerpts the interviewer is introduced as I and the child witness as C. Where present, a social worker is introduced as S/W, mother as M, and father as F.

As stated above, the research began before the introduction of the *Memorandum of Good Practice* and thus, the early experience of working with interview material was from anonymous statements. This experience was worth while in familiarising the authors with the interview procedure and the likely contents of such an interview and gave them the opportunity to begin to tease out linguistic areas where the child and interviewer were succeeding and indeed those areas where they were experiencing difficulty.

## VIDEO-RECORDED INTERVIEWS AND THE INTERVIEW SUITE

It was decided, however, for the purpose of this book, that the focus would be on the video interviews that have been conducted in North Wales since the introduction of the *Memorandum of Good Practice*. Once appropriate consent was obtained the authors were able to view a copy of some of the video-recorded interviews on police property. At no time were the videos taken away from police property and they were watched on a basic video-recorder machine which allowed them to be played, rewound and forwarded only.

North Wales has specially designed interview suites which are used whenever possible to interview vulnerable people. The authors have been to one of the houses, when an interview was not on-going and thus, are familiar with the typical layout of the interview room, medical room and other facilities. They have also spent time in a monitoring room so that they have an understanding of how the recording equipment and cameras work. The authors have not been in any of the houses during an interview.

# THE TRANSCRIPTS

Approximately 180 video interviews have been viewed but the book has as its database 100 transcripts of video-recorded interviews with children in the age range 3–12 years conducted during the period 1994–1997. There is one transcript from a 3-year-old girl and then between 12 and 15 transcripts from each age year from 4 to 12 years.

All the interviews were conducted in English and there are approximately even numbers of boy and girl witnesses. The majority of the interviewing, in the corpus, was done by a policewoman, in fact there is only one transcript involving a male interviewer. In about 50% of the transcripts the policewoman was alone with the child and there were two professionals in the monitoring room. The child's supporter (who might be a friend, parent or sibling) was waiting downstairs in a lounge area. In the other 50%, the child's supporter was in the room with the policewoman, in about 80% of these cases the supporter was the child's social worker (there are both female and male social workers) and in the rest of the cases the supporter was usually the witness' mother.

The majority of the transcripts are of interviews with young children in cases of alleged sexual abuse; a few, however, concern physical assaults. The authors have focused particularly on interviews concerning alleged sexual abuse because, in these cases, there is often no corroborating evidence and thus the child's account of the alleged incident is of paramount importance when investigating his case (a point returned to in Chapter 1).

To the best of the authors' knowledge, all of the children are able-bodied and do not have any known disability. There are no transcripts of interviews with children who have a hearing impairment, visual impairment or severe learning disability, for example. The only data from an interview with a witness with a learning disability are with a 16-year-old girl (data which are referred to, briefly, in Chapter 6).

The authors have analysed those video-recordings which were made available to them. These do not represent all the interviews with children that were carried out in North Wales during the period 1994–1997 but simply those which were stored at the police location to which they had access. It is not known what proportion of the transcript interviews went on to court nor the success or otherwise of those that did. The aim was simply to examine, linguistically, the initial interview transcripts and to suggest some guidelines for professionals on expectations they might have concerning children's language ability. The progress of the video-recorded interview through the Crown Prosecution Service and on to court and the child's ability to cope linguistically with the cross-examination is the focus of a current research project which is funded by the ESRC.

As stated above, the transcripts are from approximately equal numbers of boy and girl witnesses, but for ease of reading when the gender is not obvious *he* is used to refer to the child witness, and *she* for the interviewer, because in the corpus the interviewer tends to be female.

In addition to the transcript data, the authors also draw upon findings from a survey conducted with interviewing police-officers in Wales (Aldridge & Wood 1997a) and a variety of other research studies. In all these studies, the authors have designed and played language games with assumed non-abused schoolchildren in an attempt to learn more about relevant aspects of children's language skills. These experimental findings are reported fully elsewhere (e.g. Aldridge, Timmins & Wood 1996, Aldridge & Wood 1996, 1997b, and forthcoming, and Aldridge, Timmins & Wood 1997) but, here the authors highlight aspects of their findings which relate to interview practice.

## OUTLINE OF THE BOOK

Following on from an introductory chapter (Chapter 1), the next chapters (2–5) trace the phased approach to the interview as outlined in the *Memorandum of Good Practice*. The final chapter (6) examines language issues involved when interviewing children with special needs.

## Chapter 1 – Talking and Listening to Children

This chapter offers a brief historical account of the events leading up to the introduction of the *Memorandum of Good Practice* and then summarizes its aims. The discussion then focuses on the strengths and weaknesses of the Memorandum as reported in a number of surveys. The current information available to professionals concerning children's language development and abilities at differing ages is then evaluated. Lastly the chapter reflects on the need for professionals to receive training on language and communication issues related to interviewing young children in particular.

## Chapter 2 – Establishing Rapport

This chapter focuses on the first phase of the interview as laid down in the *Memorandum of Good Practice*, namely that of establishing rapport. It considers issues such as the interview setting in terms of the time of the interview and who should be present and then moves on to evaluate different ways of building rapport with the child. Issues such as effective opening topics, the advantages and disadvantages of different types of toys, different ways of assessing the child's development, different ways of explaining the purpose of the interview and the camera equipment, and different ways of establishing that the child knows the difference between truth and lie and fact and fantasy are discussed. Each issue is supported with examples from the video interview data and the chapter concludes with a suggested list of dos and don'ts and a self-assessment sheet with which the reader can evaluate various aspects of the rapport phase in any interviews conducted.

## Chapter 3 – Free Narrative Phase: Listening to Children

Chapter 3 examines issues relating to the free narrative phase. It discusses some of the difficulties which can arise in eliciting free narrative accounts from children (e.g. children's lack of familiarity with this type of conversation), and ways in which the child can be encouraged to provide a fuller account are considered. In particular, the chapter focuses on how adequate opportunities for narration can be provided and on ways in which the interviewer might support the child's narration in a non-leading way. The discussion is supported by examples from the interview data and from a language game with assumed non-abused children. The chapter concludes with a checklist of dos and don'ts and a self-assessment sheet.

## Chapter 4 – Asking Questions

Chapter 4 focuses on the questioning phase of the interview. It reviews the purpose of this phase as laid down in the Memorandum and considers the types of questions available for interviewers to use to elicit information. It considers how children acquire an understanding of different types of wh-questions (e.g. *what* and *when*) and examines previous research findings in relation to children's ability to answer questions in the evidentiary setting. The chapter concludes with a checklist of which question types to use and which question types to avoid when interviewing children, together with a self-assessment sheet.

## Chapter 5 – Interviewing Observed: Child Language and Development

This chapter focuses on children's ability to understand the words that are likely to be used in this type of investigative interview. There are, for example, sections on children's understanding of legal terms (e.g. *police-officer* and *court*), body part terms (e.g. words for sexual body parts), expressions of emotion (e.g. fear and coercion), prepositions (e.g. *in* and *under*), temporal terms (e.g. *before* and *after*) and pronouns (e.g. *he* and *it*). In each section, examples are given from the interview data of how misunderstandings have occurred through the child witness not fully understanding (or not understanding at all) the word(s) used by the interviewer. Where appropriate, guidelines are offered on the words interviewers can expect children to understand by certain ages. A checklist of dos and don'ts and a self-assessment sheet appear at the end of the chapter.

## Chapter 6 – Interviewing Children with Special Needs

This chapter focuses on the needs of two populations who might be considered as special in linguistic terms. First, it focuses on children who have a disability which impacts on language or some other aspect of the interview experience and it considers how the needs of disabled children might be accommodated within the interview. Findings from the authors' survey of interviewing professionals (Aldridge & Wood 1997a) are also reported in relation to the interviewing of disabled children. Second, the chapter reviews the needs of bilingual children and minority language users and considers how these might be accommodated. Again, the authors also report on findings from their survey of interviewing professionals (Aldridge & Wood 1997a). The chapter concludes with a list of contact details for a variety of organizations which represent disabled children.

# ACKNOWLEDGEMENTS

We have been very fortunate to enjoy the full support and encouragement of the North Wales Police who have given us access to (and viewing facilities for) the video data included within these pages. We would especially like to thank Inspector Chris Corcoran, Detective Chief Inspector Lorraine Johnson, Inspector Gerwyn Lloyd and Chief Superintendent Elfed Roberts for their full co-operation and expert advice which has enabled us to complete this work. We would also like to thank Neil Heginbotham and Alan Welsh for their considerable efforts in accommodating our data collection.

The financial support of the British Academy, the Economic and Social Research Council, the Leverhulme Trust and Research Centre Wales has enabled us to carry out the language games with presumed non-abused children which have been invaluable in providing experimental data to compare and contrast with our transcript data. We are very grateful for this funding.

Finally, we wish to thank everyone who has been involved in the interviews for allowing us to share their experiences. We fully acknowledge the difficult task the children, families and interviewers have when engaging in a video interview and we sincerely hope that our linguistic knowledge offered here might, in some small way, ease the burden for everyone in the future.

We could not have written this book without the full collaboration of the Interagency Unit of the North Wales Police but any errors or misinterpretations within the text are the authors' sole responsibility.

# DEDICATION

We wish to dedicate this book to our families. In particular Michelle would like to name her parents, Sylvia and John Aldridge, her husband, Alun Waddon and their son, Luke. Joanne would like to name her parents, Gill and Chris Wood and her brother, Andrew. To them all we owe a huge debt of gratitude and thanks for all their support.

# 1

# TALKING AND LISTENING TO CHILDREN

An interview of any sort can be a stressful experience. When questioned, we struggle to find the right words, we forget information, we become tongue-tied and so forth. The occasion isn't easy for the interviewer either. She tries to formulate questions to tease answers from the interviewee, she searches for ways to prompt appropriately for additional information and thinks of ways to fill gaps formed by the interviewee's silence.

As adults, we are probably familiar with the above scenario, most typically in a non-legal setting such as a job interview, where the topics under discussion are unlikely to be particularly emotive. The situation is potentially much more difficult when children are being interviewed, where the setting is evidentiary in nature and the content of the interview is emotive and may be the only evidence. As noted by Spencer & Flin (1990) this must rank as one of the most demanding of interview situations, and yet children can become involved in the legal process for a variety of reasons. They may, for example, be involved in custody issues or be the perpetrators of, or witnesses to, crime (Perry & Teply 1984). Thus, it is not that uncommon for young children to be interviewed for evidentiary purposes. In real terms, we have all seen media reports in recent years of criminal cases involving child witnesses. Josie Russell (the sole survivor of an attack, in 1995, in which her mother and sister were murdered) and the perpetrators in the James Bulger murder case (1993) are, perhaps, amongst those most readily recalled.

This book, however, focuses on the interviewing of children in cases of alleged child abuse. In fact, most of our discussion will be focused on alleged child sexual abuse since in these cases, the child witness' account is often the only source of information about the alleged incident (Saywitz, Geiselman & Bornstien 1993, Coulborn-Faller & Corwin 1995). In this situation the child's verbal evidence is crucial if the video-recorded interview is to be used as the evidence-in-chief and if the child's case is to be heard in court. This is because the child often presents with no physical evidence and there are unlikely to be other witnesses. Where other witnesses do occur, they tend to be co-abusers or other children (Coulborn-Faller & Corwin 1995) and thus, they cannot necessarily corroborate the child witness' account. As Saywitz, Geiselman & Bornstien (1993) observe, it is therefore in everyone's interest that an accurate account is obtained from the child witness so that justice may be achieved. The child's ability to recount the event(s) and the interviewer's ability to obtain all the relevant information is therefore pivotal to the success or otherwise of the investigation.

The majority of child abuse cases are now being investigated within the guidelines set out in the *Memorandum of Good Practice* (1992, henceforth Memorandum or MOGP) and we aim, therefore, first, to trace the child's experience within this phased video interview, paying particular attention to how the child copes linguistically in the evidentiary setting and second, to suggest ways of facilitating the process of talking and listening to young children in the age range 3–12 years.

This chapter provides the following information:

- A brief historical account of the events leading up to the introduction of the Memorandum.
- A summary of the aims of the Memorandum and discussion of the results of a number of surveys (e.g. Davies et al 1995 and Aldridge & Wood 1997a), plus an assessment of the advantages of interviewing children within these guidelines.
- A discussion of findings from the above studies in relation to the problems associated with the Memorandum, including a review of certain statistics, media reports and professionals' opinions.
- An examination of the operational problems associated with carrying out an interview within the Memorandum guidelines.
- An examination of the language problems experienced when interviewing children.

We also provide:

- An evaluation of the information currently available to professionals concerning children's language development.
- A discussion of training issues.

Readers interested in further information on and opinions about the Memorandum are referred to Westcott & Jones (1997); a comprehensive multidisciplinary evaluation of the document written by practitioners and academics.

## EVENTS LEADING UP TO THE INTRODUCTION OF THE MEMORANDUM

Since the Cleveland inquiry (1987) and reports from Rochdale and Orkney which resulted from allegations of the widespread sexual abuse of children, relevant professionals and the public alike have been aware that investigative interviews are being conducted, and need to be conducted, with very young children. Since the mid-1980s, there has been a growing awareness not only of the large numbers of children who are, allegedly, being abused mentally, physically and sexually but also that their problems can be compounded by the ways in which any disclosure by, or on behalf of, the child is investigated.

Prior to the 1990s, the investigative procedure simply was not geared towards children's differing cognitive and linguistic abilities. For example, no consideration was given to how children might feel when coming face to face with the accused in court, how frightened children might be by the strange appearance of court personnel, nor how confused they might be by the strict conversational procedure found there. The fact that the investigative procedure might intimidate children and make them less likely to be able to recount their alleged experience was completely overlooked. And yet, for different reasons, the credibility of children (particularly very young children) as witnesses was a contentious issue. For example, their right to be heard and believed, the reliability of their memory and their suggestibility was the focus of considerable debate and dispute. Indeed, for decades, there was a general feeling that children simply were not capable of giving reliable accounts. In brief, as noted by Davies (1991: 178–9) children were treated as second-class citizens in the eyes of the law and, not surprisingly, only a small proportion of offenders who sexually abused children were successfully prosecuted.

Fortunately, the last decade has seen substantial changes in the UK criminal justice system and similar developments world-wide (see Goodman & Bottoms 1996 and Davies & Wilson 1997 for a review) which have attempted to address the need to obtain evidentially valid accounts from child witnesses in a way which is less stressful. For example, some of the formal aspects of the investigative procedure have gone such as the competency test, the corroboration requirement and the special caution from the judge to the jury in cases of children's evidence

(Spencer & Flin 1993) and it is now more accepted that a child can be a reliable witness given appropriate questioning and legal procedures that take into account the age and vulnerability of the witness (Goodman & Helgeson 1988).

As noted in the Memorandum (1992: 1), the 1987 report by Lord Justice Butler-Sloss on child abuse in Cleveland made a number of recommendations about the investigation of alleged offences against children and the conduct of interviews. The report recognized that the key to effective action was a close working relationship between all professionals involved and a multi-agency approach, combined with Butler-Sloss' guidance on interviewing children. This was explained in the joint Government departments' interagency guide *Working Together*. Following on from a general review, the Criminal Justice Act (1988) sought to address the problems experienced by young witnesses by permitting, for the first time, children in criminal cases to give their evidence from outside the courtroom via a special television link. While not all the Pigot committee's report recommendations (Home Office 1989) were accepted, the Criminal Justice Act (1991) did allow videotaped interviews to be used as the child's evidence-in-chief. The idea was that a high quality video-recording would be made of the interview proceedings. The interview should be conducted by a specially trained police-officer and/or social worker and should take place in a specialist interview suite (often within a designated house rather than a police station) designed to be comfortable and child-friendly.

Although the video evidence can be submitted to court as the child's evidence-in-chief, it is still necessary for the child to be present at court for live cross-examination. This can take place via a live link television system so that the child does not have to come face to face with the accused but those present in the courtroom can see and hear the child via television screens and the child, too, has a small television which allows him to see the questioning counsel.

The changes within the 1991 Act were implemented in order to spare children the ordeal of giving evidence in court and, in October 1992, the Home Office introduced the *Memorandum of Good Practice*, a set of guidelines designed to assist interviewing professionals in the conduct of initial video interviews. The Memorandum, for example, suggests an upper time limit of one hour for each interview and a phased approach to interviewing. This consists of rapport building (where the interviewer asks general questions, for example, about the child's hobbies), a free narrative phase (where the child is given the opportunity to give an account of the event at his own pace), a questioning phase (where the interviewer asks the child specific questions about alleged events), and a closure phase (where the interview is summarized and the child is invited to ask the interviewer any questions that he may have).

# THE AIMS OF THE MEMORANDUM

## Summary of the Memorandum

The philosophy of the Memorandum was based on the spirit of the Working Together Act of 1987 in that interagency teams should work together to enable children, as far as possible, to tell their own story assisted by prompts and questions of gradually increasing explicitness. The Memorandum contains advice on technical aspects of the interview, discusses legal issues surrounding making a video-recording which will be used as the evidence-in-chief and outlines the so-called phased interview. As the Memorandum states on page 1, its main purpose is to help those making a video-recording of an interview with a child witness where it is intended that the result should be acceptable in criminal proceedings.

The Memorandum begins with a four page introduction and is then divided into four main parts. Part 1 offers general advice on when and where to make a video-recording for criminal proceedings, it comments on suitable equipment to use and sets out the legal conditions which must be satisfied before a criminal court can accept a video-recording of an interview with a child witness. Part 2 focuses on planning the interview. The joint investigating team is asked to consider, in advance, the child's cognitive, linguistic, emotional, social, sexual, physical and other development and to come to a decision whether or not, in principle, the child is likely to be able to give a coherent account of the events under investigation. The team is then asked to plan the length and time of the interview and who should conduct it. Part 3, the main part of the document, outlines in one chapter the phased approach to the interview, and in the next, the legal rules which should be observed in order to produce an evidentially acceptable video-recording. So in part 3A, advice is given in sections on how to conduct phase 1 – rapport; phase 2 – the free narrative account; phase 3 – questioning; phase 4 – closing the interview and factors to consider when deciding whether or not further interviewing is necessary. Part 3B considers the legal constraints and outlines the conditions that the video must meet, such as avoiding leading questions, if it is to be considered as the child's evidence-in-chief in criminal proceedings.

In part 4, advice is given about the storage, custody and destruction of the video-recording and about its viewing by others, including for training purposes. Finally, the appendices A–L contain a glossary of terms, details of the Criminal Justice Act (1988), a list of sexual offences, a list of the legal elements of the main sexual and violent offences, Crown Court rules, technical guidance, admissibility of video-recording under other provisions of the Criminal Justice Act (1988), specimen information sheets on video-recorded interviews and a copy of the warning label for videotapes.

It is made clear that the use of the Memorandum in video-recorded interviews with child witnesses for criminal proceedings is voluntary but "save in wholly exceptional circumstances, no-one should undertake any interview with a child witness which is to be video-recorded for the purposes of criminal proceedings unless he or she is properly conversant with this memorandum" (MOGP 1992: 3).

## The Advantages of Interviewing Children within the Memorandum

Let us now consider professionals' views of the advantages of interviewing children within the Memorandum's guidelines. We report on the findings of two studies: Davies et al (1995) and Aldridge & Wood (1997a).

An evaluation of the first two years of the use of the Memorandum was commissioned by the Home Office and carried out by Davies et al (1995). They questioned professionals involved with child protection (mainly the police and social workers) and professionals involved within the courts. In our discussion, here, we focus solely on the reactions of the child protection professionals as the court arena is outside the scope of our current discussion. Davies et al's (1995) study was longitudinal; they questioned police and social workers (in February 1993) about their attitudes towards the Memorandum prior to experience of working with it and again (in August 1994) once they had some experience of working with it. They received 117 responses from the police and 75 from social workers in 1993, and 76 from the police and 42 from the social workers in 1994. Their findings were that in 1993 both the police and social workers gave almost unanimous support for the introduction of the Memorandum and videotaped evidence and their major concerns were the need for adequate training and supervision. By August 1994, their enthusiasm was largely undiminished and there was less of a need expressed for training although just under one-half felt that the training could be improved or made a continuing process. Thus, as Murray had also reported in 1993, the professionals involved (police-officers and social workers) generally viewed the 1991 Act and subsequent Memorandum as introducing improvements for children within the legal system.

Moving on to Aldridge & Wood (1997a). We sent out 200 questionnaires to interagency departments in Wales and received 41 returns from police-officers. The questionnaire elicited the respondents' experience of, and attitudes towards, the guidelines set out in the Memorandum and our main findings are reported below:

- 100% of the respondents are currently conducting video interviews with children.
- 95% said that they had been introduced to the MOGP at a training course. In most cases this course was three days long and was a joint investigative course with social services.
- 73% said that they had attended at least one training course and up to three courses from a list comprising a three-day joint investigation course with social services, a week's video interviewing course, an interview development course, a two-week course in child protection, a sex offenders course and a cognitive interviewing course. Most of the professionals had received about seven training days in total.
- 27% said that they had received no actual training but had been given a copy of the Memorandum to read and to practise daily.

In terms of interview experience, the following information was reported:

- 20% reported that they had conducted fewer than 10 video-recorded interviews.
- 27% reported that they had conducted between 10 and 29 interviews.
- 27% reported that they had conducted between 30 and 49 interviews.
- 7% reported that they had conducted between 50 and 69 interviews.
- 19% reported that they had conducted 70 or more such interviews.

Our findings support those expressed in the Davies et al (1995) study in that reactions to the Memorandum were favourable. To illustrate this, consider the following findings:

- 95% said that there were advantages to video interviewing.

Examples of the advantages they gave include:

- 44% said that videoing the interview is much quicker than writing down the questions and answers.
- 37% commented that the child's emotions can be seen and this is likely to make an impact on the jury.
- 24% said that the video opportunity provides a much more relaxed atmosphere for the child which helps build rapport and helps the child talk more freely.
- 24% said that the video prevented the child from having to give a statement several times.
- 19% said that the video meant the child does not have to appear in court for his evidence-in-chief.
- 17% said that the video offers a visual impact for the Crown Prosecution Service which helps it decide whether or not the child will make a reliable witness in court.
- 17% said that the video provided better quality evidence because the interviews are more structured, the volume and depth of information can by far exceed what can practicably be obtained by written statements and, with the video, the first account is made available.
- 12% said that the video is less impersonal than writing a statement and gave a better opportunity for the child's account to be heard in his own words.
- 12% said that everything is videoed, so there is nothing to hide. They commented that the video shows the impartiality of the interviewer and safeguards interviewing officers.
- 7% said that seeing the video helps the child's memory when it is time for cross-examination.
- 5% commented that the video should cut down the amount of cross-examination necessary and therefore make the whole investigative procedure much less traumatic for the child.

The results of both studies (Davies et al 1995 and Aldridge & Wood 1997a) illustrate that the majority of the professionals working in child protection have found the introduction of the Memorandum to be beneficial in terms of reducing the stress for the child witness and for improving the quality of the child's account. The police, especially, find the Memorandum and its specific guidance to be a useful contribution to improving the skills and effectiveness of the interview. They appreciate, for example, the fact that for the first time, they have a formal framework within which interviewing can take place (Butler 1997) and they certainly feel that a video-recording provides better evidence than contemporaneous note-taking and a statement (Brownlow & Waller 1997).

It has also been reported (Davies et al 1995) that most of the child witnesses prefer to give their evidence via a video-recording rather than at trial and it is reported (e.g. Sharland et al 1995) that children do value justice through formal processes.

From reports such as Holton & Bonnerjea (1994) and Davies et al (1995) it is noticeable, however, that social workers are a little more cautious about the success of the Memorandum. They feel, for example, disempowered by its introduction and they are concerned that the welfare needs of the child are being overlooked in favour of producing data suitable for a court hearing.

Indeed, when we look more closely at the facts it is very apparent that a number of difficulties still surround the interviewing of young children for evidentiary purposes and these difficulties manifest themselves in many ways including in the statistics of successful cases to and in court, in media reports and in professionals' experience of the Memorandum.

## PROBLEMS ASSOCIATED WITH THE MEMORANDUM

First, let us reflect on some stark statistics.

## Statistics

As noted earlier, there is reason to believe that large numbers of children are victims of abuse. For example, a report by the NSPCC & Tower Hamlets ACPC (October 1996) suggests that a total of 1 million children, in the UK, are abused each year. Moreover, figures for instances of child sexual abuse, in the UK, indicate a 12-fold increase in registered cases between 1983 and 1988 (Fielding & Conroy 1992). A similar picture has emerged in the USA where in 1976, 6000 cases of child sexual abuse were reported whereas estimates of cases for 1993 indicate a 55-fold increase to 330 000 reported cases (Coulborn-Faller & Corwin 1995). It is clear, then, that a large number of children are being abused both in the UK and elsewhere and it is hoped that many of these children will have the opportunity to recount their experiences to a trained professional in the quest for justice.

Sadly, the number of children having the opportunity of being video-interviewed is alarmingly low. For example, in the year to October 1993, from an estimated 1 million cases only 14 000 video interviews were conducted with children in the UK. Even more problematic is the finding that less than 6% of these reached court and the percentage resulting in conviction was even smaller (Social Services Inspectorate 1994). The evaluation of practice under the Memorandum by Davies et al 1995 came to the same conclusion, reporting that very few of the thousands of videos made each year are ever used in court proceedings. More specifically, Davies et al (1995) report that of the 1199 trials that took place in England and Wales during the 21-month period from October 1992 until June 1994 involving child witnesses, 53% included an application to show a video-taped interview, 73% of these applications were granted and 43% were played in court. In brief, a tape-recorded interview was played in court in 17% of the total number of trials during the period in question. Similarly, Brownlow & Waller (1997) report that in 1994 only 40% of the video-recordings made in Leicestershire were submitted to the Crown Prosecution Service and less than 3% of these went on to be used in criminal proceedings.

These statistics suggest that video-recorded interviews with children are not as successful as they might be and while the number of video-recorded interviews being admitted to court is increasing it is apparent that the submission rate is still very disappointing. As well as the statistics, of course, we are aware of regular media coverage of unsuccessful interview cases involving child witnesses. The following, selected from many possible articles, illustrate the point.

## Media Coverage of Child Witnesses Cases

*The Guardian*, 4 February, 1998: Boys cleared of rape of girl aged nine.

"Two boys aged 10, who were charged with raping a girl of nine during the lunch break at their primary school were yesterday formally acquitted at the Old Bailey. They still face indecent assault charges. The trial judge, Mrs Justice Bracewell, instructed the Jury to return verdicts of not guilty on both rape charges. She also told them to acquit a third boy, also 10, who was accused of acting as a lookout and who had been facing a charge of indecent assault. The judge said she was instructing the jury to return not guilty verdicts on rape for two reasons. First, the alleged victim, who is now 10, had not positively identified one of the accused. But there is a much more fundamental flaw in the evidence, said the judge. When [the girl] was interviewed and video-recorded by the policewoman, she was interviewed for some 45 minutes. Throughout that interview she did not make any allegation of rape and the policewoman left the room at a time when, to all intents and purposes, the interview had ended. The policewoman returned and then asked a question that was both leading and wholly improper, which, in effect, put words into the girl's mouth."

*Community Care*, 5–11 February, 1998, Jo Waters: Courts deny video link to child abuse victims.

"Child abuse victims are still not getting special treatment to help them give evidence in court, says a new report by the Crown Prosecution Service Inspectorate. The report reveals that not all relevant cases are being correctly identified as qualifying for protective provisions under the Criminal Justice Acts of 1988 and 1991, which allow witnesses to give evidence via either closed-circuit television or video-recording link."

*Independent on Sunday*, 5 March, 1995: Satanic abuse/the child's story: Cleveland, Orkney and Rochdale child abuse scandals: Social worker pushed a doll into my face.

"One of the eight Ayrshire children who were taken into care for five years after their parents were wrongly accused of sexual abuse tells her story of how social workers tried to bully her into making allegations against her mother and father. The girl describes how the social workers did not produce detailed evidence of the alleged abuse but, instead, relied on interviews they had conducted with the other seven children taken into care, who were relatives. The girl reports that it was as if the social worker wanted her to say certain things, the girl continues, 'I knew I would not give in, but my cousins were younger and I remember worrying that they might say something daft just to please her or to stop her asking so many questions.'" (The girl was 10.)

*The Guardian*, 14 January, 1995, Martin Wainwright: Guidelines on children's video evidence to be re-examined.

"The Government is to re-examine guidelines on children's video evidence following a critical academic report and the collapse of the Bishop Auckland ritual abuse case, which depended heavily on videoed allegations. John Bowis, Junior Health Minister, announced a departmental inquiry yesterday but said guidelines would continue in force pending the outcome of the review and a study, already begun, of children's responses to video-recording. During the year-long investigation into the Bishop Auckland allegations, police and social workers carried out almost 240 hours of interviews with three boys aged 12 and two girls aged 10 and seven. The collapse of the case came as a Social Services Inspectorate study showed that only 6% of the 14 000 interviews filmed in a year were used in court. Brian Waller, chairman of the Association of Directors of Social Services Children and Families Committee said, 'It is totally unacceptable that so many children are being put through a process which is both wildly inefficient and damaging to them.' Mr Bowis said that the

Government was trying to find a balance between easing the way for children to give truthful evidence and respecting the rights of adults accused of abuse, 'We can't guarantee that children will always tell the truth.' Allan Levy, QC, chairman of the inquiry which found that children in the care of Staffordshire County Council were subjected to an illegal 'pindown' system, called the present video system, used for evidence-in-chief but not cross-examination of children 'half-baked' and said that alleged child victims should not have to face the ordeal of open court. The Chief Constable of Gloucestershire, Tony Butler, the Association of Chief Police-Officers' spokesman on children, said that Home Office and National Children's Home research showed the recording had little detrimental effect on children."

These reports illustrate that there are continued problems concerning the interviewing of children. Moreover, professionals, too, are reporting that they find certain phases of the Memorandum difficult to cope with especially when they are interviewing young children, which again suggests that the guidelines are not as thorough and practical as they might be.

## Professionals' Opinions

Consider our respondents' replies to the following questions:

1.  Do you find any particular phase of the MOGP interview difficult? If so, which phase and why?
2.  Is there a particular age group which you find difficult to interview? If so, which age group is this and why do you find them difficult to interview?

In response to the first question, 33% of interviewing officers said that they did find certain phases difficult and mentioned the following areas in particular:

*   29% said that establishing whether the child witness knew the difference between truth and lie was very difficult.
*   44% said that establishing whether the child witness knew the difference between fact and fantasy was very difficult.

These replies were qualified with the following type of comment: "When I mention these, I think the children think I expect them not to tell the truth". In addition to the difficulties reported in connection with truth and lies and fact and fantasy, the following areas of difficulty were also reported:

- 22% said that they found the rapport phase difficult because it is hard to get the child to speak when he is nervous, the introductions do not always run smoothly and it is not always easy to assess a child's ability.
- 15% said that they were often concerned about the closed questioning as the balance of getting all the information from the child without leading him was difficult to maintain.

In response to the second question 63% said that they did find certain age groups difficult and qualified their answer in the following ways:

- 5% said that children under 3 years of age are difficult to interview because of their short concentration span.
- 54% said that 3–5-year-olds are the most difficult to interview due to their short concentration span, their small vocabulary and their limited comprehension. These respondents commented that they found it difficult to speak at the children's level. "It's hard not to put words into their mouths," one respondent added.
- 15% said that children under 6 years of age were difficult to interview and said that this age group may have difficulty expressing themselves. They further commented that disclosure needs to be worked at much more in cases where the child doesn't want to tell due to embarrassment.
- 12% said the under 7-year-olds were the most difficult to interview because it is difficult to focus the child, their attention span is very limited, language difficulties often occur and it is difficult to establish if they know what truth means.
- 8% said that children under 8 years of age were difficult to interview as initially it is not always easy to gauge their level of linguistic ability. These respondents continued that children's understanding, coupled with short concentration span made young children very awkward interviewees. One respondent suggested that with children under 8 years of age much more time must be spent building rapport.
- 8% said that children are usually a pleasure to interview.

Two respondents added that teenagers are more difficult as they expect you to know what they are talking about and have difficulty understanding that they have to tell everything that they know. They continued by reporting that teenagers are often shy when it comes to disclosing intimate information.

These figures suggest that communicating with young children is an ongoing problem, particularly when considered in conjunction with their qualifying comments.

It is clear, then, from the statistics, the media coverage and professionals' anxieties that aspects of the video interview are not as effective as was first hoped. Of course, some of the difference between the number of videos made and the number reaching court can be accounted for by the video prompting the perpetrator to return a guilty plea and consequently there being no need for the video evidence to be shown in court. This explanation, though, cannot account for all those cases not reaching court and other explanations must be sought. From the various reviews and surveys it is apparent that the likely explanations fall within two broad categories. First, those which are general in nature concerning the mechanisms of carrying out a video interview and second, those that relate specifically to communicating with young children in an evidentiary setting. Let us look at these in turn, reporting from the studies of Davies et al (1995) and Aldridge & Wood (1997a).

## OPERATIONAL PROBLEMS ASSOCIATED WITH THE MEMORANDUM

The most frequently cited problems associated with carrying out an interview within the MOGP guidelines in the Davies et al (1995) study are listed below:

- One-third of interviews were of no evidential value and thus Davies et al recommend more careful pre-interview screening. This finding supports the observation made by Tissier (1995) that there is some ambiguity about the circumstances in which interviews should be conducted.
- Some professionals felt that the document contains too little detail about the procedural framework which is needed to organize an interview involving interagency collaboration and too little detail about matters such as when the interview should be conducted. As a result, many inconsistencies in the application of the Memorandum across the country have been reported and it is felt by many that uniformity must be achieved.
- Another frequently cited difficulty, when trying to work within the guidelines set out in the Memorandum is the interview time limit of one hour which many professionals regard as insufficient time for disclosure to take place.

- Some professionals felt that the time lapse between the initial interview and trial (an average of 20 weeks) is too long.
- Some professionals felt that the video-recorded interview gives defence lawyers more opportunity to discredit the way in which evidence was obtained and that police-officers and social workers giving evidence would come under fierce attack about the conduct of the interview.
- Some felt that because, within the guidelines of the Memorandum, the evidential requirements of the criminal investigation are the main concern, the philosophy expressed within the Children's Act that the welfare of the child is paramount has been lost.
- Some social workers felt that the interview had become too police led.
- Some professionals felt that child witnesses were still receiving inadequate preparation for court.

In Aldridge & Wood (1997a), 54% of respondents felt that there were some disadvantages to video interviewing and the types of observations they made include the following:

- 37% of the respondents were concerned that everything is on video – mistakes and all. A typical comment was, "It's stressful for the interviewing officer who is open to criticism by all who view it".
- 22% felt that it was unfair to expect the child to settle in a false setting in unfamiliar surroundings. They felt that taking a child to a strange place and expecting him to disclose the most intimate occurrences in a specified time is totally impractical.
- 17% of the respondents said that the child can be inhibited by the camera and it can be even more embarrassing for the children to have to describe sexual activities in front of a camera.
- 15% of the respondents felt that some police forces experienced storage problems with the videos.
- 15% of the respondents felt that editing the tapes is technically difficult and the problem is compounded by the fact that requests to edit come at short notice and are often urgent.
- 15% of the respondents commented that the courts do not seem very happy with videos as evidence.
- 15% said that the distance the child often has to travel to and from the interview suite is distracting.
- 5% of the respondents felt that the interview structure is sometimes too formal.
- 5% of the respondents reported that the equipment does not always work.

- 5% of the respondents said that some children "perform" for the camera.
- 5% of the respondents said that it can be frustrating that once the child has been interviewed he cannot be re-interviewed unless it is about another offence.

It is clear that the same types of concerns are reported in both studies (Davies et al 1995, Aldridge & Wood 1997a) and elsewhere (e.g. Department of Health 1994) and that work still needs to be done to improve the operational aspects of the interview. However, for many, a far more critical problem is the difficulties encountered when trying to communicate with children in an evidentiary setting.

## LANGUAGE PROBLEMS ASSOCIATED WITH INTERVIEWING CHILDREN

A major concern that comes through in all the studies is whether or not a child is capable of being a reliable witness. Of course, in the interview situation there are three possible barriers to a successful interaction. One is that the child is unable to be an effective witness, second, there is the possibility that the adult fails to be an effective questioner and third, there could be both an ineffective child witness and an ineffective adult questioner.

Professionals have raised concerns about children's ability to act as reliable witnesses particularly from the point of view of having the linguistic skills necessary to produce adult-like evidence and professionals, academics and child witnesses have raised concerns about adults' ability to interview young children. We will look at these points in turn.

## Professionals' Attitudes towards Child Witnesses

Professionals are aware of the problems that can arise when interviewing children. For example, in Aldridge & Wood's (1997a) survey, when the respondents were asked whether they had encountered any difficulties when video interviewing children which they felt were directly related to language difficulties 93% said yes and gave the following replies:

- Young children haven't got time to talk! They run around the interview room and have a short concentration span.

Many commented on the miscommunications that can occur and the following quotes are typical of the sentiments expressed:

- "Sometimes I have used phrases which have been clear to me but ambiguous to the child and therefore their reply has been totally unexpected."
- "Sometimes I have put a question to the child and I have expected the child to understand it but she doesn't and I don't know why."
- Many said, quite simply, that sometimes there are problems trying to understand very young children.
- Many commented on having problems when children used words they weren't familiar with.
- Many commented that the limited vocabulary of the child makes disclosure difficult (we return to this issue in Chapter 5).
- Many said that they had problems when interviewing children with language disabilities. Children with hearing impairments were reported as a frequent and difficult situation to cope with (we return to this issue in Chapter 6).

In summary, the following quote reflects the anxiety experienced: "A major problem with the video is that it clearly shows how confused the child can become". Almost without exception, then, professionals have experienced interview problems as a result of children's linguistic immaturities. They are, however, ready to accept responsibility for some of the language breakdown themselves.

## Professionals' Reflections on their own Performance

An examination of the literature provides plenty of examples of professionals commenting on the need to monitor their interviewing style. Dennet & Bekerian (1991: 356), for example, note that police authorities internationally have acknowledged the problems that interviewing techniques pose in child abuse investigations. Clarke (1994: 1), a policeofficer, makes a similar observation, noting that one aspect of interviewing children that is always discussed at some point is the need to use age-appropriate language or to take account of the child's linguistic ability. It is apparent that professionals are acutely aware of their own shortcomings when interviewing children and many would appreciate specific training in this area. A point we return to shortly. Let us consider first academics' views on the skills of interviewers.

## Academics' Reflections on Adult Interviewers

Academic research consistently emphasizes the crucial importance of an awareness of the fact that the language ability of young children is essentially different from that of adults and challenges the assumption that adult interviewing methods and language will be effective when dealing with children. In countless articles the point is made that interview problems can arise if the interviewer is unaware of developmental changes in language ability and cognition. The following quotes illustrate the point:

> "An untrained interviewer may misinterpret a child's words or may use age-inappropriate language that will confuse the child" (Yuille et al in Goodman & Bottoms 1993: 98).

> "The credibility of the child witness is systematically destroyed by a combination of language devices and questioning styles" (Brennan 1994: 53).

> "Communication failures obscure the fact-finding process and derail the court of justice" (Saywitz, Geiselman & Bornstien 1993: 59).

> "The real question of children's linguistic competence in evidentiary settings belongs not to the children but to the adults. . . . There is still a lack of knowledge on the part of professionals as to the linguistic abilities of young children and this lack of knowledge is a serious oversight which presents the opportunity for untold mischief . . . language is the lynch-pin for all these investigations and for their applications in the court"(Walker 1993: 78–79).

Professionals and academics alike, then, are aware of the dangers of inappropriate interviewing skills. Child witnesses, too, have also commented on this matter and we report here from Westcott & Davies' (1996) study.

## Child Witness' Reflections on Adult Interviewers

Westcott and Davies (1996) have evaluated sexually abused children's and young people's views on a variety of aspects of investigative interviewing. In a study involving retrospective evaluation by 14 children and young people (aged 6–18 years) aspects of the investigative interview such as location and duration were considered. In addition, the children and young people raised a number of concerns of their own. Foremost of these concerns was difficulties with the language used by some interviewers. In fact, 11 out of 14 (79%) of the children and young people suggested that the language used by the interviewers was problematic. They referred specifically to "long and complicated words and sentences". A comment by a 6-year-old girl is particularly revealing. When asked what would have made the interview easier for her, she said that the interviewer should, "Put the questions a little bit smaller. They kept talking longer then smaller so I couldn't keep up with it, and they kept talking a question then a different question before I answered" (Westcott & Davies 1996: 18). Even a 13-year-old reported finding the language difficult to cope with. She recalls particularly the fact that she was being asked to talk about a difficult topic and yet the interviewer was using long words in her questions. For further discussion of children's perspectives on investigative interviews, see Wade & Westcott (1997).

## EVALUATION OF INFORMATION CONCERNING CHILDREN'S LANGUAGE DEVELOPMENT

Clearly then there is a consensus regarding the difficulties that can occur when interviewing children in an evidentiary setting. An obvious question to ask is what advice about children's language development is available to help professionals communicate appropriately with children? We thus turn our attention to published child language guidelines.

It is not surprising that professionals are anxious about their ability to cope with children's linguistic immaturities because, having surveyed the current literature on child language guidelines, it is striking that they are limited in number and that the information available is rather vague and therefore inadequate. This point is also made by academics such as McGough & Warren (1994: 19) who comment:

> "Many guidelines written for workers who interview alleged victims of child abuse suggest that the language used in the interviews should be age-appropriate . . . however, these interview guidelines make no specific suggestions regarding what constitutes simplified, age-appropriate language."

Professionals such as Clarke (1994: 1) make the same point:

"Information about the most appropriate language to use or the aspects of language which need to be altered to help a child understand adult speech are frequently not forthcoming."

Looking through the literature the following quotes are typical of the advice to be found:

"In any interview situation, a variety of circumstances and factors will promote effective communication, at the same time, others may hinder it. The lawyer's principal communication tasks in an interview are to minimize or avoid those situations that block, mislead, and discourage communication and to utilize or stress the skills that facilitate, encourage and motivate" (Perry & Teply 1984: 1375).

"The best approach is to reduce the questions or explanation to the most basic and concrete terms" (Perry & Teply 1984: 1383).

"Once the interview has begun, the interviewer should focus initially on the level of linguistic development shown by the child when discussing everyday matters so as to be able to adjust his/her use of language to the needs of the particular child" (Bull 1992: 7).

"Talk with the child in age-appropriate language . . . with words that are not confusing to the child" (Rappley & Speare 1993: 340).

"To establish accurate communication with the child, interviewers should use developmentally sensitive language. Specifically, interviewers should initially gauge the child's linguistic and cognitive skills, avoid complex and jargonistic questions and be alert to signs the child may not have understood a question" (McGough & Warren 1994: 23/4).

"Recommendation: That we adapt our language to the child. We can make a habit to use basic words and clear sentences" (Walker & Warren 1995: 161).

And from the MOGP:

"Knowledge of the child's linguistic development is particularly important to enable the joint investigating team to plan how best to communicate with the child. Younger children are likely to have a limited vocabulary and language style and may use words and phrases not in common parlance, particularly in relation to sexual activity and genitals. The interviewer will need to listen to the child and to adjust his or her language accordingly" (1992: 9–10).

"Simple sentence constructions should be used, avoid double negatives and other potentially confusing forms" (1992: 18).

"It seems likely that young children in particular may be more willing to respond to yes/no questions with a yes response" (1992: 20).

While the above advice is accurate, it is not clear that these recommendations are especially useful as working guidelines. More specifically, how are professionals to know, for example, which situations block, mislead and discourage communication, how do they know how to reduce the questions or explanations to the most basic and concrete terms, or how do they know how to adjust their language, as some of the above advice suggests?

Moreover, this advice is scattered in published books and journals and it is not obvious that these are available to professionals. Our reason for saying this is based on our respondents' replies to the request to briefly outline the training they have undergone relating to children's language ability:

- 80% reported having no specific training on children's language ability even though 60% of these commented that they had asked for such training several times.
- 20% felt that children's language had been covered in the initial training sessions and they could remember points such as the following:

  Use age-appropriate language
  Speak at the child's level
  Avoid leading questions
  Ask open questions
  Do not ask more than one question at a time
  Assess the child's ability regarding his level of communication

It is interesting to note that, without exception, these points are those mentioned in the Memorandum which indicates that this document might well be the only source of information available to professionals concerning children's language development.

It is obvious that if we are to improve the success rate of video-recorded interviews being accepted as the child's evidence-in-chief we must work on ways of eliciting the fullest account from the child in a non-leading fashion. There is little, if anything, anyone can do to change the child witness' linguistic immaturities but there are ways in which professionals can be trained to facilitate the child's reporting.

# TRAINING

The Memorandum places great stress on the need for professionals to understand the complexities of child language development and children's cognitive capacities in relation to time and memory. This emphasis led to recognition that the introduction of the Memorandum had training implications and study days for professionals began to be held around the country. Many different circulars, workshops, speakers, briefings at Hendon Police College and training work packs, such as the Open University's (OU) (1993) pack for social workers, have been employed with varying degrees of success. For example, some police-officers believe that the OU pack is too rudimentary (Hughes, Parker & Gallagher 1996). As we saw earlier, most professionals have received training and advice on how to work with young children but in all the surveys there is an overriding feeling that more training is needed. To be more specific, 43% of our respondents (Aldridge & Wood 1997a) thought that the training they had received was adequate, but many of those said it was only adequate and no more. The need for more training is reported in numerous documents as the following quotes illustrate:

"More training is needed so that there can be better planning of the interview based on the child's age and development" (Brownlow & Waller 1997).

"The various professional bodies involved with interviewing children – lawyers, police-officers, social workers and psychologists have agreed that 'training . . . has been identified as an essential requirement if the interviews are to succeed'" (Westcott 1992a: 78).

"There is a need to improve interviewer training so that a greater percentage of such interviews will comply with the guidelines provided in the MOGP" (Davies et al 1995).

"There is no doubt that children who have been the victims of physical or sexual abuse receive a better response from police-officers and social workers as a result of the guidelines in the Memorandum. There are also opportunities to further improve that response. The source of those improvements, however, is more likely to be achieved by professionals developing the state of their knowledge and skills rather than a re-writing of the Memorandum" (Butler 1997).

And indeed many professionals are asking for more training. In our survey, for example, many identified the need for refresher courses so that their information on recent legislation, modifications of good practice and recent research findings might be constantly updated. Many asked for information about child development, especially language development and many said that some form of assessment was needed. They also asked for constructive criticism on their interviews and felt that videos should be audited to eliminate bad practice. For a further discussion on training issues the reader is referred to Hendry & Jones (1997).

# SUMMARY

The facts then are clear, both interviewers and interviewees recognize the role that language use plays in the interview setting and the difficulties that inappropriate language use can present, especially when the interview is video-recorded. There is a consensus, though, that the process of video-recording is no more stressful than other procedures that currently exist for interviewing children and it is indeed felt by many to be the best all-round alternative that has been devised to serve the interests of the child and the criminal justice system (Butler 1997). We can, therefore, assume that the video interview (and the MOGP, perhaps in a modified form), is here to stay as a method within which children are interviewed for evidentiary purposes. Throughout this chapter, the advantages of video interviews and the MOGP are apparent. Although many difficulties have been identified it is clear that with appropriate planning and training many of these can be overcome. We have also been heartened by professionals' willingness and indeed, desire for more training, information and evaluation.

We have noted that the child language information that professionals require in order effectively to address many of their communication difficulties with children is largely unavailable. The only exception to this, in our opinion, are the guidelines produced by Walker (1994) which concentrate largely on court language.

The aim of this book, then, is to provide child language guidelines to help professionals when interviewing children. To the best of our knowledge, the book contains the first set of guidelines to focus in depth on individual aspects of language use which have been identified as being problematic in the video-recorded interview which is to form the child's evidence-in-chief. The following chapters, then, take in turn each of the first three phases of the staged interview as set out in the MOGP. The fourth phase – closure – is referred to at the end of Chapter 4 on questioning. We focus on language issues at each stage with the aim of filling in the gaps in professionals' knowledge concerning children's language development. It is hoped that this book can be used as a working manual and thus each chapter offers advice and there is a self-assessment section where the interviewer can check his/her performance against a list of dos and don'ts and then add evaluative comments about his/her performance to assist preparation for the next interview.

We go forward then with the words of Lamb, Strenberg & Esplin (1995: 446) in mind:

> "The demonstrable fact that investigative interviews with young children can be rendered worthless by inept practice should not blind us to the substantial literature demonstrating that reliable information can be elicited from young children who are competently interviewed."

In the following chapters, ways of competently interviewing young children are explored.

# ESTABLISHING RAPPORT

The main focus of this chapter is the first of the *Memorandum of Good Practice*'s (1992) recommended phases; the rapport phase. In addition, we consider issues related to the interview setting such as:

- What is the best time and place for an interview to be recorded?
- Who should be present at an interview?

Methods of getting the interview under way are also addressed. For example:

- At the start of the interview, how can the interviewer most effectively communicate information such as the time and date that the interview is taking place?

We then focus on the first of the Memorandum's recommended phases – the rapport phase – and consider:

- How can rapport best be established?
- What are the most appropriate toys to use in an interview?
- What are the best indicators of the child's social, emotional, cognitive and linguistic development?
- How can the interviewer explain clearly to the child why the interview is taking place?
- What is the best way to ensure that the child understands the function of the video equipment, microphones and the interviewer's earpiece?
- How can an interviewer give the child the best opportunity to demonstrate that he knows the difference between the truth and a lie?
- What is the best way to check that the child can differentiate between fact and fantasy?
- What is the best way to ensure that the child understands that it is OK to say that he hasn't understood a question or that he doesn't know the answer to a question?

We begin by examining aspects of the interview setting.

## TIMING THE INTERVIEW

The Memorandum (1992: 6) recommends that a video interview should be made "as soon as proper planning and the child's interests will allow". This is clearly sound advice in that it takes account of the needs of both the child and the justice system. However, there are some rather more mundane, practical matters which it would also be useful to consider. These involve taking account of the child's routine to ensure that he is comfortable with the timing of the interview. For example, interviews which commence late in the morning may intrude upon the child's usual lunch time. Hence, we have seen examples such as the following:

(1)    From an interview with a 9-year-old boy:
       C:      My belly's rumbling now.
       S/W:    All our bellies are rumbling.

This exchange is taken from an interview which started just before noon. Clearly, a child who becomes hungry during an interview may, as a consequence, lose concentration. The possibility (or suspicion) of this or of the child rushing to get an interview finished should be avoided. Breaks can be taken but this may not satisfy a child whose lunch time routine is broken. Just as routine is important in children's lives, so too are some school-based events. One child, for example, took part in an interview when her school Christmas party was due to take place later the same day. In instances such as this, the possibilities of lack of concentration and a desire to get the interview finished quickly arise and thus such timing is best avoided, where possible.

## LOCATION OF THE INTERVIEW

Our own experience and data are drawn from interviews which have taken place in purpose-built suites and we therefore have little comment to make on the location of interviews since we have seen few problems arise. However, two points can be noted. First, for some children, the distance from their home/school to the interview suite can be greater than they are used to travelling on a day-to-day basis. This concern was also raised by some of the interviewers who responded to our survey (Aldridge & Wood 1997a reported in Chapter 1). One child was clearly disorientated by her journey as the following exchange illustrates:

(2)     From an interview with a 6-year-old girl:

C:      Mum said we were coming to [place name].
I:      This is [same place name].

Of course, the Memorandum (1992: 7) notes the potential "adverse effect and inconvenience to the child of a lengthy journey". In fact, the actual length of the journey should probably not be the focus but the child's perception of his journey should be considered. As adults, we are often used to travelling to, from and within work, sometimes for significant times and distances. In contrast, some children will only have day-to-day experience of a short journey to school and thus the journey to the interview suite may seem long. In some cases, it may therefore be appropriate to offer reassurance to the child. This could be given in conjunction with checking that the child is happy to begin the interview and could be along the lines of the following:

I:      Well, you've had to spend a bit of time in the car to get here but, if you're ready now, we can start.

Another area that some children may need reassurance about is the ownership of purpose-built suites located in houses. In a number of cases, children have thought that the interviewer lives in the house. For example:

(3)     From an interview with a 6-year-old girl:

C:      Is this your house?
S/W:    No, it's not my house, I just come here sometimes.
C:      Whose house is it?
I:      It just belongs to the police.
C:      Whose toys are these?
I:      Theirs, the same. The toys are here for any children who come to talk to us.

Other children have sought to clarify that the house is not where they live. For example:

(4)     From an interview with a 6-year-old boy:

     I:       Home with mummy and daddy. That's where you live, isn't it?

     C:     Yeah, I don't live here.

     I:       You don't live here, no. Nobody lives here, in this house, only the toys.

These examples illustrate the potential need for clarification of this matter. The more comfortable the child feels, the more confidence he will have and thus he will be in a better position to give a full and reliable account of events.

## WHO SHOULD BE PRESENT AT AN INTERVIEW?

An early decision which needs to be made is who will be in the interviewing room during the interview. The possibility of a supportive adult being present in addition to the child and interviewer needs to be considered. Below we review who might be best placed to fulfil this role.

Clearly, as the Memorandum (1992: 13) states, "a suspected offender should never be present" at an interview. The Memorandum (1992: 13) also suggests that "normally, no-one else should be in the room".

We would echo this comment too in terms of what we will refer to as an "attached" adult presence (by this we mean the presence of any adult who has a personal attachment to the child but who is not a suspect). In contrast, we report on instances where the presence of a social worker (who we refer to as a "detached" adult presence) may be helpful. We consider each of these circumstances in turn.

## Attached Adult Presence

There are a number of reasons why an attached adult presence can be problematic for both the adult and the child and, indeed, for the evidential quality of the video.

First, from the point of view of an adult, it can prove too tempting to provide information in response to the interviewer's questions and to correct factual errors in the child's responses. Such temptation clearly overrides the Memorandum (1992: 13) recommendation that "the accompanying adult will need to be clear that he or she must take no part in the interview". We have seen, for example, the following exchanges:

(5)    In an interview with a 6-year-old girl:

  I:      So, who's your best friend in school?
  C:     [Name].
  I:      [Name] and does she live near you?
  C:     Quite near.
  M:     Up the road, doesn't she?

(6)    In an interview with a 5-year-old girl:

  I:      Can you tell me your name?
  C:     [Name].
  I:      All right, have you got any other name?
  C:     [Shakes head].
  M:     Yes, you have! Oh, sorry.
  I:      It's all right, mum's helping us isn't she?

Later in the same interview:

  I:      And how old's your sister then?
  C:     Five.
  I:      And you're five?!
  M:     They're twins.
  I:      OK.
  M:     In case you get confused.
  I:      And what about [name of child's brother]? How old's he?
  C:     Four.
  M:     Nearly.
  C:     Nearly.

In these cases, the maternal interventions are innocuous. Nonetheless, they highlight the (often) overwhelming temptation for an attached adult to offer information/clarification. A similar problem arises for the child in that he can become reliant on the attached adult to provide information. It is very hard for children to understand why this is inappropriate given that, in other circumstances, it is entirely natural to check information with mum, dad or teacher. Hence, we have the following example:

(7)    From an interview with a 7-year-old girl:

  I:      And do you know when your birthday is?
  C:     My mum does.
  I:      Your mum does, I'm sure, but can you try and remember when your birthday is?
  C:     [Shakes head].

(8)    In another interview with a 7-year-old girl:

    I:    And when was the last time this happened?
    C:    The last time we went there.
    I:    When was that?
    C:    Don't know, when do you think it was, dad?
    F:    The last time we went there was August.

Later in the same interview:

    I:    Right, who else is there?
    C:    Just [name of cousin] really, isn't it? 'Coz I sleep with him, isn't it?
    F:    Well, I don't know, it's up to you to say.
    C:    Well, I sleep in the same room as him.
    I:    OK, so what I want you to do, I know you're looking at your dad, have you told your dad about it?
    C:    [Nods].
    I:    Right well, do you know what I want you to do?
    C:    No.
    I:    I want you to forget that you've told dad about it.
    C:    Em.
    I:    And just tell me about it. Forget what you've told other people 'coz there might be a bit more that you've forgotten about, mightn't there?

As examples (7) and (8) illustrate, it is very difficult for a child to appreciate that the normal rules of interaction (if you're not sure about something – ask an adult) don't apply. It is especially difficult for the child to understand this in circumstances where they know that the adult is aware of the piece of information that is needed (e.g. the child's birth date or the timing of an event like a visit to relatives).

A further problematic feature of an attached adult presence is that this can place an additional emotional burden on both the adult and the child. For example, in an interview with a 5-year-old girl, the combination of a fidgety child who wasn't keen to disclose plus an upturned drink caused the mother to shout at the child which in turn caused the child to cry and thus the interview was brought to an abrupt conclusion. We also see the following exchanges:

(9)    In an interview with a 7-year-old girl:

    I:    And what is it that you don't like?

| | |
|---|---|
| C: | What he does, what he looks like. You're going to cry [to dad]. |
| F: | I'm not, no, honestly, I'm not, princess, promise. |
| C: | You cried the other day. |
| F: | Who did? |
| C: | You. |
| F: | Did I? |
| C: | Yeah, remember? |
| F: | Why did I? |
| C: | 'Coz of what happened. |
| I: | And why did daddy cry? |
| C: | 'Coz he likes me so much. |

(10)  In an interview with a 5-year-old girl:

| | |
|---|---|
| C: | Why are you crying? |
| M: | Mummy's all right, sweetheart. |
| I: | Are you all right, mum? |
| M: | [Nods]. |

In both these cases, we see how distressing it can be for an attached adult to be present when the child is interviewed. In turn, this also places an additional burden on the child who may conclude that it is his disclosure which has upset the adult and that therefore the best solution is to say no more in order that the adult is not upset any further.

Finally, we have observed that an attached adult presence may also not be in the interests of evidential quality. We have, for example, the following exchanges:

(11)  In an interview with a 5-year-old boy:

| | |
|---|---|
| I: | Right and which room were you in? |
| C: | Mum's room. I was in a different room and now I swapped. When I was in school, mum and [name] swapped. |
| I: | Ah, you swapped bedrooms, did you? |
| M: | I used to sleep downstairs 'coz I couldn't face the bedroom. |

(12)  In an interview with a 10-year-old boy:

| | |
|---|---|
| I: | OK, I think that I've asked you everything but I'll just ask [name of officer in the monitoring room] if I've missed anything out. Is there anything mum wants to ask? |
| M: | Can I say something here or will that invalidate what [name of child]'s said? |

> I:      Well, can we leave anything else for another day if we've
>         not discussed it already here today.
> M:     Fine.

In example (11), the mother's comment reveals the difficulties that existed between herself and the child's father (in this case the suspect), thus she exposes her own biases and brings her own motives (and possibly the child's too) into question. In example (12), the implication that what the mother wants to say will invalidate (presumably contradict) the child's account clearly calls into question all that the child has said.

## Detached Adult Presence

In contrast to the potentially problematic presence of an attached adult, our observations suggest that the presence of a detached adult (e.g. a social worker) can sometimes be helpful. For example, we have seen instances where reticent children have found playing with playdough or using colouring books with the social worker whilst being interviewed comforting. In these cases, the play activity had a settling effect on the child and the social worker's presence enabled the interviewer to concentrate fully on asking questions.

## GETTING THE INTERVIEW UNDER WAY

The Memorandum (1992: 15) recommends that the interview should start with an introduction of those present and a statement of the date and time of the interview. Our data suggest that this can sometimes be problematic. Consider, for example, the following exchange:

(13)   From an interview with a 3-year-old girl:

> I:      This is a videotaped interview taking place at the [venue].
>         I am WPC [name]. In the room as well is [name of child]
>         [date of birth]. The date today is [date] and the time is
>         [time].
> C:     I can't put them in [referring to toy].
> I:      The other persons present are [name] in the monitoring
>         room and [name], social worker also in the monitoring
>         room. [Name of child]'s mum is also in the building with
>         [name] social worker.

C:     Ah, can't put that in.
I:     Now then [name of child] let's see what we've got there. Which one can't you put in?

Similarly, consider the following exchange:

(14)   From an interview with a 6-year-old boy:
C:     [Waves at the camera] hello camera.
I:     I am WPC [name] of [place] police. I'm stationed at [name of unit] at [place].
C:     What does that say?
I:     The time is now Tuesday, sorry, the time now is 11.20 a.m. on Tuesday.
C:     Who are you talking to?
I:     Tuesday [date] and the location is [location].

In both these exchanges, the children try to gain the attention of their interviewer. However, understandably, the interviewers are unable to give the children their attention because of the need to provide key information before the interview commences. The first few minutes when the child and interviewer enter the room are vital both in settling the child and in beginning to establish a rapport. Once they have been effectively ignored, children lose concentration and as a result become less co-operative.

As a solution to this initial difficulty, we have seen a practice whereby either the interviewer or monitoring room officer initially go into the interview suite alone and give much of the detail on camera before the child enters the room. The date and time are displayed clearly on the video picture thus giving a clear indication that there is no inexplicable break between the information being presented and the child being interviewed. Details such as the child's name can be confirmed during the interview but the initial burden is removed. The following examples illustrate this practice:

(15)   From an interview with a 4-year-old girl:

       [Interviewing WPC enters the interview room alone].
I:     Hello, I'm WPC [name] of the [name] unit [name] police. We're at the [name] suite and it's [time] and [date]. I'm about to do a video interview with a little girl who's 4 years old by the name of [name], known as [abbreviated

form of child's name]. In the video monitoring room is
[name], social worker and [name] operating the equipment. So, I'm going to get [name of child] now and she
will be the next person into the room.
[WPC leaves the room and re-enters with the child]

I:      In here, that's right, you found it straight away. There we
        are.
C:      There's the playdough.
I:      Yeah, what are we going to have a play with then?
C:      These [pointing to tubs of playdough].
I:      OK.

Similarly, we have the following example:

(16)  From an interview with an 8-year-old girl:
        [WPC enters the room]
WPC:  I'm WPC [name] and I'm at [location]. The date today is
        [date] and the time is [time]. Today, I'm going to monitor a
        video interview between WDC [name] and [name of
        child]. In the monitoring room with me will be social
        worker [name], [name of child]'s mother [name] and her
        father [name]. The next people to enter this room will be
        [name of child] and WDC [name].
        [Child and interviewer enter the room]
I:      Right then, OK?
C:      [Nods].
I:      What do you fancy doing?
C:      [Silence].
I:      Shall we get some paper out?
C:      [Nods].
I:      Right, do you know where it is?
C:      [Nods].
I:      Let's have a look.
C:      Colouring books.
I:      Right, which one do you like?
C:      I'll need some pens.
I:      Do you want the felt pens out or just the pencils?
C:      Pens.
I:      Right and there's one underneath I think as well, isn't
        there? Right then, there we go, do you want this one as
        well?
C:      [Nods].

> I:      Shall I sit there? Do you want to sit there?
> C:      [Sits down].

If we contrast the above two exchanges (15 and 16) with the previous two (13 and 14), we clearly see how much easier it can be when the preliminary information is dealt with before the child enters the room. Instead of being burdened by giving information to the camera, the interviewer can begin by putting the child at ease, by making the child the centre of attention and ensuring that he is settled with an appropriate activity. Notice that in the second two exchanges, the children are guided towards very suitable toys (the playdough and colouring books, respectively). Left to their own devices, children will often choose less suitable toys. We will return to the issue of appropriate toys later in this chapter. Our attention now turns to the first of the Memorandum's recommended phases: the rapport phase.

## THE RAPPORT PHASE

The Memorandum (:15) states that "the main aim of the first phase of the interview is to build up a rapport between the interviewer and the child in which the child is helped to relax and feel as comfortable as possible in the interview situation". To facilitate this, the Memorandum (:16) suggests that "with younger children, a rapport phase may involve some play with toys, drawing or colouring to help the child relax and or to interact with the interviewer". In addition, the Memorandum (:15/16) suggests a number of additional functions which this phase can fulfil. It is suggested that these functions include:

- supplementation of "the interviewer's knowledge about the child's social, emotional and cognitive development and particularly about his or her communication skills and degree of understanding" (:15/16),
- explanation of the reason for the interview,
- reassurance that the child has done nothing wrong,
- explanation of the camera equipment,
- emphasis of the need to speak the truth, and
- indication of the "acceptability of saying 'I don't know' or 'I don't understand'".

We will now address each of the above functions of the rapport phase in turn:

# Building an Effective Rapport

The need for an effective rapport phase is clearly justified if we consider the burden that an interview places on the child. Often, the child will be unused to talking for such a length of time, particularly to a relative stranger. The setting will be unfamiliar (however comfortable) and the information to be conveyed to the interviewer is often both distressing and embarrassing. Given these factors, it is vital that an effective rapport is established between the interviewer and the child. As we have already suggested, one way that this can be achieved is by ensuring that the child is the central focus of the interviewer's attention right from the start of the interview and that play activities are chosen together. What other factors contribute to effective rapport building?

## *Discussion topics*

A key factor to consider is the topics that might be discussed during this phase. Our data suggest that there are a number of topics that children can respond well to and these can be useful in the rapport phase. As with adults, productive topics of conversation depend very much on the individual. For example, one person might like watching football and so be happy to talk about their team's last win, another might enjoy line dancing, whilst another may have no particular interests. If possible then, part of the interview planning should include eliciting (perhaps from caretakers) information about what the child enjoys doing, whether the child has any pets and whether or not the child enjoys school. Such information will allow the interviewer to identify a productive topic of conversation for use with an individual child. In the following examples, we see how different topics of conversation work well with different children.

*School*
In the following interview, we see that the topic of school is particularly productive:

(17)   From an interview with an 8-year-old girl:
      I:        What do you like doing in school?
      C:      Colouring.
      I:        Colouring?
      C:      Drawing.

| I: | And drawing? So, you're good at drawing are you? You'll have to draw me a picture after, won't you. Do you think you could do that? |
|----|----|
| C: | Yeah. |
| I: | So, what other things do you like doing in school? |
| C: | Doing stories. |
| I: | Reading stories? |
| C: | Doing them, writing them. |
| I: | Writing them, that's good. What kind of things do you write about? |
| C: | Do adventure stories. |
| I: | You do adventure stories. Do you do those yourself, do you? |
| C: | [Nods]. |
| I: | I wish I could do that. |
| C: | I give them to my teacher as well to read. |
| I: | Oh do you? Does she read them out to the class? |
| C: | Sometimes. |
| I: | So, you like reading and writing and drawing. |
| C: | Yeah. |
| I: | What about, are you any good at maths? |
| C: | [Nods]. |
| I: | Yeah? 'Coz I saw your school report, didn't I? |
| C: | I'm almost on book four of those books. |
| I: | Are you? That's good, isn't it? And how many As did you have in your report? |
| C: | 16. |

Notice that in the above exchange, the interviewer reveals that she has seen the child's school report. The child has been doing very well in school and is clearly proud of her achievements. However, this enthusiasm for school will not be apparent with all children as the following extract shows. Therefore, an idea of how the individual child feels about school prior to the interview may well be useful.

(18)  From an interview with a 9-year-old boy:

| I: | Right. So, what do you think about missing this afternoon's school? |
|----|----|
| C: | Good. |
| I: | I see, don't you like school? |
| C: | No. |
| I: | You don't? |
| C: | It's boring. |

Where children do not enjoy or are reticent about discussing school, other topics of conversation need to be explored.

*Friends*
Again, the effectiveness of this topic will depend to a large extent on the individual child. Some, for example, may claim to have no friends as the following extract illustrates:

(19)   From an interview with a 3-year-old girl:
       I:      Have you got any friends?
       C:      No.
       I:      Haven't you?
       C:      No.

In contrast, other children will have large circles of friends. The boy in the following extract has two close friends who he is keen to talk about:

(20)   From an interview with a 7-year-old boy:
       I:      All right then, what are your friends at school called?
       C:      Got loads of friends.
       I:      Have you? Have you got a best friend?
       C:      Yeah [name] 'coz he lives next door to me.
       I:      Oh.
       C:      And he's seven and he's in my class as well.
       I:      Oh, that's good, isn't it? Do you go to school with [name]?
       C:      I take him on my bike.
       I:      Oh.
       C:      And he comes on his bike and I go to his house and then I
               got another friend and he just hops on to my bike and then
               I take him on the back.

*Toys and hobbies*
Many children will have favourite toys that they will be keen to discuss. Again, prior, "insider" knowledge can be helpful here as the following extract (where the interviewer has visited the child's house and has seen his toys) shows:

(21)   From an interview with a 9-year-old boy:
       I:      Well, you know I went to your house this morning and I
               talked to your mum and you were in school, weren't you?
               Do you know where I saw in your house?

C:    No.

I:    Your bedroom and I saw all the things in there, so I know you like to play with action man, don't you?

C:    [Nods].

I:    What else do you like to play with?

C:    Power Rangers.

I:    Oh, I didn't see the Power Rangers. I saw the action man 'coz he was in his jeep and I saw a guitar there as well, what can you tell me about that?

C:    I play songs on it sometimes in the summer holidays.

I:    That's good. So, what other things do you like to do?

C:    I like to go out and play football with my friends.

I:    Yeah.

C:    Play on my Sega.

Similarly, some children will have particular hobbies which can be a fruitful topic of conversation.

(22)   From an interview with a 9-year-old boy:

I:    And what sort of things do you like doing when you're not in school?

C:    I go to football on Thursday and I play a match, not every Sunday. Like last week, I just went training.

I:    So, which football team do you support?

C:    Manchester United.

I:    Do you?

C:    My room's full of the posters. I've covered my wardrobe. I'm just starting on my door.

I:    Golly!

C:    And I've still got three books with lots of posters in.

I:    You must be a real fan. Who's your favourite player?

C:    Giggs and my favourite goalkeeper is Peter Schmeichel.

Of course, not all children have specific interests and in these cases a productive topic can be television and videos.

*Television, videos and films*
The majority of children will have a favourite television programme or video that they like to watch so this can be a useful topic where little is known about the child.

(23)   From an interview with a 5-year-old girl:

I:        And what sort of tapes do you watch?
C:       *Dumbo* and *Mickey Mouse* and *Ghost*.
I:        And what's the best bit in *Dumbo*?
C:       Where, er, he flies.
I:        Yeah?
C:       Birds make him fly.
I:        And what sort of animal is Dumbo?
C:       An elephant.

*Pets*
Often children who have pets will be keen to talk about them.

(24)   From an interview with a 9-year-old boy:

I:        Who is there in your house?
C:       My mum and [name of brother].
I:        Just the three of you?
C:       And some birds.
I:        And some birds? What birds have you got?
C:       Five.
I:        What birds are they?
C:       I've got a baby chick, two love birds that had the baby chick, a few eggs and two budgies.
I:        Have you? And where do you keep those?
C:       In a cage, in the house.
I:        And have you got names for them?
C:       Yeah.
I:        And what do you have to feed them on?
C:       Birdseed.

*Holidays and Christmas*
At the appropriate times of year, holidays and Christmas can also be productive topics of conversation.

(25)   From an interview with a 7-year-old boy:

I:        Have you been on holiday this year?
C:       Yeah.
I:        Where've you been?
C:       To [place].
I:        And where's that?
C:       In [place].

| I: | Oh, how did you get there? |
|---|---|

I:      Oh, how did you get there?
C:      By car, with a caravan on the back.
I:      Oh right, is it your caravan?
C:      Yeah.
I:      Bet that was good fun, wasn't it? Is it good fun sleeping in a caravan?
C:      Yeah.
I:      I've never slept in a caravan.
C:      I slept in the bunk bed this year.
I:      Which bunk did you sleep in?
C:      The top bunk.
I:      Oh, was it a long way up?
C:      [Nods].
I:      Yeah? Weren't you frightened of falling out?

(26)    From an interview with a 5-year-old girl:

I:      Have you got a Christmas tree up at home?
C:      Yeah.
I:      Has it got anything on it?
C:      Decorations up and Christmas lights.
I:      And who put that up?
C:      My mummy and me.
I:      And you?
C:      Yeah.
I:      What did you do? Which bit did you do?
C:      The bit, the bit where there was a Santa on it.

There are three general points to note with reference to these types of exchanges. First, personalized comments from the interviewer can be good for establishing rapport. For example in (17) the interviewer says she wishes she could write adventure stories like the child. Similarly, in (25) the interviewer says that she's never slept in a caravan. Where appropriate, these comments can help to keep the conversation going and also help the child to feel that it is not just he who is revealing details about himself.

Second, some older children (e.g. 10 years and above) may feel that the rapport phase is a waste of time. In the following exchange, for example, the child is clearly impatient to tell his story and go home!

(27)    From an interview with a 10-year-old boy:

I:      This interview is being recorded at [place]. My name is WPC [name]. Would you like to give your name?

S/W:   My name's [name] and I'm a social worker with [place]
       social services.
C:     My name's [name].
I:     I'm just going to give the time and date. The date is [date]
       and the time is [time]. OK, so it's [name] have you got a
       middle name [name]?
C:     [Name].
I:     [Child's full name]. Right, OK.
C:     I was wanting to move in with my dad.
I:     Oh, it's a bit quick actually, I was going to just ask you a
       few general questions first.
C:     OK, go on then.

Later in the same interview:

I:     The cameras might move a bit if we move at all but don't
       be put off by it through the interview.
C:     It won't be long, will it?
I:     Well, no but if you want to go out to have a drink.
C:     No, I'm alright, we won't be that long.

Clearly, in a case such as this, the rapport phase needs to be minimized
so that the child is not discouraged from telling his story.

A third point to note is that often conversation topics such as school,
friends and holidays are only effective with older children. There are
two key reasons for this. First, some topics (e.g. school and hobbies) are
unfamiliar for some younger children (i.e. some under sixes) as these are
outside their experience. Second, this type of interaction isn't common
for young children. Hence, we have seen exchanges such as the
following:

(28)   From an interview with a 3-year-old girl:

I:     Do you want to tell me a bit about yourself?
C:     No.

For such a young child, this kind of interaction based on an open topic
(effectively, "tell me *anything* about yourself") is inappropriate because
it is not the type of interaction that she is used to. Therefore, with
younger children (the under sixes) a discussion about the "here and
now" – a more familiar type of interaction for younger children – is
likely to be more productive. By a "here and now" interaction, we mean
a conversation based on what the child is doing at the time of the

conversation rather than on a more abstract or open topic. One way to facilitate this kind of interaction is through the use of toys. In the following exchange we see that a discussion about playdough facilitates rapport building:

(29)   From an interview with a 4-year-old girl:

      C:     There's the playdough.
      I:     Yeah, what are we going to have a play with then?
      C:     These.
      I:     OK.
      C:     These are all.
      I:     Has it gone hard?
      C:     These are all mixed up.
      I:     Oh, it's OK, that one's a bit mixed up as well but we can have a play with them anyway, can't we?
      C:     Yeah.
      I:     And there's some pens, we can have a play with those later.
      C:     We can make a cake with it.
      I:     Yeah.
      C:     Couldn't we?
      I:     That'd be good.
      C:     Roll it.
      I:     You're very busy there. What kind of cake are you going to make?
      C:     A little cake. Oh, look at that there.
      I:     So, do you like this house then?
      C:     Yeah.

In this interview, it is the initial game with the playdough which breaks the ice and is a key to the establishment of a rapport between the child and the interviewer.

## Using toys to facilitate rapport

Our recommendation that toys can be useful is not, however, uncon-ditional. There are instances where toys can be unhelpful. For example, children can become engrossed in some toys (e.g. puzzles) and this can lead to lapses in concentration. Similarly, cupboards full of toys can be a distraction and can cause children to move back and forth selecting one toy after another. In one instance, we saw a child play with 11 different toys (ranging from jigsaws to building blocks) in a single interview.

A further point to consider is whether the toy is suitable for the child's age. In one interview, we saw a 3-year-old girl becoming increasingly frustrated by jigsaws and puzzles which were beyond her because they were clearly designed for older children. When she was unable to cope with an unsuitable toy or puzzle, she became increasingly frustrated:

(30)   From an interview with a 3-year-old girl:

    C:      Jigsaw.
    I:       Is it a jigsaw? I think that's a difficult game. Let's have a look at it. Do you know who these people are?
    C:      Yeah.
    I:       Who's that?
    C:      No.
    I:       It says here that that's Mr Tickle.
    C:      What do you have to do with them?
    I:       This looks like a difficult one, you know. I think you take those little counters out.
    C:      Yeah.
    I:       And then, I think, you have to go like this, look.
    C:      Yeah.
    I:       Like that.
    C:      Yeah.
    I:       It's called tiddlywinks, it's a bit difficult to do though, isn't it?
    C:      No, do you have to put them.
    I:       Do you want to get something else?
    C:      This.
    I:       Come on then, let's have a look at that one.
    C:      What them for?
    I:       I think those are called paper-clips, they're for sticking things together, like that.
    C:      Let me, like that? Like this?
    I:       It's a bit difficult to do, isn't it?
    C:      Put them back.

Later in the same interview, we see how the child's struggle with difficult toys distracts her from the interviewer's questions which, in turn, distracts the interviewer from pursuing her questions:

    I:       Well, who lives with you then?
    C:      Can't do this [jigsaw].
    I:       Shall I have a go for you?

C:      And me can do this, where this go?

I:      You might not be able to fit that one in yet.

Moments later . . .

I:      So, who's come with you today then?

C:      My nanny. Oh, I can't put that [jigsaw].

I:      Who's come with you today, to here today?

C:      My nanny.

I:      Your nanny?

C:      Can't do it.

I:      Shall I do it then? Oh, it doesn't fit, does it? We need another piece for there. Let's see what we can do here. I tell you what, let's see if we can find any more pieces like that. Any more pieces with red on, like that.

C:      I do [becoming frustrated].

I:      OK, you do it [child wanders off to toy cupboard] don't you want to finish this one first?

C:      Then we can do this one, yeah?

I:      You want to do this one?

C:      Yeah.

I:      I think for this one, you need a special board that we haven't got but, we can have a look at some of the letters.

C:      No, we don't want to do that.

I:      You don't want to do that?

C:      Want to do them.

I:      I tell you what, do you want the paper and pencils?

C:      Want to do that.

I:      Come on then.

C:      No, don't want to do them, want to do that drawing.

I:      Can you manage? Shall we draw your house?

C:      You have to draw, yeah?

I:      Right, you tell me what you want to draw then.

C:      No, I draw first.

In this case, age-inappropriate toys have an unsettling effect on the child and she becomes increasingly frustrated which is clearly counter-productive. We would suggest that toys such as colouring books (suitable for different age groups and with suitable colouring materials, e.g. simple pictures with chunky crayons for younger children, more sophisticated pictures and felt-tips or pencils for older children), jigsaws (again a variety for different age groups) and soft toys are amongst the most appropriate. We would also suggest that it is often helpful if the interviewer guides the child towards an age-appropriate toy rather than giving the child a free choice of a large number of toys (some of which will be too sophisticated for him to cope with). Unsuitable toys include those which demand too much of the child's attention (as in the above exchanges) and noisy toys such as wooden building bricks played with on table tops. An illustrative example of the problems such toys can present can be seen in the following:

(31)   From an interview with a 4-year-old girl:

      I:     And how old's [name of child's sister]?
      C:    Six [dropping building blocks onto a wooden topped table].
      I:     I don't think we'd better do that! Do you remember [names] are in the monitoring room, next door?
      C:    Yeah.
      I:     Well, they're in that room next door where the telly is and if we drop those bricks on the table, we're going to deafen them, aren't we? We'll make their ears hurt.

Of course, in addition to the problems of noisy toys which the interviewer points out in the above exchange, they also obscure the sound recording and thus should be avoided. We now focus on the additional functions of the rapport phase (listed earlier) and we address each of these in turn.

## Assessing Development

As we noted earlier, the Memorandum highlights the role of the rapport phase in supplementing the interviewer's knowledge about the child's social, emotional, cognitive and communicative development. Interviewers need to be able to gauge the child's ability in order to ensure that appropriate questions are asked and appropriate interpretations of the child's responses derived.

In our data, the most frequent methods of gauging the child's cognitive development are assessments of colour naming and arithmetical ability. Certainly, it is true that these are indicators of cognitive development but, are they the best indicators of the aspects of development which are important in an interview and to which the interviewer needs to tune in? Our data suggest that, in fact, these indicators may not be the key to assessing the child's ability as an interviewee and certainly, there are other clues to more relevant aspects of the child's development which

would be a better focus for interviewers. In the following exchanges, we
see both arithmetical ability and colour naming tested:

(32)   From an interview with a 6-year-old boy:

     I:       If I have one pen and I put that down here.
     C:      Yeah.
     I:       And if I add, this is a bit tricky this, see if you can do this
             one. If I add how many more pens?
     C:      One, two, three [counting as the interviewer adds pens to
             a pile] four [giving total].
     I:       If I add three more pens, how many will there be all
             together?
     C:      Four [correct].
     I:       If I add two more pens to those four, how many are there
             altogether?
     C:      Easy, one, two, three, four, five, six.
     I:       OK.
     C:      Six.
     I:       If I take three of those pens away, how many are left?
     C:      Three.
     I:       Good.
     S/W:   You said that without even counting them.

Later in the same interview:

     I:       What are you like at colours? Do you know your colours?
     C:      That's easy.
     I:       Well, I've got some here so let's see if you can tell us what
             these colours are?
     C:      Orange [then, as interviewer shows more pens] yellow,
             blue, green.
     I:       What colour's this one?
     C:      Red, yellow, pink.
     I:       You're too good, well done.

These error-free responses to tests of arithmetical and colour naming
ability may be taken as positive indicators of ability. However, these
types of ability do not always correspond with the child's ability to give
a full account of alleged events. In this case, for example, the child was a
"poor" interviewee in that he failed to concentrate, was reticent in
discussing personal matters and made no disclosure (this was despite
independent evidence that the child had important information to

disclose). Our evidence also suggests that, conversely, a child who gives a poor performance on an arithmetical test is not always a poor interviewee:

(33)   From an interview with a 9-year-old girl:

| | |
|---|---|
| I: | What about tables? |
| C: | I can do twos, fives and 10s and threes. |
| I: | Which one are you going to do for me now? |
| C: | Twos. |
| I: | Go on then, show me how clever you are. |
| C: | One twos are two, two twos are four, three twos are six, four twos are 10, five twos are 12, six twos are. |
| I: | You're getting a little bit confused there now. You've missed out one figure and you've said another figure twice. Go back to three twos are? |
| C: | Six, four twos are eight . . . eight twos are 16, nine twos are 20. |
| I: | Not quite, nine twos are? |
| C: | 16. |
| I: | What comes after 16? |
| C: | 18. |
| I: | What's the last one? |
| C: | 20. |

From the above alone, it might be assumed that this child would struggle to provide a coherent event account. In fact, this was not the case:

(34)   I:   You tell me everything you can remember and everything you want to tell me so I'll scribble some little notes down and maybe ask you some questions, is that OK?

C:   [Nods] Sometimes he [child has already stated that it is her grandfather who she wishes to talk about] makes us put our bra and knickers on and some long socks and then he, and then he says, "Stay in those" and then he says, "Put apples in them to make them look big" and then I said, "No" and sometimes he keeps dragging me in bed and he keeps kissing my lips and he keeps putting me in shorts and t-shirts.

This child also went on to perform well in the specific questioning phase, providing clear descriptions of where and how events took place.

If arithmetical and colour naming ability are not always reliable indicators of performance, how might interviewers gauge the child's ability? We would suggest that in most rapport phases, clear indicators of the child's ability as an interviewee exist without the need to resort to specific "testing". To illustrate this, we compare various extracts from two interviews. One is with a 5-year-old girl, the other with a 6-year-old girl. Both girls are reporting the same abusive event at which both were present and both were victims. Both interviews are conducted by the same interviewer. When asked arithmetical questions, both girls perform similarly well:

(35)   From an interview with a 5-year-old girl:

    I:       So, what's one add one?
    C:      Two.
    I:       What's two add two?
    C:      Four.
    I:       What's four add two?
    C:      Six.
    I:       Well done. Do you do take aways as well?
    C:      Yeah.
    I:       What's three take away one?
    C:      Two.
    I:       What's five take away two?
    C:      Three.

(36)   From an interview with a 6-year-old girl:

    I:       OK, so if I said to you what's two add two?
    C:      Four.
    I:       So what's two add five?
    C:      Seven.
    I:       So what's five take away three?
    C:      Two.

From these "test" performances, it could be assumed that the two girls will be equally good witnesses and perform equally well in the interview. In fact, this is not the case. First, we consider the girls' free narrative accounts. The 5-year-old girl provided the following account:

(37)   C:   Em, well, we went to show him our picture and he said, "Do you want to see my willy?" and I said, "Yeah". Then he said if you do and he wanted us to open it, like that and then he got his finger and he put his hand in there.

The 6-year-old provided the following account:

(38)  C:      Well, we went to [name of alleged abuser]'s with some
              pictures and we were sitting down watching TV and
              [name of other child] said, "Can we see your willy" and he
              said, "Can I see, er, yours first" and he started sniffing and
              he kept on doing that and then he did it [child has already
              said he put his finger inside her] and he went up to the
              bathroom and he did it and then he came downstairs and
              did it again and then he stopped.

In terms of length, the 6-year-old girl's account is slightly longer. More
significantly, it is the 6-year-old who provides more specific information
(e.g. she names the alleged abuser and she states exactly where the
events took place). The 6-year-old also goes on to provide better answers
in the specific questioning phase. Consider the following, for example:

(39)  From the 5-year-old:

      I:      What time was it? Do you know?
      C:      No.

(40)  From the 6-year-old:

      I:      What time did this happen?
      C:      I think three o'clock.

(41)  From the 5-year-old:

      I:      Describe, what did his willy look like?
      C:      It was big.
      I:      Was it?
      C:      [Nods].
      I:      Anything else you remember about it?
      C:      No.

(42)  From the 6-year-old:

      I:      OK, can you describe his willy? What did it look like?
      C:      Hairy.
      I:      How big was it?
      C:      About that big.

The tests of numerical ability reported earlier did nothing to indicate
that the 6-year-old would be a better witness than the 5-year-old.
However, an examination of other aspects of the rapport phase reveals
some interesting indicators of ability which highlight differences

between the two girls. First of all, if we compare the two girls' ability to answer general questions at the start of the interview:

(43)   From the 5-year-old girl:

    I:      Do you know how to tell the time?
    C:      No.
    I:      OK, well the time on my watch is four, 40 and do you know what day it is today?
    C:      [Shakes head].

(44)   From the 6-year-old girl:

    I:      Can you tell the time?
    C:      A bit, I'm learning.
    I:      Do you think you could tell the time on my watch there?
    C:      Half past three.
    I:      That's right and what day is it today?
    C:      Friday.
    I:      And do you know what the date is?
    C:      Friday the 4th.

Clearly, the 6-year-old girl is far more aware of time concepts than the 5-year-old girl. The girls' performances on questions relating to time in the rapport phase (seen in (43) and (44) above) are clear predictors of their ability to answer questions relating to time in the specific questioning phase (illustrated by the data in (39) and (40) above).

In terms of narrative ability, we also see early indicators of competence in the rapport phase. Compare the following exchanges:

(45)   From the 5-year-old girl:

    I:      Before we start talking about that, I just want to know a little bit about you really. What can you tell me about yourself?
    C:      I don't know.

(46)   From the 6-year-old girl:

    I:      So, tell me a little bit about yourself.
    C:      Well, I play a lot with [name] 'coz she lives about three houses away from me.

In (45) we see that the child is either reluctant to reveal personal details or that she isn't a particularly competent narrator. In (46) in contrast, we see that the child is happy to construct a short narrative account. These differences may be taken as indicators of the girls' differing abilities to produce the narrative event accounts that we saw in (37) and (38) above. We would suggest then that rather than using the child's arithmetical and colour naming abilities to infer interviewee competence, other indicators of likely interviewee performance are available within the rapport phase. Some of these indicators are shown in Table 1.

We turn now to a further additional function of the rapport phase.

## Explanation of the Reason for the Interview

When considering this aspect of the rapport phase, it is important to note that different children will have different initial concepts of why the interview is taking place. We can contrast the following exchanges to illustrate this:

(47)   From an interview with a 6-year-old girl:

I:      So, we've come here today for a special reason, haven't we?
C:      [Nods].
I:      Why've we come here?
C:      'Coz a boy's been bad.

(48)   From an interview with a 9-year-old boy:

I:      Do you know why you've come here today?
C:      Yeah.
I:      And why is that?
C:      Because I got attacked down an alley by a man or it could have been a teenager. He looked a little bit bigger than my dad so the policeman put down 6'1" because my dad's 6'.
I:      Right.

In these examples, the children clearly know the issues that their interviews are going to address but may not be fully aware of the evidential function of the interview. In contrast, the 6-year-old boy in the following exchange demonstrates very limited overall awareness:

(49)   I:      OK [name] do you know why you're here today?
        C:      Em.
        I:      Why?
        C:      I play with toys.

**Table 1**

| FEATURE OF THE RAPPORT PHASE | INDICATIVE OF |
|---|---|
| Questions about time and date (e.g. the time and date of the interview or of significant dates like the child's birthday) | Ability to relate when an abusive event took place in terms of time and date. Certainly, if the child is unable to say what time/date the interview is taking place it is unlikely that he will be able to say time/date of abusive incident. If child can say only when his birthday is, it is likely that he will only be able to state time/date of abusive event in relational terms (e.g. before birthday/after Christmas) |
| Questions about persons present (Can you remember who else is in the house?) | Ability to recall peripheral details. At an interview, the child may take little notice of police-officers or social workers who are going to monitor the interview or keep parents company. This may be indicative of the type of information the child will recall about abusive events (e.g. if it didn't have a direct impact on the child he might not remember it. For example, if the child is asked what mummy – in a different room at the time – was doing when an event took place) |
| Questions about location (e.g. where do you go to school?) | Ability to relate where abusive events took place. A child who finds it difficult to relate the location of his school may well find it difficult to relate location(s) of events |
| Other wh-questions | As we discuss in Chapter 4, there is a clear order of acquisition of wh-question types (e.g. *what* is understood before *when*). The interviewer should monitor the child's answers to these types of questions. If a child fails to answer why-questions in the rapport phase it is unlikely that he will be able to say why the abusive incident took place |
| Personal details | If the child is reticent in revealing personal details (e.g. who he lives with) this may well be a precursor of reticence to disclose |
| Ability to answer questions about how he feels about non-abusive events (e.g. how do you feel about your birthday or about missing school?) | Ability to answer questions relating to feelings about the abuse/abuser. A child who is unable to say how he feels about a neutral topic or who gives a general answer such as *all right* or *OK* may perform similarly when asked how he feels about the abuse/abuser. We return to this issue in Chapter 5 |

*continues overleaf*

**Table 1**  *cont.*

| FEATURE OF THE RAPPORT PHASE | INDICATIVE OF |
| --- | --- |
| Free narrative ability | A child who provides a clear "neutral" free narrative account (e.g. about what he likes to do in his spare time, or what he has done at school) has the ability to provide a clear free narrative about abusive events. Of course, the intimate nature of events to be reported may make the abusive event free narrative more difficult (and thus less productive) than the neutral free narrative. We discuss free narrative accounts further in Chapter 3 |

These children's different initial conceptions about their interviews illustrate that different approaches are often needed when explaining the function of an interview to a child. In (47) and (48) the children have made disclosures and the interviewer can therefore explain that the child is right about the substance of the interview and that the function of the interview is to discuss this matter and anything else which the child is unhappy about and with which the interviewer may be able to help.

In contrast, in (49) the child offers no indication that he is aware of the matters to be discussed (in this case, there has been prior disclosure from a sibling) and so the interviewer must be more vague in outlining the function of the interview. In this instance, she told the child that she believed (from his brother) that the child was unhappy about something and that she would like him to tell her if he was unhappy so that she could help him.

## Reassurance that the Child has done Nothing Wrong

Following on directly from the explanation of the function of the interview, it is important to reassure the child that he has done nothing wrong. In light of the data we present later (Chapter 5) this reassurance is clearly justified. In Chapter 5, we show that children often assume that because they are speaking to a police-officer, they must have done something wrong and are in trouble. Given this misperception, it is vital that, at the start of the interview, the child is reassured that he has done nothing wrong and that he is not in any kind of trouble. We return to this issue in Chapter 5 but, as examples of how the child might be reassured that he has done nothing wrong, consider the following extracts:

(50)  From an interview with a 4-year-old girl:

    I:      Lots of children talk to me and they don't worry about what they've told me and they tell me about different things that have happened to them and I won't be cross or shout at them and I won't be angry and the children are not in any trouble and you won't be in any trouble.

(51)  I:      Now, you've been brought here today to talk to me but not because you've done anything wrong. You're not in any trouble, do you understand that? You're not here because you've been naughty or anything because you haven't, OK?

    C:     Yeah.

# Explanation of the Camera Equipment

The Memorandum (1992: 16) recommends that the interview suite camera equipment should be explained to the child within the rapport phase. The importance of this explanation is emphasized by our survey results (Aldridge & Wood 1997a) which reveal that some interviewers are concerned about the presence of camera equipment in that this can make some children wary of disclosure. Intuitively, it could be argued that children are familiar with video and similar technology as part of their everyday lives and that, therefore, they should be comfortable with the interview suite equipment. However, we would voice particular concern about the potentially distressing effect of the camera equipment on those children who have been photographed as part of their abusive experience. In addition, our data illustrate the need for explanation of the camera equipment by highlighting some of the confusions about the nature and function of the camera equipment which can arise:

(52)  From an interview with a 6-year-old boy:

    C:     Who are you talking to now?

    S/W:  Still talking to the camera.

    C:     How can you talk to the camera?

    I:      Well, I've just been talking to the camera. Did you see it?

    C:     No.

    I:      Did you see me when I was talking to the camera and I was looking at it?

    C:     Yeah.

    I:      Now then, what we're going to do next.

C:     Talk to the camera again.
I:     Is em, while I'm . . . the camera can see what we're doing here in this room. I'll explain a little bit about that.
S/W:   I think he doesn't understand how it can hear.
I:     Right, you see these things here [microphones]?
C:     Yeah.
I:     These are called microphones and they send a message through to [name] in the room next door.
C:     Em.
I:     And it records everything that we say.
C:     [Goes over to the wall and shouts down the microphone!] Hello.
S/W:   I wouldn't shout too loud.
C:     [Shouts down microphone again] Hello.

Later [25 minutes into the interview]

C:     Are you going to put me in the video camera yet?
I:     Well, the video camera's working now, it's on.
C:     Already on?
S/W:   Yeah.
I:     It's already on from when we started talking, OK?

There are two sources of potential confusion about the video equipment. Firstly, the nature of the video equipment can be unclear for some children (that is, how the equipment works). For others, the difficulty lies in the function of the equipment (that is, why the equipment is working). The following extract illustrates how the nature of the camera equipment might be explained:

(53)   From an interview with a 5-year-old boy:
I:     Now I'll just explain a little bit about how this is working now, this interview. Can you see that little camera up there?
C:     [Nods].
I:     That's actually filming us now and the people in the room next door can see us through a little telly screen, yeah?
C:     [Nods].
I:     'Coz that camera joins up with that telly screen so they can actually see us now on that telly screen in the other little room, OK?
C:     [Nods].

I:  And it's recording everything that we're saying because there's two little microphones, one over there and one on that wall there and that picks up everything that we're saying as well.
C:  [Laughs].
I:  Do you think that's clever? It's good, isn't it?
C:  Yeah.

Clearly, such an explanation is facilitated by a visit to, and description of, the monitoring room prior to the interview. In terms of the function of the video equipment (and the interview itself), an explanation along the following lines may well be appropriate:

(54)  From an interview with a 7-year-old girl:

I:  Do you remember me pointing that out to you up there?
C:  [Nods].
I:  What did I say it was?
C:  A camera.
I:  A camera, that's right. Now, that camera is taking pictures of us while we're talking.
C:  Why?
I:  Why, right, because I want to ask you some questions while you're here today, OK and to save me writing them down and to save you having to repeat everything again. If we film it on camera and we make it into a video then it's there for ever, isn't it and it saves having to do it again. Are you happy about that?
C:  [Nods].

In some instances, if the interviewer is wearing an earpiece, further explanation of equipment may be required. Appropriate explanation may be along the following lines:

(55)  From an interview with a 10-year-old boy:

I:  Now, I've got this little thing here and it's called an earpiece and I didn't get a chance to show you this before, did I?
C:  No.
I:  Well, if [name of officer in monitoring room] speaks into that, I'll be able to hear him through this little earpiece here. So, if I put this to your ear and get [name of officer in the monitoring room] to speak to you, you'll be able to hear him.

C:      [Laughs].
I:      What did [name of officer in monitoring room] say?
C:      He said make something good for him.
I:      With the lego?
C:      Yeah.

# Emphasis of the Need to Speak the Truth

As noted earlier, the Memorandum recommends that the need to speak the truth should be emphasized within the rapport phase. Our data suggest that in providing this emphasis, interviewers often ask children to differentiate between telling the truth and telling lies. The difficulties which are often encountered within this strategy are highlighted by our survey results (Aldridge & Wood 1997a, reported in Chapter 1) which suggest that some interviewers consider this to be the most difficult part of the interview. In addition, our interview data suggest that this is not always a successful strategy. The following examples are illustrative:

(56)    From an interview with a 4-year-old girl:

I:      Now, I talk to lots of children but, do you know what I like them to tell me?
C:      Yeah.
I:      Only about things that have really happened. Do you know what that means?
C:      Yeah.
I:      What does it mean then?
C:      If you're naughty.

(57)    From an interview with a 5-year-old girl:

I:      Do you know what telling the truth means?
C:      Em.
I:      What does it mean?
C:      Er, talking the sense.
I:      Talking the sense, yeah. What is it when you don't tell the truth? What do you do then?
C:      You be mad.
I:      You've been mad. What about telling lies, telling fibs?
C:      [Silence].

(58)    From an interview with another 5-year-old girl:

I:      Do you know what telling lies is?
C:      It's when, it's when you're, you're not allowed to say it.

I:    OK.
C:    And you say, and you say a naughty word.
I:    Can you think of anything that would be a lie?
C:    Em . . . swearing.
I:    Em.
C:    And saying nothing, that's it, I think, I think.

(59)   From an interview with a 6-year-old boy:

I:    Do you know about telling the truth?
C:    No.
I:    Do you know what a lie is?
C:    Tigers.
I:    Tyres?
C:    Tigers.

(60)   From an interview with a 9-year-old girl:

I:    So, if I was to say, "[Name of child], when we come here, we have to tell the truth", do you know what that means – telling the truth?
C:    It's like, you tell a lie and you wanna be . . . oh, I forgot.
I:    Well, shall we start with what's a lie?
C:    Yeah.
I:    Can you tell me what a lie is?
C:    When people say there's something behind you, a monster's behind you and they be try to tell them that they want to scare them and they say, "You're a liar" like that.

From these examples, a variety of difficulties become apparent. In (57) and (58), we see that children's understanding of misdemeanours can be overgeneralized so that being naughty, swearing and lying are seen as broadly the same. In (59) the potential problem of inattention is highlighted. And in (60) we see that, even for older children, it is not easy to offer a definition of telling the truth versus telling lies. These observations are supported by experimental data from our study of 4–8-year-old children's ability to describe telling the truth and telling lies. Experimental findings from our language game suggest that it is difficult for 4–8-year-olds to provide an effective description of either telling the truth or telling lies. For example, we found that none of our 4-year-olds could provide a correct description of either of the concepts. This rose to 87.5% of 8-year-olds for both concepts. Interestingly, at the ages of 6 and 7 years, we found that the children found it easier to describe what it means to tell lies than to describe what it means to tell the truth. This corresponds with previous findings from other researchers. For example Bussey (1992) suggested that young children's appreciation of lying as "naughty" exceeds their appreciation of the value of truthfulness.

Notice also that we addressed the concepts of telling the truth and telling lies separately. That is, we didn't ask the children to describe the difference between telling the truth and telling lies. Instead, we asked them first what telling a lie means and then what telling the truth means. A comparison of our findings with those of a previous study (Pipe & Wilson 1994 where the two concepts were addressed together) indicates that it is easier for children to address these concepts separately.

However, the most significant finding from our study is that children give a much clearer indication of their understanding of the concepts of telling the truth and telling lies if they are given examples of these to identify rather than being asked for descriptions of the two. For example, although none of our 4-year-olds was able to describe correctly either telling the truth or telling lies, 37.5% of them could correctly identify an example of telling a lie and 18.75% of them could correctly identify an example of telling the truth. Similarly, 87.5% of 8-year-olds could correctly describe both telling the truth and telling lies. In contrast, 100% of the 8-year-olds could identify examples of telling the truth and telling lies.

The nature of the examples of telling the truth and telling lies that children are given to identify is also important. This is illustrated by a comparison of our experimental findings with those of the Pipe & Wilson (1994) study. In our study the children performed better in identifying examples of telling the truth and telling lies than the same age children in the Pipe & Wilson study. This may well be due to the nature of the examples given. In the Pipe & Wilson (1994) study, the children were given abstract examples (such as, "If I said you were 12 years old would that be the truth or a lie?" addressed to a 6-year-old). In our study more concrete examples utilizing toys the children were playing with were used (e.g. referring to a model classroom with children and their teacher with which we were playing, we asked, "If I said the teacher was standing up would that be the truth or a lie?"). The importance of presenting children with suitable examples of telling the truth and telling lies for identification purposes is also highlighted by extracts from our interview data. Consider, for example, the following:

(61)    From an interview with a 5-year-old boy:

        I:      If I've got this piece of paper and I rip that and I said to
                [name of officer in the monitoring room] that "[name of
                child] ripped that piece of paper" what would that be?

C:    I don't know.
I:    OK, right. Would that be good or would that be bad?
C:    Bad.
I:    OK and if I ripped that paper and I said that [name of child] ripped that paper, what would that be?
C:    Bad.
I:    OK, because I ripped the paper?
C:    [Nods].
I:    Right, if I ripped the paper and it was all right to rip the paper and I said, "OK, I'm a silly girl and I ripped the paper" and I told the truth. Would that be good or bad?
C:    Good.

(62)   From an interview with a 5-year-old girl:

I:    OK now, if I picked that cup up, right?
C:    [Nods].
I:    And the drink that's inside it, tipped it over mummy's head.
C:    [Nods].
I:    And then I went and I said to [name of officer in the monitoring room], "[Name of child] did that" yeah?
C:    [Shakes head].
I:    What would you think I was doing?
C:    You had done it.
I:    I had done it, do you think that's right to say it, to blame you?
C:    [Nods].
I:    Em?
C:    [Shakes head].

(63)   From an interview with a 6-year-old boy:

I:    OK, I'll tell you what, if I broke this pen in half and then it was in two bits and I went and told your mummy you'd done it. What would that be?
C:    Naughty.
I:    Well, yes. Why would that be naughty?
C:    'Coz you'd broken the pen.
I:    But would I be right in saying that you'd done it when I'd done it?
C:    No.
I:    So, what would that be?
C:    [Silence].

> I:      Would I be telling a lie do you think?
> C:     [Nods].

(64)  From an interview with another 6-year-old boy:

> I:      OK, if I said to you, if I said to mummy after, when we
>         had been talking, "[Name of child] broke this pen in half"
>         but actually, I broke it in half, not you.
> C:     No.
> I:      No, what do you think about that? Would that be the truth
>         if I told mummy that?
> C:     Naughty.
> I:      It is naughty. What do you think I'm saying?
> C:     You'd tell mummy.

Examples such as the above are problematic because they focus on two events, a misdemeanour – ripping paper in (61), upsetting a drink in (62) and breaking a pen in (63) and (64) – and subsequently telling a lie about the misdemeanour. The difficulty with this type of example is twofold. First, such examples require the child to focus on two separate issues which is clearly more demanding than focusing on a single issue at a time. Second, the interviewer's question along the lines of, "What would that be" is often ambiguous (does *that* refer to the misdemeanour or the subsequent lie?). The danger of examples such as these is that the child focuses on the misdemeanour rather than the lie about it. Thus, the opportunity for the child to demonstrate that he knows what telling a lie is, and that this is naughty, is lost. Worse still, by appearing oblivious to the fact that the interviewer has described an instance of telling lies and failing to point out that this is naughty, the child is left vulnerable to the suggestion that he doesn't appreciate either of these facts.

When giving examples for children to identify interviewers should ensure that these are simple and unambiguous. For example, the interviewer might proceed along the following lines:

> I:      Can you tell me what colour my jumper is?
> C:     Red.
> I:      OK, then if I said, "My jumper is blue" would I be telling
>         the truth or telling a lie?
> C:     A lie.

In this example, the child's colour naming ability is demonstrated prior to using colour terms within the truth/lie example. Alternatively, the truth/lie example could focus on toys within the room. For example, the interviewer might use the following type of example:

I:      OK, so what are you doing now then?
C:      Colouring a pirate picture.
I:      Right, so if I said you are playing football at the moment what would I be doing?
C:      Wrong.
I:      Would I be telling the truth or telling a lie?
C:      Telling a lie.

Notice that in this second exchange, the interviewer doesn't offer the child a choice of "telling the truth" or "telling lies" in her initial question but leaves it open for the child to introduce these terms. When the child fails to use the term "telling lies" the interviewer then introduces this choice. An open question format is more likely to be productive with older children (the over-7s) and a choice type question (am I telling the truth or telling lies) with the under-7s.

Other possible examples to elicit children's understanding of truth and lies involve aspects of information provided in the rapport phase. For example the following type of exchanges:

I:      So, you've told me you've got a sister and that her name is Jane?
C:      Yeah.
I:      Has she got a middle name?
C:      No.
I:      So if I said, "Your sister's name is Alison"? what would I be doing?

Or,

I:      So, you came here today in your mum's car?
C:      Yes.
I:      Now then, if I said, "You came here in a helicopter" would I be telling the truth or would I be telling a lie?
C:      Lie.

In summary then, the key points to consider when assessing children's understanding of telling the truth and telling lies are:

• Focus on telling the truth and telling lies separately, don't expect children to offer a comparative description of the two.

- Focus questions on telling lies rather than on telling the truth. Children understand about telling lies at a younger age.
- Offer children examples of telling the truth and/or telling lies as this will be a fairer test than asking them to describe either of the two concepts. This is vital for the under-7s.
- Make sure that you offer simple examples. Again, most important for the under-7s.

## Differentiating between Fact and Fantasy

An issue sometimes associated with children's understanding of telling the truth versus telling lies is their ability to differentiate between fact and fantasy. Again, our data would suggest that caution is needed in assessing this aspect of children's understanding. Fundamentally, we should consider the difference between "reality" in the adult world and "reality" in the child's world. For adults a simple distinction between existent and non-existent is inadequate for differentiating between fact and fantasy. For example, George Clooney exists (and thus he is a fact), but this is clearly distinct from any fantasies we might have about him (or do we mean his TV character – Doug Ross – in *ER*)! For children, a simpler distinction between fact and fantasy might be that if it exists it's fact and if it doesn't it's fantasy.

Of course, for the purposes of the interview, this distinction is adequate (certainly in terms of recounting a factual event). But it doesn't account for some things which exist being elements of fantasy. Therefore, it is important to utilize examples which tune into the child's conceptions of fact and fantasy. For example, for children, Mickey Mouse exists (they may have seen someone dressed up as Mickey Mouse, they may have seen a life-size Mickey Mouse in footage from Disney world, they may have a Mickey Mouse cuddly toy) and thus he may be considered to be real. Even more confusingly, characters from television soap operas are just like people in the street and thus may be considered real. We've all heard soap stars recount how (adult) fans address them in character and even offer them advice on problems the character is experiencing! Thus, we can see how difficult these fine distinctions may be for children as the following extract shows:

(65)   From an interview with a 7-year-old girl:

I:       Do you watch any videos?
C:      [Nods].
I:       What videos do you like?

C:      *Peter Pan.*

I:      *Peter Pan,* do you think that Peter Pan is real?

C:      [Nods].

I:      Yeah? Is there a real man called Peter Pan?

C:      [Nods].

I:      OK. Do you watch *Neighbours* or anything like that on the telly?

C:      [Nods].

I:      Do you? Do you think *Neighbours* is a real family?

C:      [Nods].

I:      Do you? Where do they live?

C:      Australia.

I:      They actually live in Australia. OK.

What then are fairer, more adequate and relevant ways of assessing children's appreciation of the distinction between fact and fantasy? It is important to focus on elements of the real world and fantastical events rather than fantasy characters. Thus, an exchange such as the following might be appropriate:

(66)   From an interview with a 6-year-old girl:

I:      OK, the other thing is, I want to see if you know the difference between something that's make-believe and something that's real. So, this house is real and we're here and it's real.

C:      [Nods].

I:      So, if I went to your house and I said, "I went to a house in [place] today and Mickey Mouse and Donald Duck and Pluto were there" what would that be?

C:      A lie.

I:      Is it made up?

C:      Yeah.

Notice that although this example involves fantasy characters, the child is asked about a fantasy event (the characters' presence at the interview). An even better example would be one which similarly focused on a fantasy event but which didn't potentially confuse matters by introducing fantasy characters. For example, an exchange like the following could be used:

I:      OK, the other thing is, I want to see if you know the difference between something that's make-believe and

something that's real. So, this house is real and we're here
and it's real.

C:      [Nods].

I:      So, if I went to your house and I said, "I went to a house in
        [place] today and all [name]'s family and all [name]'s
        teachers were there", would I be talking about something
        that had really happened or something that was make-
        believe?

C:      Make-believe.

We turn now to the final additional function of the rapport phase.

# When a Child doesn't Know or doesn't Understand

Clearly, it is important to reassure a child that it is OK to say that he
doesn't understand a question or doesn't know the answer to a question.
Typically, this might be along the following lines:

(67)    From an interview with a 6-year-old girl:

I:      OK, now, if I ask you a question you don't understand,
        you tell me and I'll ask it in a different way, OK?

C:      Yeah.

I:      And if I ask you a question and you don't know the
        answer, you just say you don't know, OK?

C:      Yeah.

We refer the reader to Chapter 4 for further discussion of this issue.

We conclude with a summary of some of the key issues discussed in this
chapter:

| TOPIC | DOs | DON'Ts |
|---|---|---|
| Time and place of interview | Consider the child's routine (e.g. mealtimes and "one-off" events should be accommodated) Reassure the child about the interview location (in terms of the distance travelled and ownership of the location) | Conduct interviews which interfere with the child's routine Assume that the child has an adult-like understanding of where the interview is taking place. He may well think that this is the interviewer's home |

| TOPIC | DOs | DON'Ts |
|---|---|---|
| Persons present | Consider the individual child – some children may find it easier to settle with a second adult present | Where possible, avoid the presence of an attached adult (e.g. parental presence). The emotional burden and temptation to provide information can be overwhelming |
| Preliminary details | Consider presenting these before the child enters the room. Details can then be repeated at the interviewer's convenience during the interview, thus removing the initial burden of providing key information | Ignore the child in an attempt to get key information on camera. This can be damaging to the establishment of an effective rapport |
| Establishing rapport | Try to ascertain prior to the interview some of the child's interests (e.g. does he like school? Has he got any pets?) Use this prior information to tune into topics of conversation productive with an individual child Consider topics such as school, friends, toys, hobbies, TV and video, pets, holidays and Christmas | Ask children open questions along the lines of, "tell me something about yourself", this is an unfamiliar type of interaction for children |
| Appropriate toys | Guide the child to an appropriate toy Choose toys such as colouring books and crayons/felt-tip pens, soft toys, playdough and jigsaws Choose age-appropriate toys | Give the child a free choice of toys Choose toys which are too noisy (e.g. building blocks on table tops) and those which are too distracting (e.g. complex puzzles) Choose toys which are designed for an older child (and are therefore too complex) for the interviewee |

| TOPIC | DOs | DON'Ts |
|---|---|---|
| Assessing development | Focus on indicators of ability such as ability to state time and date of interview and date of birth, recall of "peripheral details" (e.g. other persons present in the interview building), ability to answer different types of wh-questions, ability to express feelings about non-abusive events, ability to give a non-abusive event account (e.g. about an event such as a school day or Christmas party) | Rely on colour naming and arithmetical ability as indicators of interviewee ability |
| Reason for interview | Explain that the interview is taking place to discuss anything the child is unhappy about (the precise wording will depend on the extent of disclosure prior to interview)<br><br>Reassure the child that he has done nothing wrong | Assume that the child (even one who has made a prior disclosure) knows why the interview is taking place |
| Function of equipment | Explain how and why the video equipment is working | |
| Truth and lies | Address truth and lies separately<br><br>Focus on lies first (this is an earlier conceptual development)<br><br>Provide identification tasks with examples of telling the truth and/or telling lies<br><br>Give simple examples addressing only one issue | Ask children to think about the two concepts together. Therefore, avoid questions such as, "Do you know the difference between telling the truth and telling lies?"<br><br>Ask solely for descriptions<br><br>Use examples which focus on a misdemeanour plus subsequent telling of a lie |

| TOPIC | DOs | DON'Ts |
|---|---|---|
| Fact and fantasy | Use alternative terms such as real and make-believe Focus on events rather than characters and give examples for the child to identify as fact or fantasy | Use characters from soap operas or cartoons as examples |
| Don't know and/or don't understand | Offer reassurance that these answers are acceptable | |

## SELF-ASSESSMENT SHEET

(1)   Where was the interview held?

(2)   What were the strengths of the interview room?

(3)   What were the weaknesses of the interview room?

(4)   Were the right people present? If not, what was the problem?

(5)   Was the interview at the right time of day?

(6)   Did the child settle? If yes, what helped the child to settle? If no, what could have been done to help the child settle?

(7)   Did the child seem concerned about the cameras? If yes, how might you alleviate the child's fears next time?

(8)   Did you reassure the child that he had done nothing wrong? If so, how did you broach this matter?

(9)   How did you elicit the child's understanding of truth/lie? Did this work? If not, what strategy would you adopt next time?

(10)  Did the child appreciate that "Don't know" answers are OK? How did you broach this matter?

Any other comments concerning the rapport phase of the interview?

# 3

# FREE NARRATIVE PHASE: LISTENING TO CHILDREN

In this chapter we turn our attention to the second of the Memorandum's recommended phases: the free narrative phase. The purpose of the free narrative phase is for the child to be "encouraged to provide *in his or her own words* and at his or her own pace an account of the relevant event(s)" (MOGP 1992: 17).

We therefore examine characteristic features of children's free narrative accounts and suggest ways in which the Memorandum's objective of encouraging the child to provide an account of events can be achieved. Drawing upon our own data both from video interviews and from an experimental language game with assumed non-abused children (Aldridge & Wood, forthcoming), as well as on previous research findings, we examine some of the difficulties apparent in obtaining an account of events from the child. We then suggest ways in which the child can be encouraged, by the interviewer, so that a full and accurate account is given. This chapter includes discussion of the following issues:

- The importance of the free narrative phase.
- How the free narrative phase is intended to proceed.
- Children's lack of familiarity with this type of exchange.
- Children's reticence in providing free narrative accounts.
- The quantity problem: the provision of short free narrative accounts.
- The quality problem: the provision of unhelpful information.
- Children's memory skills.
- The influence of linguistic development on children's provision of narrative accounts.
- Problems presented by over-hasty entry into specific questioning.
- The provision of adequate free narrative opportunities.
- The provision of support for children's narratives.

# THE IMPORTANCE OF THE FREE NARRATIVE PHASE

Clearly, this is an evidentially crucial phase as it is the child's chance, as the Memorandum suggests, to tell of his experience(s) in his own way. In fact, the Memorandum (1992: 17) refers to the free narrative phase as "the heart of the interview". Ideally, within this phase, the child will produce a full and clear account of the alleged incident which will be evidentially adequate and not open to criticism in terms of the (potential) influence of direct questioning. This is important because Dent & Stephenson (1979) and Powell & Thomson (1994) – amongst others – have reported that young children are likely to be more vulnerable to adult suggestion when exposed to specific questioning strategies. Furthermore, there have been some reports (e.g. Shuy 1986 reported in Bull 1992) that juries may find free narrative accounts more persuasive than the fragmentary testimony achieved by specific questioning techniques. Given its importance within the interview, we now consider how this phase is intended to proceed.

# HOW TO PROCEED

The free narrative phase should proceed with the interviewer asking "only the most general, open-ended questions . . . for example 'Why do you think we are here today?', 'Is there anything that you would like to tell me?'" (MOGP 1992: 17). In response to this type of questioning, it is hoped that the child will make a disclosure and, in fact, the second question which the Memorandum suggests (Is there anything that you would like to tell me?) may not be ideal for this purpose in that it may meet simply with a yes/no response. However, let us assume that an account is given and consider what the account might be like.

The account may be a full account containing answers to the main questions that we might have about an event. That is an account which says *what* happened, *who* was present, *where* an event took place, *when* an event took place, *how* an event proceeded and perhaps some explanation of *why* the event took place. Of course, these pieces of information can be provided with differing levels of detail. To illustrate this point consider the two accounts below:

(1)     Yesterday, I went shopping, with Siobhan, in York, to look for paint.

(2)     Yesterday, I went to Sainsbury's Homebase, in York, with Siobhan – a friend of mine. She's planning to redecorate her lounge so we looked at different brands of yellow paint to try and figure out which would be the best buy.

Both accounts (of the same event) contain answers to the main wh-questions. However, the second account offers more detailed information than the first. That is, it offers more precise answers to the questions we might have about an event. For example, if we consider the information in the two accounts about who was present. Both accounts identify the speaker and another person (Siobhan) as being present but the second account tells us something more about who Siobhan is. Similarly, if we consider the information in the two accounts about where the event took place, we see differing levels of detail. In the first account, the (shopping) event is simply described as taking place in York whereas, in the second account a more precise location (Sainsbury's Homebase, in York) is given. Of course, adults have an intuitive understanding of what level of detail is required and they know that the level of detail required is dependent on a variety of factors. For example, the identity of the listener can be influential. If we consider the two accounts above, if the listener is known to the speaker then the listener probably already knows that Siobhan is the speaker's friend. Hence, the level of detail in the second account would be redundant. Given an evidentiary interview where the listener (the interviewer) knows little about the speaker, this greater detail is highly salient. Children may be less adept at identifying the level of detail required in a particular situation. Thus it is likely that the child may disclose events by summarizing them. A typical exchange involving this type of disclosure would be along the following lines:

(3)   I:    Why do you think you are here today?
      C:    Because [name] has done bad things to me.

From this kind of summarized disclosure, the interviewer can proceed to obtain a fuller event account by asking questions such as, "Can you tell me what happened? Please tell me more." The MOGP would recommend that questions such as, "Can you tell me what happened?" are used in the questioning phase. But, given that this type of question is used to elicit a narrative from the child, we include discussion of the use of open questions (which prompt narration) in this chapter. Chapter 4, although dedicated to the questioning phase, gives limited attention to open questions – concentrating instead on more specific questioning techniques.

Turning our attention to children's ability to provide free narrative accounts; what are the difficulties that arise within this type of exchange? First of all, this type of exchange may not be familiar to the child. A possibility which we discuss below.

# CHILDREN'S LACK OF FAMILIARITY

Eliciting a free narrative account may appear to be a straightforward task: ask the child a single open-ended question and let him tell his story. Given a little more thought, our intuitions about this phase may well change. If we stop and think about our own conversational exchanges with children in day-to-day settings, we will probably begin to appreciate how difficult this phase can be. Certainly, many of us will have experience of exchanges with children along the following lines:

(4)    Adult: What've you been doing at school today?
       Child: Nothing.

(5)    Adult: How did you get on at school today?
       Child: OK.

In terms of conversational experience, children are more used to being asked specific questions: "Did you finish the story you were working on, at school, today?" "What did you have for your lunch?" "Did you give Mr Brown the note about going to the dentist?" This is not to say that children are unable to narrate accounts. In fact, research findings suggest the contrary, for example, Preece (1987) suggests that 5- and 6-year-olds produce many different types of narratives with those of a personal nature predominating and possibly accounting for as many as 70% of all narratives with fantasy stories being relatively rare. However, the data that Preece (1987) provides is taken from conversational exchanges between young children and their peers rather than between children and adults. In terms of frequency of usage in exchanges with adults, children are more used to adults asking them specific rather than open questions. Given that free narratives are an unfamiliar type of con-versational exchange for children, it is unsurprising that a variety of problems have been reported in connection with children's free narratives. We turn now to a discussion of some reported problems.

# CHILDREN'S RETICENCE

Children's frequent reticence to provide free narrative accounts is a central concern when considering their performance within the free narrative phase. In our experience, where children are reticent they are often unwilling to provide any narrative account. This may be simply that they are determined not to disclose or, more often, their reticence may be triggered by fear of disclosure. To exemplify this fear of dis-closure, we have seen exchanges such as the following:

(6)    From an interview with a 4-year-old girl:

    I:       OK, so do you know the day the taxi was late, who was looking after you?

    C:     Not telling you.

    I:       Have you told anyone about it?

    C:     Yeah.

    I:       Who've you told about it?

    C:     Let's pretend I ring you [reaching for play telephone].

    I:       You don't want to talk about this do you?

    C:     No.

    I:       Why don't you want to talk about it?

    C:     I don't.

    I:       Do you think somebody will be in trouble if you talk about it?

    C:     Yeah.

    I:       Who would be in trouble?

    C:     My teacher.

In this example, the child admits that fear of the effect of disclosure on the alleged abuser is what prevents her from providing a free narrative account. A further factor which can prevent children from providing a free narrative account is shyness or embarrassment. We see this in the following exchange:

(7)    From an interview with a 9-year-old boy:

    I:       OK, perhaps you could tell [name of social worker] and I.

    C:     [Shakes head].

    I:       Is there a reason why you can't say?

    C:     [Nods].

    I:       OK, so what's the reason?

    C:     [Silence].

    I:       It'd be helpful to [name of social worker] and I if we knew why you were finding it difficult to say 'coz we'll be able to help then.

    C:     [Silence].

    I:       Is it something that you're a bit shy to talk about?

    C:     [Nods].

    I:       Well, we understand that 'coz we speak to lots of boys and girls.

Later in the same interview:

    I:       OK, do you remember telling mum something about what he'd done?

C:     Yeah, I can remember that.
I:     OK, all right. Tell us about that then. Can you remember now?
C:     [Shakes head].
S/W:   Right, so you can remember but you don't want to say?
C:     [Shakes head].
S/W:   Right, is it worrying you?
C:     [Shakes head].
I:     What made it that you don't want to say then?
C:     I'm embarrassed.
I:     OK, well, we understand that.
S/W:   Yes, we do.
C:     Nobody does.

In these instances it is important to reassure the child that he has nothing to fear from disclosure and that his embarrassment is perfectly understandable (as we see the interviewer doing in the above exchange). Further examples of reassurance can be seen in the following exchanges:

(8)   An example of a reassurance about fear of disclosure taken from an interview with a 6-year-old girl:

I:     Are you worried about telling us about the hospital?
C:     [Shakes head].
I:     'Coz you don't have to be. As we say, this room is where children can come and they can say what they like and there's nothing to worry about 'coz nobody's going to get upset, nobody's going to get angry with them or anything like that. Do you understand that?
C:     [Nods].

(9)   An example of a reassurance about embarrassment taken from an interview with an 8-year-old girl:

I:     Do you think you'd be able to tell us what those wrong things were?
C:     I can't remember.
I:     I know it might be a little bit embarrassing and there might be things that you don't want to say 'coz you think they're not things that you say out loud normally and they are a bit embarrassing. But, [name of social worker] and I have heard all sorts of words and we've spoken to all sorts of children who've told us about all sorts of different things so you don't have to be embarrassed at all. While

you're in this room, you can say anything you want to is
that OK?

C:      [Nods].

I:      So you can feel completely safe 'coz that's what this room
is for and this whole house as well.

Sometimes, then, when a child fails to produce a free narrative account,
it is not because he has no story to tell or because he is incapable of
producing an account. It is simply the case that he is determined not to
disclose, is fearful, shy or embarrassed. Any or all of these factors can
prevent the child from giving an account of events and, as we have seen
in the above examples, reassurance needs to be offered. Children need to
be told that they should not be fearful of, or embarrassed by, what they
have to say.

Of course, some children's reticence in providing a free narrative account
may not be triggered by fear or embarrassment related to the specific
events to be recounted. Some children are simply naturally reticent or shy.
Evans (1987: 171), for example, notes that quiet or reticent children are
"estimated to comprise 14% of the elementary school population". We can
therefore expect that at least some of the children who present for
interview are naturally reticent and therefore "disinclined to speak"
(Evans 1987: 171). In fact, we might expect reticent children to be over-
represented in the interview population. This is because, as Evans (1987:
171) notes: "Feelings of shame and low self-worth which may undermine
the confidence to speak up have also been noted among shy people". Of
course, such feelings are often noted as one of the possible consequences
of abusive experiences (see, for example, some of the accounts of abusive
experiences in Renvoize 1993). Clearly then free narrative accounts can be
adversely affected by reticence for a variety of reasons. One way to
support reticent children is to concentrate on building a rapport with
them in the initial stages of the interview. Of course, this strategy is
dependent upon early (perhaps, pre-interview) identification of reticent
children. Having addressed the issue of reticence, we turn now to some of
the problems apparent when children do produce free narrative accounts.

## THE QUANTITY PROBLEM

A significant difficulty which has been reported in relation to children's
free narrative accounts is their length (or rather lack of it!). That is, when
children do respond positively to a free narrative opportunity their

accounts are often very short. As McGough & Warren (1994: 16) note: "research has repeatedly and consistently demonstrated that younger children typically provide much less information than older children or adults in free recall of events". Or, as Powell & Thomson (1994: 208) state: "Although free reports provide highly accurate information among children of all ages, the amount of completeness of the information provided is very age sensitive. Young children provide relatively little information during free recall compared with older children and adults . . . and the amount of information increases steadily up to preadolescence".

A variety of experimental research findings (e.g. Baker-Ward et al 1993, Cole & Loftus 1987, Davies et al 1989, Dent & Stephenson 1979 and Ornstein, Gordon & Larus 1992) offer support for these comments. However, although all these studies show that children often provide an incomplete account they also show that what children do say tends to be accurate. The limited length of children's free narrative accounts is also demonstrated by our own video interview data. In the following examples we see how short children's accounts often are:

(10)  From an interview with a 4-year-old girl:

       I:    So, besides being sick and breaking your arm, have you
             hurt anywhere else on your body recently? Have you had
             anything else?
       C:    Yeah, [name of alleged abuser] put his fingers in my
             private.
       I:    I see. Who is [name of alleged abuser]?

(11)  From an interview with a 6-year-old girl:

       I:    All right then, do you want to tell me?
       C:    Nanny and grandad they pick on [name of child's sister]
             and me.

(12)  From an interview with a 10-year-old girl:

       I:    It's OK to tell me.
       C:    He said lie down for a minute and I said no and then I lied
             down and he got it in and he put it in here and he turned
             me over and licked my bum and that's all of it.

We have seen similarly short accounts produced in a language game with assumed non-abused children (Aldridge & Wood, forthcoming). In this study, we asked a group of 60 school children aged 5–10 years to recount the events of their school Christmas party. Our data collection took place 3 months after the party had taken place and our aim was to elicit free narrative accounts from the children about a neutral event. We then compared our experimental data from this setting with the accounts produced in the real-life evidentiary setting.

Our complete findings are available elsewhere (Aldridge & Wood, forthcoming) and we therefore summarize the main points here. Firstly, in terms of the amount of information produced, there is little difference between the free narratives produced by children in evidentiary interviews compared to those accounts about neutral events in an experimental setting. This would suggest that it is not only factors unique to the evidentiary setting (e.g. the unfamiliar surroundings or the intimate nature of events to be recounted) which constrain children's narrative accounts. Instead, the similarities between the same-age children's accounts across both settings would suggest that developmental factors prevent children from offering longer narrative accounts. A similar pattern emerges when we consider the quality of children's free narrative accounts.

# THE QUALITY PROBLEM

A further difficulty with children's free narrative accounts is that they often not only contain insufficient information but also the information that they do contain is not always helpful – a comment which echos Richardson's (1993: 133) concern that: "beginning forms of narratives do not contain the kind of detail that the justice system finds necessary for legal resolution of disputed events". For example, we often see accounts where, as Walker & Warren (1995: 159) note: "The critical knowledge needed by the adult interviewers – all of the detail in the middle – [is] missing".

We refer to these accounts which lack crucial details as "empty sandwich" accounts. They have a beginning and an end but no middle and are therefore like a sandwich with no filling. Examples of these "empty sandwich" accounts include the following. Example (13) is taken from Walker & Warren (1995) and examples (14) and (15) from our own data:

(13)  I:      Can you tell me what he did the other time?
      C:      He pulled me inside my house and then, and then I fell asleep on my couch.

(14)  From an interview with a 5-year-old girl:

   I:     Can you tell me what happened?
   C:     He went downstairs and me and my dad and that was all.

(15)  From an interview with a 6-year-old girl:

   I:     OK then, tell us what happened.
   C:     I came home from [name of pub]. My dad sent me up to
          go in the bath. I got out the bath and my dad gave me a
          towel. He said, "Go downstairs and get dry". I dried
          underneath me and there was all blood on the towel.

In all these accounts, we see that the children omit the middle sections;
the key information-giving sections. In (13), for example, what happened
between the child being pulled into the house and falling asleep on the
couch? In (14), what happened between the child and her dad? And in
(15) what happened to the child between coming home from the pub
and drying herself and finding blood on the towel?

Furthermore, children sometimes produce incoherent free narrative
accounts as the following examples demonstrate:

(16)  From an interview with a 6-year-old boy:

   I:     Do you think you'd be able to tell me what you saw?
   C:     I was lying in bed and I heard [name of alleged abuser]
          come up the stairs 'coz I knew mum had gone out. Well, I
          was in the bedroom and he had his hand there [round
          neck] and then he lifted it up.
   I:     On who now?
   C:     [Name of child's brother].

In this case, we might assume, from the child's narration, that the
alleged abuser had his hand around the child's neck. In fact, as the
interviewer's question clarifies, the alleged abuser had his hand round
the child's brother's neck. Having already interviewed the child's
brother (the victim of the assault), the interviewer was alert to the
confusion within this account. In other cases, it may not be so easy to
either identify or clarify this type of confusion. In the following example,
for instance, the child's account is all the evidence the interviewer has
and she has to tease whatever information she can from him.

(17)  From an interview with a 7-year-old boy:

   I:     Can you tell us as much as you can remember?

C:      Well, I was in the bath. I was getting out of the bath. No, I
        had a quick bath, I was getting out then my dad come up
        and he had a sweet wrapper and, em, I dried myself and
        then no, he squeezed, no, sorry.

I:      Take your time.

C:      I stayed in the bath for half an hour, I came out, had a
        quick bath, dried myself, he squeezed my willy very tight
        and he smacked me for no reason.

In this case, various aspects are unclear. For example, how many times
did the child go in the bath and how long did he bathe for? These
examples indicate that children can have difficulty not only in knowing
which information to include but also in effectively organizing the
information that is included.

Interestingly, a comparison of narrative accounts from the interview
setting with accounts from the same-age children in our language game
(Aldridge & Wood, forthcoming) suggests that the evidential narratives
are little worse than the experimentally elicited accounts in terms of the
quality of information provided. If we compare two accounts from 10-
year-old children in the two different settings, this point is clearly
illustrated. In (18) below we see an account from a 10-year-old girl from
our experimental study and in (19) an account from an evidentiary
interview with a 10-year-old girl:

(18)  I:     Can you tell me what happened at your school Christmas
             party?

      C:     We had musical statues and I won two of them. I won
             sweeties and we watched *Secret Garden* and Mr Bean, and
             Father Christmas came and gave us presents.

(19)  I:     Can you tell me what happened?

      C:     He told me to come upstairs with him to see his rats and
             so I saw his rats and then he shut the door and then he
             started to do things to me.

In both quantitative and qualitative analyses, these accounts (and many
others in our study) proved remarkably similar. A more detailed
discussion of these analyses can be found elsewhere (Aldridge & Wood,
forthcoming). However, the general and important conclusion to be
drawn is that developmental factors clearly play a significant role in
shaping these accounts. Thus some of the deficiencies within them may
be traceable to developmental rather than environmental sources. We
turn now to aspects of the child's development which are likely to

influence the ability to produce a free narrative account and we discuss children's memory and language skills.

## CHILDREN'S MEMORY SKILLS

Clearly, the child must have a clear memory of the relevant events if she is to recount them successfully and, in fact, research findings are very positive in terms of children's memory skills. Studies by Cassel & Bjorklund (1995), Flin et al (1992) and Goodman et al (1991) – to name a few of many – all show that children's memory ability is sufficient to provide an adequate account of events. This is certainly the case in terms of central rather than peripheral information (e.g. the child is likely to remember a man coming into a room but not necessarily the colour of his shoes) and of personally experienced events, rather than those observed as a bystander (Saywitz, Geiselman & Bornstien 1992). Of course, in this arena, it is central information and (most often) personally experienced events which are of most interest and evidential value. Unfortunately, this evidential interest will often conflict with what is important to the child. A child who has been through an abusive experience is unlikely to feel that the details of when and where an event took place are important and he is therefore unlikely to report these details spontaneously.

In addition to memory skills, other skills, such as language skills, are likely to be influential in the provision of an adequate free narrative account. An issue which we address in the following section.

## THE INFLUENCE OF LANGUAGE SKILLS

A number of previous studies have highlighted the influence of language development on the recounting of events. A quote from Ornstein, Larus & Clubb (1991: 165) is illustrative: "A child's level of language competency can have a strong effect on the recovery of stored information". In fact, we would suggest that language competency is influential in a number of specific ways and that children's limited linguistic skills may constrain their accounts in the following ways:

- The type of information children are able to provide may be constrained by their limited language skills.
- Children may be constrained in their ability to link pieces of information together because of limited language skills. That is, they

may not be able to use the types of words needed to link ideas together.

- Children may be constrained in the level of detail they include in their accounts because of limited language skills. In particular, children may find it difficult to provide evaluative comments about the information they report.
- Children may be constrained in the level of detail they report because they lack the linguistic skills to provide very specific information.

We discuss each of these points in turn.

## Type of Information

The type of information reported may be constrained by children's limited language skills. A number of previous studies have offered analyses of the type of information which children report in their free narrative accounts. Fivush and colleagues (Fivush, Gray & Fromhoff 1987, Fivush & Hamond 1991, Fivush 1994), for example, calculated the amount of information reported by children in terms of "informational units". These units included each unique mention of any one of the following: a person, an activity, an object, a descriptor or a location. Thus, consider a statement such as:

(20)   John bought a pint of beer at the bar.

We can divide this statement into the different types of informational unit present. Hence we have the following analysis:

(21)   John – a person,
         bought – an activity,
         a pint of – descriptor,
         beer – object,
         at the bar – location.

Information about children's language development would suggest that they may be less capable of providing certain types of information because of the aspects of language needed to convey the information. For example, prepositions (such as *under* and *behind*) can be problematic for children (see Chapter 5 for further discussion of prepositions and also Berman & Slobin 1994). We would therefore predict that location information which is likely to require the use of a preposition would be more difficult for children to provide than other types of information. This view is supported by data from our language game (Aldridge and Wood, forthcoming) and from real-life data from evidentiary interviews.

First, let us consider evidence from our language game (described earlier) and examine which types of information the children tended to omit from their accounts of their school Christmas party. As we report fully elsewhere (Aldridge & Wood, forthcoming), when we asked the children in our language game about their school Christmas party, the type of information most likely to be omitted was location information. That is, the children failed to mention in which rooms the various party events took place. This is somewhat surprising in that the interviewer was unfamiliar with the school (and the children in the study knew this) and the party events took place in a number of different rooms (e.g. the children made party hats in their classroom, ate their party food in another room and moved on to various rooms around the school building for party games and dancing). Given the interviewer's lack of familiarity with the school and the changes of location during the event being reported, it might be expected that this information would be reported. In fact, across age groups (5–10 years) location information was frequently omitted.

Second, when we applied the same type of analysis to our video interview data for children in the same age range we found that the pattern was repeated. That is, the type of information that the children most frequently failed to provide was any indication of location. They did not say where the events they were reporting took place. This is despite some of the children providing quite detailed information about other aspects of the event.

Taken together, then, the findings from our language game and from our video interview data would seem to suggest that linguistic skills affect the type of information that children are able to provide within their free narrative accounts. That is, children may not provide information about where an event took place because to do so they would need to use an aspect of language (i.e. a preposition), which is difficult for them.

Armed with the knowledge of which aspects are likely to be omitted (e.g. location information) interviewers can be more alert to the types of follow-up questions they are likely to need to ask. In the case of location information follow-up where-questions are likely to be necessary (we return to further discussion of different types of questions in Chapter 4).

# Linking

The effectiveness with which pieces of information are linked together may be constrained by limited language skills. If a narrative account is to be cohesive (that is if all the points made are to be linked together effectively) then the speaker's utterances must flow naturally one after another. Smooth delivery of our ideas is achieved through the use of words known as conjunctions (for example *and* or *but*). Of course, our skills in using such words develop with time, and adults are much more adept than children at using these aspects of language.

In fact, the research literature suggests that children employ two different strategies when organizing their ideas. These strategies have been referred to as "centring" and "chaining" (Applebee 1978). First, children begin to organize their accounts by the use of centring. This is where an account centres on a certain aspect of an event. Later, children develop chaining strategies where a series of features of an event are linked together. The following examples illustrate this developmental trend.

(22)   An example of centring from a narrative account from a 5-year-old boy:

   I:      Can you tell me what happened?
   C:     [Name of alleged abuser] put mummy's tights on.

In this case, the child's account is centred on a key feature of the event to be recounted (i.e. the alleged abuser putting on the tights).

(23)   An example of chaining from a narrative account from a 9-year-old girl:

   I:      So, I think you told your mum something that happened, about something that happened at the fete, at the stall, yeah?
   C:     Yeah.
   I:      Tell me what happened there.
   C:     I was sitting on the van and what he done, he touched my bum and then after that he put his hand under my shirt, this shirt.

Clearly, if a child is to use a chaining strategy (as in (23) where the child links together a series of events: sitting on the van, being touched on her buttocks and being touched under her shirt), then he or she needs the linguistic skill to use conjunctions such as *and* or *but* effectively. In fact, our language game findings (Aldridge & Wood, forthcoming) and previous findings from others (e.g. Liles 1987) suggest that younger children make much less (accurate) use of conjunctions. Thus, their accounts are limited because they have not got access to the strategies which would allow them to link different pieces of information together. Of course, this is not to suggest that children are unable to recount multiple facts about an event, simply that they need to recount these facts in smaller chunks. We address ways in which the interviewer might exploit this ability to recount in small chunks in the last section of this chapter.

# Evaluating

Children's ability to evaluate the information they provide may be constrained by limited language skills. Bamberg & Damrad-Frye (1991: 696) report that "the overall use of evaluative comments increases significantly with age". What this means is that evaluative and descriptive information is increasingly incorporated into children's accounts as they get older. By evaluative or descriptive information, we mean comments such as those italicized in the following examples:

(24)   I watched TV last night, *I wanted to see the interview with the Prime Minister.*

(25)   I'll get the bus into town, *there's never anywhere to park.*

(26)   I got out of the meeting earlier than I'd expected, *it was only two o'clock.*

(27)   Pam showed me her new car earlier, *it's a Toyota.*

In (24) the comment *I wanted to see the interview with the Prime Minister* explains why the speaker watched television. Similarly, in (25) the comment *there's never anywhere to park* explains why the speaker will travel by bus rather than car. In (26) the comment *it was only two o'clock* adds information about what time the speaker left the meeting and in (27) the comment *it's a Toyota* tells us more about Pam's new car. Evaluative and descriptive comments such as these clearly offer more information than the rather bland corresponding statements of fact which we see in (28) to (31) below:

(28)   I watched TV last night.

(29)   I'll get the bus into town.

(30)   I got out of the meeting earlier than I expected.

(31)   Pam showed me her new car earlier.

In terms of children's use of the kind of evaluative and descriptive comments highlighted in (24) to (27) above, these are generally only apparent in older children's accounts (that is, the accounts of children over 7 years of age). Hence we see the following examples:

(32) An account from an 8-year-old girl taken from our experimental data. The evaluative comment is italicized:

    I:   Can you tell me what you did at your school Christmas party?
    C:   We made party hats, *mine wasn't very good.*

(33) An account from an 8-year-old girl taken from our interview data. Again, the evaluative comment is italicized:

    I:   Can you tell me what happened?
    C:   Dad pulled me off the chair, *it hurt.*

Of course, the use of evaluative comments tends to strengthen the impact of an event account as they help to provide more detailed information. They also eliminate the need for so many follow-up questions. It is therefore unfortunate that the very children who would benefit from less direct questioning (i.e. the under-7s) are the ones who may need to be subjected to direct questioning because they are unlikely to provide evaluative or descriptive information spontaneously. In the final sections of this chapter, we will address some ways in which children may be encouraged to offer further information via free narrative accounts.

## Being Specific

Children's accounts may be constrained by their inability to provide specific information. However, with increasing maturity, various aspects of the accounts tend to become more specific. Berman & Slobin (1994), for example, report that general purpose verbs with multiple meanings such as *get out* are replaced, with increasing maturity, by more specific verbs like *escape.* This increasing specificity is not limited to the choice of individual words. Entire statements, too, become more specific. Hence, a statement such as (34) is likely to be replaced by (35):

(34) I went on holiday.
(35) I went skiing in Switzerland.

The impact of this for the interview setting is clear: older children's accounts are more likely to contain more specific details than younger children's accounts (by "older" and "younger" children, we mean those over 7 years of age and those under 7 years of age, respectively). The following examples from interviews with younger and older children illustrate this contrast:

(36)  From an interview with a 4-year-old girl:

   C:      He touched my leg.

(37)  In contrast, from an interview with a 9-year-old girl:

   C:      He rubbed my leg.

(38)  From an interview with a 5-year-old girl:

   C:      [Name of alleged abuser] put his fingers in my private.

(39)  In contrast, from an interview with an 8-year-old girl:

   C:      He pushed his fingers into my mary.

Firstly, if we consider examples (36) and (37), we see that the general verb *touched* (in 36) is replaced with increasing maturity with a more specific verb, *rubbed* (in 37) indicating the kind of touch. From other older children we see alternative replacements for the verb *touched* such as *stroked*. We see a similar development if we contrast examples (38) and (39) where the general verb *put* is replaced with the more specific (and at the same time more graphic) verb *pushed*. Also in these exchanges we see the general term *private* replaced by the more specific term *mary*. We return to a discussion of children's general and specific names for parts of the body in Chapter 5. Other examples of increasingly specific statements include the following:

(40)  From an interview with a 3-year-old girl:

   C:      He smacked me.

In contrast, we see the following more specific statement from an older child:

(41)  From an interview with a 9-year-old boy:

   C:      He kicked me three times in the ankle and on the back of my leg.

In (40) we see the 3-year-old's simple statement that she was smacked by
someone (in this case *he* refers to her grandad who the child has already
mentioned). She gives no information as to how many times she was
smacked or where she was smacked. In contrast, in (41), the 9-year-old
boy says he was kicked by someone (again the child has already stated
who kicked him). But unlike the 3-year-old girl, he goes on to provide
further details. Similarly, we can contrast the levels of detail in the
following two statements:

(42)    From an interview with a 6-year-old girl:

        C:      We were sitting down and watching TV

In contrast, we see the following statement from an older child:

(43)    From an interview with a 9-year-old boy:

        C:      We were watching *Power Rangers* on TV and he made us
                sit on the other chair by him.

In (42) the 6-year-old girl makes a statement about two activities –
sitting down and watching TV. She doesn't say where these activities
took place or offer any further details. In contrast, the 9-year-old boy
provides more detailed information. He says where he was sitting and
what was being watched on the TV.

Clearly then, a variety of aspects of language development (including
those we have outlined above) can be instrumental in the provision of
free narrative accounts. Accordingly, a variety of techniques can be
adopted to support children's narratives and to compensate for the
absence of later linguistic developments and we report on these in the
final sections of this chapter. Prior to our discussion of methods of
supporting children's free narrative accounts, we turn to issues concerning the provision of adequate free narrative opportunities.

## OVER-HASTY ENTRY INTO A SPECIFIC
## QUESTIONING PHASE

In relation to children's free narrative accounts, it has been reported that
sometimes children are not given an adequate opportunity to provide
their account. Davies et al (1995: 3) report, from their review of video
interviews in the UK, that "the free narrative phase was frequently
omitted and some children were judged to have been rushed into the

questioning phase". Our own data offer only partial support for this finding. More specifically, our data would certainly not support the claim of frequent omission of this phase. In only a handful of interviews (where spontaneous disclosure occurred in the rapport phase) have we seen no free narrative phase included and we would emphasize the difference between noting a phase is non-existent (Davies et al's finding) and that it is unproductive (our own finding). Our data would, however, support Davies et al's (1995) finding in terms of some children being rushed into a questioning phase. We have seen, for example, exchanges such as the following from our own data:

(44)   From an interview with an 8-year-old girl:

I:      Do you think you can tell me what happened?
C:      [Silence].
I:      It's OK, this thing that happened, do you think you could tell me when it happened?
C:      Yesterday night.
I:      Yesterday night?
C:      [Nods].
I:      And where were you?

In this case, after only a single unproductive attempt at eliciting a free narrative account, the interviewer asks the specific question, "Do you think you could tell me when it happened?" From this point onwards, the interviewer continues to elicit information via specific questions. No further direct opportunity for a free narrative is offered to the child although some indirect prompts such as echoing (e.g. *yesterday night* in the above exchange) do occur. Similarly, we see the following exchange from an interview with a 6-year-old boy:

(45)   I: Will you tell me about it then, tell me what happened?
C:      Put mummy's favourite on.
I:      What's that? What's mummy's favourite?
C:      Dancing.

In this case, we see that after a very short account from the child, the interviewer immediately seeks to clarify an aspect of what he has said via a specific question. As an alternative to the specific question, "What's that? What's mummy's favourite?", the interviewer could, more effectively, have asked the child to tell her more (e.g. she could have said, "OK, you put mummy's favourite on, what else happened?"). Instead, as this interview proceeds we see no return to the free narrative phase and information is elicited from the child via direct questioning only.

It would appear to be the case, then, that some children are indeed rushed into a questioning phase. Our experimental findings would suggest that this is inadvisable and in support of this, we report below on the success of providing a "second chance" free narrative opportunity.

## PROVIDING ADEQUATE FREE NARRATIVE OPPORTUNITIES

In our recent experimental study (Aldridge & Wood, forthcoming), we investigated the effectiveness of providing children with a "second chance" free narrative opportunity. That is, we gave each child a first opportunity to provide a free narrative account by asking: "Can you tell me what happened at your school Christmas party?" Then, once the child had provided a free narrative in response to this question, we asked a follow-up question which gave the child a second chance to produce a further free narrative. We used two different follow-up questions. Half the children were asked: "Can you tell me any more about your school Christmas party? Tell me anything you can remember", and the other half were asked: "What happened just before X?" (X, here, stands for the last reported event. If, for example, the child said, "I made a party hat and played musical chairs" the follow-up question would be "What happened just before you played musical chairs?")

These questions were selected because they reflect two of the techniques from the Cognitive Interview protocol (Geiselman et al 1984). The Cognitive Interview is a technique for enhancing the recall of events which was originally used with adults but which has been experimentally adapted for use with children (an adaptation process which has not been entirely successful cf. Geiselman & Padilla 1988). The original Cognitive Interview protocol utilizes four different techniques to enhance recall:

1. Encouragement to report everything regardless of perceived importance (i.e. "be complete")
2. Recounting events in a variety of orders (i.e. change order)
3. Reporting events from a variety of perspectives
4. Mental reinstatement of context

Our selection of techniques (1.) "be complete" and (2.) "change order" reflects the suggestion that, of the four Cognitive Interview techniques, these two are likely to be the most effective when used with children (Saywitz, Geiselman & Bornstien 1992).

Our findings suggest that giving children a second chance to produce a free narrative account is highly effective. We found that for all age groups, the second chance was effective for some children. In an average of 60% of cases (across all the age groups; 5–10 years) we found that a second chance free narrative opportunity resulted in the provision of further information. A more detailed picture of the effectiveness of this second chance emerged when we looked at the different age groups individually. When we focused on the different age groups, we found that the effectiveness of a second chance free narrative opportunity increases with age. That is, for the 5-year-olds the second chance produced further narration in 30% of cases and in 50% of cases for the 6-year-olds. For the 10-year-olds, the second chance free narrative resulted in the provision of further information in 80% of cases.

Of course, these additional narrations are only useful if the information they contain is accurate, and previous research findings would suggest that persistent probing for further information can result in the provision of inaccurate information. For example, Leichtman & Ceci (1995) have shown that if a child is repeatedly asked a misleading question his or her recall may be distorted. Hence the Memorandum (1992: 17) cautions against the use of too many prompts for an event account.

However, our data would suggest that a second free narrative opportunity does not result in the provision of inaccurate information. In all cases, within our experiment, the children who responded to a second free narrative opportunity did so with further accurate information. This is not necessarily a contradiction of previous research findings. Within our study, we prompted only twice for information. Many previous studies which have reported children's vulnerability to suggestion in repeated questioning or probing were far more relentless in their repetition of questions and/or prompts.

In addition, we occasionally see the effectiveness of a second chance free narrative opportunity within our evidentiary interview data. For example, we have seen the following exchanges:

(46)   From an interview with a 7-year-old boy:

    I:       Can you tell me what happened?
    C:      This man, this, em, boy, this big boy, he came to babysit me.
    I:       Yeah.

C:  And he got into my bed and, em, I didn't like it and he just, em, tumbled over on to me when I was fast asleep and woke me up and just started saying "horsey, horsey" and I got on top of him and he started on "horsey, horsey" again.

In this instance, after the child's initial narration and subsequent silence, the interviewer prompts for further narration simply by the use of, "Yeah" which results in further narration from the child. Of course, after the child's initial narration, it would have been all too easy to have asked a direct question (for example, "Who is this boy who came to babysit you?"). Instead, by refraining from asking a direct question, the interviewer obtains further spontaneous information from the child. Similarly, we see the following exchange:

(47)  From an interview with a 9-year-old girl:

I:  OK, what I'd like you to do, if you can, is to tell me, in your own words, everything you can remember about grandad. Not to leave anything out, if you can. You might not think it's very important but it might be very important to me and what I'd like is for you to tell me your own story in your own words and maybe I'll write some little notes down and ask you some questions after. Do you think you'll be able to do that?

C:  Yeah.

I:  So, you tell me everything you can remember and everything you want to tell me and then I'll scribble some little notes down and maybe ask you some questions. Is that OK?

C:  [Nods].

I:  So, you do that first then, yeah?

C:  Sometimes he makes us put our bra and knickers on and then he, erm, and then he says, erm, stay in those and he says put apples in them to make 'em look big and then I said no and then, em, sometimes he, er, he keeps dragging me in bed and he keeps putting me in shorts and t-shirts.

I:  Yeah?

C:  And then he, when it was bedtime, he kept touching my fanny and putting his fingers in it and he kept putting his willy on my leg and he kept rubbing and bouncing it up and down and then he, white stuff came out and he rubbed it on my leg.

I:       Yeah?

C:       And he puts rude films on while we're in the bath and when we get out he keeps them on.

Again, simply by the use of "Yeah" the interviewer prompts, successfully, for further narration from the child. Of course, as with the exchange in (46) it would have been all too easy for the interviewer to have asked a direct question after the initial narration (for example, "Who are you talking about when you say 'us'?" or "When/where did this happen?"). We see a further example of the effectiveness of prompting for a further free narrative in the following exchange:

(48)    From an interview with a 10-year-old girl:

I:       Now, I've explained to you that I've asked you here so that we can have a little talk. What I'd like you to do is explain to me about everything that you've told your [step]daddy and mummy, OK. And I want you to try and start at the very beginning and try and not to leave anything out, if you can. All right?

C:       [Silence].

I:       OK, do you think you could perhaps start and say why I've asked you to come here today, what it's about?

C:       About what [name of alleged abuser – her father] has done to me.

I:       OK, you tell me about what [name of alleged abuser]'s done to you.

C:       Mum was in work one morning, yeah, and [name of alleged abuser] asked me to make a cup of tea, so I made a cup of tea and I took it upstairs and he said, "Could you get me a fag?" So, I got him the fags, went upstairs and then he goes, there was a paper and I gave it to him and he was cuddling me and he just got me into bed.

I:       Right, go on.

C:       And he was drinking his cup of tea and he was smoking his fag and then once he's read the paper, he kept on cuddling me.

I:       OK, go on.

C:       And he got hold of me and he put me on top of him and he tried to tickle him and he started to tickle me then, I tickled him 'coz he asked me to and I said, "No" and then he just forced me to tickle him.

In this case, the interviewer prompts twice for the child to continue with her account. Both prompts result in the production of further information.

Both experimental data and data from real-life interviews suggest that a second chance free narrative opportunity often results in the production of a further narrative. Furthermore, our experimental findings suggest that, if a second free narrative opportunity is offered and further narrative information produced, this information is accurate. Our experimental findings do not extend to the effectiveness of more than two (sequential) narrative opportunities (i.e. where more than one opportunity is presented immediately after another) and we therefore cannot comment on how accurate any information provided in more than two (sequential) narrations would likely be. Therefore, our recommendation is that all children are given a second chance to produce a free narrative account before direct questioning is undertaken.

## HELPING TO SUPPORT CHILDREN'S NARRATIVES

A number of previous studies have reported that children need adult support to facilitate their narrative accounts. For example, Hamond & Fivush (1991: 435) state that "younger children can recall as much information as older children but they need more external support in the form of more questions, probes and prompts from the adult than do older children". Hamond & Fivush (1991: 446) continue: "younger children need more adult guidance in order to recall information than older children". These comments are supported by examinations of exchanges in day-to-day settings where narrative opportunities are provided. As Foster (1990: 127) notes, when children do provide free narrative accounts in day-to-day settings, adults often "scaffold early stories, allowing children to produce a more complex sequence of ideas than they are able to convey unaided". To exemplify, Foster (1990: 128) reports the following exchange between a boy aged 2 years 6 months and his mother:

(49)  C:      Sometimes.
      M:      [She looks at him].
      C:      Ross come out bed bed come out my.
      M:      What are you talking about? What about the bed at night?
      C:      Mm.
      M:      What did you say?
      C:      In a dark.

M:      In the dark.
C:      Ross, em Ross runs in a dark.
M:      Run in the dark.
C:      Ross runs.
M:      You get out of the . . . you got out of the bed in the night,
        did you, and ran around in the dark?'

We see a similar pattern occurring if we look at the neutral free narratives which occur in the rapport phase of some interviews. Consider the following exchange:

(50)    From an interview with a 10-year-old girl:

I:      OK well, I don't know much about you at all. Tell me a
        little bit about yourself, which school do you go to?
C:      I go to [name of school].
I:      Do you like school?
C:      Yeah.
I:      Yeah?
C:      Sport and I like tennis.

Looking at these exchanges, it becomes clear how adults provide the scaffolding upon which children build their free narrative accounts. By echoing what the child has said (with comments such as, "In the dark, run in the dark" (in 49) and prompting, for example by the use of "Yeah" (in 50)), the adults are encouraging the children to continue with their accounts. If children's free narratives are supported by adults in neutral settings then it would be helpful if the interviewer could provide similar (non-leading) support within the interview setting. There are a number of ways in which this might be achieved and we outline some possibilities below.

## Provide a Framework for the Child's Narration

One possibility is for the interviewer to provide a framework for the child to base his narrative upon. This echos Walker & Warren's (1995: 161) recommendation "that the child be provided with a framework for reporting what has happened. We can direct the child's attention to the topic under discussion at the moment and inform her when topics have changed. We can also provide the chronological structure for the child's report."

## Presenting information in a logical order

In terms of supporting the chronology of the child's account (i.e. helping
the child to present information in a logical order), the interviewer can
suggest that the child starts at the beginning within his account and
proceeds through to the end. Typical exchanges of this sort might be
along the following lines:

(51)   From an interview with a 6-year-old girl:

    I:    OK then [name of child] what I want you to do now is to
tell me why you've come to talk to me and I want you to
start at the beginning about what happened, take your
time and tell me what happened.

    C:    Well, first I went out on my bike and I was only out for
five minutes until a boy came.

(52)   From an interview with a 9-year-old boy:

    I:    Right now, I tell you what I'd like you to do. Can you
think hard about what happened that afternoon and why
you came to be out. The best place to start, I think is the
beginning and try and remember as much as you can –
don't leave anything out. Just take your time and tell me
everything that happened. Do you think you can do that?

(53)   From an interview with another 9-year-old boy:

    I:    OK, do you think you'd be able to tell me from the start to
the finish what happened?

    C:    I was lying in bed and it was about 10.30 and I'd just fell
asleep then [name of alleged abuser] burst in the door
slagging my mum off and then she burst out going to call
my nan and I think it was the police as well. Then, he
came upstairs and he said, "You get to sleep" then he
grabbed hold of my arm, twisted it.

As we see in (51) and (53), by suggesting that the child starts at the
beginning and proceeds event-by-event to the end, he is encouraged to
give a chronological account of events.

## Directing the child towards salient types of information

A second method of supporting the child's narration is for the interviewer to steer the child towards the type of information to be provided.

This is important because, as Saywitz, Nathanson & Snyder (1993: 71) note, "children do not necessarily remember less than adults but they are less proficient at producing . . . the kind of information and level of detail relevant to the questioner in the forensic context".

For example, children sometimes stray into providing peripheral rather than central information. In these cases, it is important for the interviewer to guide the child towards concentrating on the central information. Peripheral aspects of the account can always be returned to in later, separate narrations. The following exchange shows how the child can stray into peripheral aspects of the account and how the interviewer can intervene to correct this:

(54)   From an interview with a 9-year-old boy:

    C:      I came home from school – I can't remember what time it was – we went past the shop and mum had forgotten to get potatoes so, when we got in, she asked me to get potatoes so I went back to the shop. So, as I came to the alley there was this lad with a hat on which I've drawn.
    I:      Right, we can talk about what he was wearing in a bit more detail afterwards. But, first of all, can you go back to when you left home and go through it slowly. Take your time.

In this instance, the child gives his account of events up to the point where he was approached by his attacker in an alley. The child then refers the interviewer to the drawing that he has done of his attacker's clothes and ends his narration. At this point, the interviewer has a number of options. She could start to ask direct questions or she could prompt for further narration. On this occasion, the interviewer not only avoids the temptation of early entry into direct questioning by prompting for continued narration, she also neatly directs the child's narration. She suggests that he concentrates his narration on what happened next rather than on the specifics of what his attacker was wearing. By doing this, the interviewer succeeds in steering him towards central aspects of the event allowing later, separate, narration about specific aspects of the account (in this case, the clothes the attacker was wearing).

Given that we recommend two (rather than more than two) free narrative opportunities, this steering of the child's free narrative can be especially important with older children who tend to provide a lot of peripheral information at the start of their accounts. For example:

(55)   From an interview with a 10-year-old boy:

    I:      So, whenever you're ready, you start and tell us what happened.

    C:     Well, [name of alleged abuser] before, he was a nice man 'coz every time he came to clean windows he would let me help him and one night when I was in my pyjamas, ready for bed, I wanted him to see the cinema I'd made out of a cardboard box.

In this case, the child's initial narration has concentrated very much on background information. It is only half way through his account (when he says, "and one night") that the child starts to provide information about the events in question. Given that even older children's narratives are relatively short and that we recommend two narrative opportunities are given, the interviewer needs to make sure that the child's continuation of the account is focused on central aspects of the event. This can be done by using a follow-up prompt such as: "OK, now can you tell me what happened next?" By using this prompt, the interviewer focuses the child's attention on proceeding from when he wanted the alleged abuser to see his model cinema. Similarly, we see the following exchange:

(56)   From an interview with a 9-year-old boy:

    I:      Right, OK, do you want to start telling me about it?

    C:     Well, the very first day I saw him, he took me to his house. My mum knew. Then, a couple of weeks later, he said, "Do you want to sleep" and my mum said I can but that was the day when we went to book the swimming baths and [name] was upstairs. That was nothing to do with it, like, and that day I went to the toilet and I didn't know he was already in there and he was already in there and he wouldn't go out so I just went to the toilet and he said, "You've got something wrong with your privates" and he was like playing with it like a piece of plasticine.

Again, it is at least half way through his narration before the child starts to outline central events and it is again vital that in his second free narrative opportunity he is prompted to expand on these issues rather than peripheral information.

A further circumstance where it is necessary for the interviewer to steer the child's account towards a specific topic is where the child is talking about more than one abusive event. In this type of case, it is often hard to differentiate between aspects of the child's account which occurred on separate occasions. We see exchanges such as the following:

(57)  From an interview with a 7-year-old boy:

I:      OK, tell me what happened.

C:      So I fell asleep again and then someone gave me a fright and I woke up and seed who it was and I just got under my covers again and came up and I saw who it real was then and it was [name of alleged abuser] and he gave me a fright.

I:      What happened next?

C:      I went to sleep and he just left me and then he started coming up the stairs again.

I:      OK and what happened next?

C:      He got into bed. Took his shoes off and got under the covers.

S/W:    You said, "Again", let me just make that clear 'coz I'm getting a bit confused. Does that mean he came twice into your room?

C:      [Nods].

S/W:    Twice? Two times?

C:      Two times and he heard my dad come through the gate so he ran back downstairs quick. The light came on, my dad could see through the door then when the light came on. He got downstairs just in time.

In this instance, the child has already given an account of events earlier in the interview in which there is no indication that the alleged abuser came into the child's bedroom twice in the same evening. It is only in this later narration that the child's use of, "he started coming up the stairs again" alerts the social worker to the fact that the child has been talking about two separate events (although these are to some extent related both in nature – the alleged abuser repeated the same activities with the child on both visits to the child's bedroom, and timing – both visits to the child's bedroom took place on the same evening). In this type of case, it is important, for the sake of clarity, for the child to be guided towards talking about one reported event at a time. This is even more important when we consider the possibility that events may be reported in a jumbled way because they are remembered in a jumbled way. That is, as Ornstein, Larus & Clubb (1991: 152) note: "It seems likely that the repeated nature of the abuse . . . would have led the child to acquire generalized expectations and even to confuse the details of one particular episode with another". To help the child differentiate between different occurrences of repeated events, the interviewer may need to intervene and try and get the child to concentrate on one episode at a time. So, for example, in response to the above exchange where the child has disclosed the alleged abuser visited his bedroom twice, the interviewer might proceed along the following lines:

(58)   I:      OK, can you tell me any more about the first time [name of alleged abuser] came into your bedroom?

By providing guidance like this the interviewer "take[s] the responsibility for naming the topic . . . and for providing the chronological scaffold that holds the topics together" (Walker & Warren 1995: 159). By so doing, the interviewer facilitates the child's narration in a number of ways. First, in a series of specific ways (by helping the child to establish a chronology for recounted events or by helping the child to focus on one event at a time). Second, the child's account is also facilitated because, by using these specific strategies, the interviewer makes the interview situation more like an everyday interaction for the child (by providing the kind of scaffolding that, as we have noted above, is reported to be provided by parents in day-to-day interactions with their children).

## The Use of Props

A further method of supporting and facilitating children's free narrative accounts is via the use of props. In a recent survey of interviewing police-officers in Wales (Aldridge & Wood 1997a) 78% of the interviewers said that they found props useful. More specifically, they suggested that the most useful props include drawing materials (to allow the child to indicate the layout of a room), dolls – not anatomically correct ones – to indicate exactly what happened including the relative positions of child and abuser, and a toy telephone (in which to tell embarrassing or secret information).

Our own data also show that these props can be useful. We have seen examples where it has been unclear how a child was held by an abuser or whereabouts in a room an incident took place. The use of dolls and drawing materials, respectively, clarified these issues. Similarly, there are some issues which some children are either too embarrassed to describe or lack sufficient linguistic skills or awareness to disclose. An obvious example is where the child needs to describe an erect penis (an issue which we return to in Chapter 5). In this situation, some children are unaware of the significance of this, others do not have adequate linguistic skills to allow them to provide a description whilst others are simply too embarrassed to use the word erection. In this situation, it can be very useful if the child can draw what he has seen.

In terms of indicating sexual matters it might be suggested that anatomically correct dolls are useful (this is certainly the view of many practitioners – see Renvoize 1993, for example). However, our recent survey (Aldridge & Wood 1997a) reveals little support, amongst interviewing police-officers in Wales, for the use of anatomically correct dolls. Only 25% of the interviewers felt that these are useful. Many felt that any potential usefulness was overridden (particularly in an evidentiary setting) by the risk of suggestibility and by the possibility that a non-abused child could be adversely affected by their use. Research findings are inconclusive with regard to the use of anatomically correct dolls (see Goodman & Aman 1990) and more evidence is needed before they are accepted for evidentiary purposes. However, neutral props (such as drawing material and ordinary dolls) can be useful in supporting children's free narrative accounts. This is especially true where limited linguistic skills preclude a verbal explanation.

In addition to the strategies that we have outlined above, a number of other potentially facilitative strategies are being investigated. Findings in relation to these innovative strategies are, as yet, incomplete. However, the investigation of such strategies is indicative of the lengths that we may need to go to if we are to maximize the free narrative accounts produced by children. Innovative strategies currently under investigation include the following.

### The Cognitive Interview with practice session

Saywitz, Geiselman & Bornstien (1992) studied the effectiveness of the Cognitive Interview technique (a technique which we outlined earlier) with 7–12-year-old children. In particular, they investigated the effectiveness of providing the children with a "practice run" with the cognitive interview retrieval techniques. That is, children were given an explanation of the techniques and a practice run at using them to recount a neutral event. Findings suggest that giving children a practice run at recalling event details can be useful in two ways. First, it gives the child an opportunity to get used to the task of event recall and to manipulate different recall strategies (e.g. they can practise recalling events in different orders). Second, it gives the interviewer an opportunity to explain to the child the level of detail which is required. Types of information that have been omitted can be noted and these can then be pointed out to the child. A further innovative technique which aims to equip children with the skills they require to be successful narrators is narrative elaboration.

## Narrative elaboration

The narrative elaboration technique (Saywitz, Nathanson & Snyder 1993) is designed to improve the level and saliency of detail provided in children's free narrative accounts. The narrative elaboration technique relies upon the use of a series of picture cards which highlight for the child the type of information they should include in an event account. The children are presented with a set of picture cards depicting different types of information. For example, a card depicting a stick person represents "who" information and a card depicting a house and yard, "where" information. Children are offered an explanation of the cards and a practice run at using them to narrate a neutral event prior to the real interview. Within the real interview the cards are present and act as reminders to the child of the type of information they need to provide. Preliminary findings are positive for this technique but further investigation of its validity is required.

## Felt boards

Poole (1992) and Sattar & Bull (1994) (both reported in Bull & Davies 1996) have investigated the potential facilitative effects of an innovative technique using felt boards. The felt board technique involves using a board with two heads outlined. These heads represent the interviewer's head and the child's head respectively. Coloured felt triangles are used to represent pieces of information. At the outset of the interview, these felt triangles are placed in the outline of the child's head and the interviewer head outline is empty. As the child provides information, within a narrative account, the triangles are transferred from the child's head to the interviewer's. This technique is designed to show the child that initially the interviewer knows nothing about the events in question and to highlight the amount of information that has been transferred as the interview progresses. This technique is intended to counter the mistaken view (held by many children) that adults know everything, and is used to encourage the child to provide a full account of the event. As Bull & Davies (1996) report, research findings to date suggest some effectiveness of this technique but further investigation is required.

## Playing back the child's initial account

A further technique investigated by Poole (1992) and Sattar & Bull (1994) (again reported in Bull & Davies 1996) is the audio recording and playing back of the initial recall attempt to the child. The idea behind this technique is that hearing what the child has already disclosed may help him to recall further information. To date, findings from Sattar & Bull (1994 reported in Bull & Davies 1996) suggest that this may well be a useful technique. Again, however, further research is needed before this technique could be considered for use in real-life interviews.

Looking to the future, a variety of potentially facilitative techniques are undergoing development and we look forward to further evidence of their effectiveness. Clearly, a lot of attention is focused on facilitating children's free narrative accounts which once again highlights their evidential importance.

We conclude with a summary of recommendations together with a self-assessment sheet.

| DOs | DON'Ts |
|---|---|
| Remember that children may not be used to providing free narrative accounts for adults. They may be more accustomed to being asked more specific questions | Don't be too disheartened if the child doesn't respond too well to a free narrative opportunity |
| Remember occasions where you've asked children open questions in more neutral settings and the responses you've received (e.g. "What have you been doing at school today?" Answer: "Nothing") | Don't assume that the child is necessarily incapable of responding to a free narrative opportunity. Consider other ways of prompting |
| If a child fails to provide a free narrative account, explore the possibility that this is due to fear or embarrassment. If this is the case, offer reassurance that the child has nothing to fear and/or that he has no need to be embarrassed | Don't assume that the child has no story to tell and avoid the temptation of entering too quickly into asking the child specific questions |
| Do remember that some children are naturally reticent or shy and that even in neutral settings shy children provide only small chunks of information at a time. Try and identify shy children in pre-interview | Don't assume that a brief narration contains all the information the child has to tell or that the child can remember |

| DOs | DON'Ts |
|---|---|
| preparation and concentrate on rapport building with any children identified as reticent | |
| Remember that even for children who are not reticent, it is likely that they will provide only a short narrative account | Again, don't assume that this is all the child has to tell or all the child can remember. Use prompting and support strategies |
| Remember that "empty sandwich" accounts are common. Children often provide accounts with key information missing | Don't assume that an account which lacks central detail is indicative of an inconsequential event. Use prompting and support strategies to elicit further information |
| Remember that research indicates that children have good memories for central (as opposed to peripheral) information and for events which have been personally experienced (rather than those observed as a bystander) | Don't go directly into specific questioning immediately after a short account. The chances are that the child's memory is good enough to allow for further recounting if he or she is given a further free narrative opportunity |
| Consider linguistic factors. There are certain types of information which children are disinclined to provide because they are constrained by limited linguistic skills. In particular, it is likely that the accounts of those under 7 years of age will lack specific detail (the child will say he was touched but not where or what kind of touch it was). Accounts will also be constrained by the child's limited access to cohesive devices; so the under 7s, in particular, will provide any information in small chunks. They don't have the linguistic skills effectively to link pieces of information together | Don't assume that the child can't remember in any greater detail. He may just need further opportunity or support to provide more detailed information spontaneously |
| Make sure that children are given adequate opportunity to provide a free narrative account | Don't enter too quickly into a specific questioning phase |
| Remember that children will offer a limited amount of information and this may include scant detail. Therefore, offer a "second chance" free narrative opportunity where the child is likely to provide further information | |

| DOs | DON'Ts |
| --- | --- |
| Given that children find it difficult to provide free narrative accounts, support their narration as far as you can without leading. For example, you can encourage a logically ordered (chronological) account by suggesting that the child starts at the beginning and goes through to the end without leaving any information out. Similarly, you can direct any second narration by highlighting central information from the child's initial narration and asking him to tell you what happened next, or, what happened just before an event he has mentioned. You can also help children to differentiate between repeated abusive events by encouraging them to tell you about one occasion at a time | |
| Do consider the use of props (e.g. drawing materials or ordinary dolls). These can assist the child in describing complex matters such as the layout of a room or the relative positions of different people. These can also help the child depict things which he or she is too embarrased to name or describe. Once drawn, naming or description may well be facilitated | Don't rule out the use of props. These do not have to be used to the exclusion of a verbal account. They can, in fact, be a useful tool to support a verbal account |

# SELF-ASSESSMENT SHEET

(1)  How did the child respond when you offered him an opportunity to give an account of events?

(2)  Why do you think he responded in this way? For instance, if he failed to respond to the opportunity, do you think he was perhaps shy or embarrassed?

(3)  If the child didn't respond well to the opportunity to provide an event account, did you reassure him that he had nothing to fear from disclosure or to be embarrased about? If so, how did you explain this?

(4)  If the child did provide an account, how good was it? For example, how long was the account? How much information did it include?

(5)  Considering the information in any account provided, what (if

anything) was missing? Did the child provide answers to the main questions we might have about an event (i.e. answers to what, who, where, when, how and why)? Make a list of the pieces of information that were missing.

(6)  How well did the child link together the information he was reporting?

(7)  Did the child try and evaluate any of the information he provided? That is, did he offer any comments about why an event (or aspect of it) took place or say how he felt about any of the events reported?

(8)  How much detail did the child provide in his account? Were general words (e.g. *put*) or more specific (graphic) words (e.g. *pushed* or *forced*) used?

(9)  Did you give the child an adequate opportunity to provide a full account? That is, once he had reported information, did you enter in to direct questioning or offer him a second free narrative opportunity? If you offered a second chance free narrative opportunity, what happened (i.e. did the child provide further information)?

(10) Did you try and help the child to structure his account in any way? Did you suggest he start at the beginning and continue to the end, for example? Or, did you help the child to focus on particular aspects of an event? If so, how successful were these techniques?

# 4

# ASKING QUESTIONS

In the previous two chapters, we have looked at the early phases of the interview and have examined ways of establishing rapport (Chapter 2) and of giving the child the opportunity to recount his words in a free narrative style (Chapter 3). We now move on to look in detail at the third phase of the interview – questioning. The aim of this chapter is to provide practical information which can be used when training interviewers or as a reference when embarking on a child interview. It is hoped that by working through the following sections the reader may be more informed about the types of questions which can be used appropriately with children of various ages. The chapter is organized into the following sections:

- Difficulties encountered when questioning children.
- The purpose of the questioning phase as laid down by the Memorandum.
- The types of question which are available for adults to use to elicit information.
- Published research findings: children's acquisition of the understanding of different question types.
- Published research findings: what is known about children's ability to answer questions in the evidentiary setting.
- Published research findings: advice given to professionals when interviewing children.
- Current practice: an analysis of our transcript data.
- A checklist of recommended question types and those to avoid when interviewing young children.

## DIFFICULTIES WITH QUESTIONING CHILDREN

We have devoted a complete chapter to questioning because this part of the interview is a crucial phase and a stage which, many (e.g. Dent & Stephenson 1979) have suggested, causes problems for the interviewer. This, of course, should come as no surprise to us as we may have experienced similar problems in everyday situations where children are reluctant to answer questions. For example, when parents ask their children what happened at school or at a friend's party, they typically receive the answer "nothing". These non-informative responses to open-ended questions are very common among young children as parents can attest and it is therefore not surprising that in the much less familiar environment of an evidentiary interview the child is likely to be relucant to give information.

Indeed, the task ahead of the child in an evidentiary interview violates what he knows about conversations in a number of ways (Bull 1992). For example:

• Children believe that adults know everything and thus children ask questions not adults.
• Very young children often assume that because one adult (the perpetrator) knows what took place, other adults must already know (Toglia, Ross & Ceci 1992).
• Many children are warned not to speak to strangers and it is likely that, at best, the child will have met the interviewer once or twice before the interview.
• Children are generally instructed not to talk about certain topics, sex included, in public and here the whole conversation may be of an intimate nature.

In fact, difficulties in questioning children from the interviewer's and child's perspective and a call for training are prominent features of the research literature. Aldridge, J. (Dent & Flin 1992), for example, notes that research findings consistently implicate the questioning techniques used with children as greater sources of distortion to their testimony than any underlying deficits in their cognitive ability. She suggests that poor questioning strategies (e.g. over-reliance on leading questions and lack of attention to the child's developmental level in question structure) may result in incomplete responses which lack clarity and are con-taminated by suggestion. Of course, research has demonstrated that inappropriate questioning can bias the replies of adults as well as children but younger children's replies have sometimes been found to be particularly biased by poor questioning (Bull 1992). The following quotes illustrate this point:

"The accuracy of a child's account clearly depends on the interviewer's skill and sensitivity to children's special vulnerabilities to questioning" (McGough & Warren 1994: 14).

"Insufficient developmental sensitivity by professionals (as a result of lack of training or the adversarial role) can frustrate children trying to answer questions that they are not yet capable of understanding. Often children are questioned in language too complex for them to comprehend about concepts too abstract for them to understand" (Saywitz, Nathanson & Snyder 1993: 60) (a quote made with reference to in court questioning but which can be applied equally to the initial interview).

"The skill of questioning is a key issue in effective interviews with children" (Toglia, Ross & Ceci 1992).

Indeed, children's comments from Westcott & Davies' (1996) study of young people's perspectives on investigative interviews illustrate the stress questioning can cause. The young people in the survey reported that the interviews were often too long and contained too many questions which caused distress. For example, when a 6-year-old girl was asked what would have made the initial interview easier for her she answered, "Put the questions a little bit smaller. They kept talking longer then small, so I couldn't keep up with it, and they kept talking a question then a different question before I answered". Even some 16-year-olds commented on the question style (the following comments came from two different speakers): ". . . if she asked a question, she like went on about it for ages and then she goes, what do you think? I'd completely forgotten what on earth she was going on about", "well they were questioning me about dates and that, and I couldn't remember, that got to me, and times, I mean you don't remember that sort of thing really. How long it went on for an' all that".

From our own data, we also observe the problems interviewers can have when questioning young children. The following are examples where the children fail to respond to the interviewer's questions, respond inappropriately or contradict themselves. First, let us consider a few examples of non-responsive children:

(1)    From an interview with a 3-year-old girl:

I:      What sort of toys have you got?
C:      [Silence].
I:      Do you want to come and have a chat with me now?
C:      [Silence].
I:      Shall we have a little talk?
C:      No.

(2)    From an interview with a 4-year-old girl:

I:      We were trying to remember what sort of clothes you were wearing when it happened?

C:      Em.

I:      Do you think you had your daytime clothes on or your nightie?

C:      [Silence].

I:      What do you think you were wearing?

C:      I want a wee.

(3)     From an interview with a 4-year-old girl:

I:      Have you been to hospital?

C:      Yes.

I:      Was it big or was it small?

C:      Big.

I:      Who did you see at the hospital?

C:      [Silence].

I:      Did you see doctors?

C:      No.

I:      Did you see nurses?

C:      No.

I:      So why is your sister in hospital?

C:      Don't know.

(4)     From an interview with a 5-year-old girl:

I:      Can you remember her name?

C:      Yes.

I:      She asked you some questions yesterday, didn't she?

C:      [Nods].

I:      What did she ask you?

C:      Don't know.

I:      You don't know, well you told her something didn't you?

C:      [Nods].

I:      Will you tell me?

C:      No.

(5)     From an interview with a 4-year-old girl:

I:      Where do you do painting and glueing?

C:      I'm not telling you.

I:      Why aren't you telling me?

C:      'Coz I don't like telling people.

I:      So who teaches you at school?

C:      I'm not telling you.

I:      And what are the names of the children in your class?

C:      I'm not telling you.

    I:      We're not going to have much of a chat if you won't tell me anything!

    C:     I bored. Play those, pretend you are my friend and I've come for tea.

In each of these cases we see that the children fail to respond to the interviewers' questions. The questions posed are met with silence or refusal to respond. An additional problem is where the children provide inappropriate responses. Consider, for example, the following:

(6)    From an interview with a 3-year-old girl:

    I:      What shape is it?
    C:     No.
    I:      What do you think it is?
    C:     Red.
    I:      Red?
    C:     No, orange.
    I:      Do you know what shape that is?
    C:     Green.

(7)    From an interview with a 6-year-old boy:

    I:      Is there anything you would like to ask me or [name of social worker]?
    C:     [Nods].
    I:      What would you like to ask?
    C:     I go to school and I work on colouring.
    I:      Now, I've only met your family for a short time so perhaps you could tell [name of social worker] and me a little bit about your family, OK?
    C:     Yeah, but not yet.

(8)    From an interview with a 5-year-old girl:

    I:      What happened?
    C:     [Name] in my school and she smacked me in the tummy.
    I:      And how old is [name]?
    C:     Five.
    I:      But that's not why you're here is it?
    C:     No.

(9)    From an interview with a 6-year-old boy:

    I:      What else does he do?
    C:     He throws walls and houses.

I:     Walls and houses! That's not right is it?
C:     No.

In each of the above cases, the child responds inappropriately to the questions asked. In (6) the child clearly does not understand what is being asked when the interviewer asks about shape and responds instead by answering a question (which hasn't been asked but which she can understand) about colour. There are two issues to consider in this case. First, the child doesn't understand the word *shape* (we return to the issue of the child's limited knowledge of words in Chapter 5) and second, the child answers the question as if information she is able to provide has been requested (we return to the issue of children's response strategies to questions they don't understand later in this chapter).

We turn now to examples where the child contradicts himself:

(10)   From an interview with a 5-year-old boy:

I:     Do you like him looking after you?
C:     Yeah.
I:     I understand that [name of child's brother] doesn't like [name] looking after him, does he?
C:     No, I don't like him looking after me.
I:     You don't?
C:     No.
I:     Why don't you like [name] looking after you?
C:     Don't know.

(11)   From an interview with a 6-year-old boy:

I:     How do you know that he had a knife?
C:     Because he always hides a knife in his back pocket.
I:     Have you seen him with a knife in his pocket before?
C:     No.

(12)   From an interview with a 7-year-old girl:

I:     Did he put them on over his trousers?
C:     Yeah.
I:     Or not?
C:     Yeah.

In the first example, (10) above, we see that initially the child says he doesn't mind the alleged abuser looking after him, however, when the interviewer mentions that the child's brother feels differently, the child changes his mind and admits that he doesn't like being looked after by the alleged abuser either. In (11), we see a similar contradiction. The child initially says that the person in question "always hides a knife in his back pocket". When the interviewer probes for further information, the child concedes that he has never seen the person with a knife in his pocket before (thereby contradicting his earlier claim that a knife was *always* carried). Finally, in (12) the 7-year-old girl first claims that something was put on over someone's trousers and then confirms the interviewer's suggestion of the opposite.

We also find examples of questioning breaking down because the child takes a literal approach to the question being asked and won't be swayed into another way of thinking as the following example illustrates:

(13)   From an interview with a 3-year-old girl:

> I:     Do you know where you do a wee-wee from? Do you know where that is?
> C:    Toilet.
> I:     Can you show me on here [pointing to herself] where you do a wee-wee from?
> C:    No, can't find toilet here.

In this case, the child initially takes the interviewer's question literally and responds to a where-question with a geographical location. When the interviewer tries to prompt the child into giving a location on the body, the child ignores this and again interprets *where* as needing a geographical response.

These are, of course, a few examples from many and we are sure many readers will be familiar with these frustrating types of responses. To state the obvious, it really is not easy to question children. As noted by Walker & Warren (1995: 154) adults often converse with one another with, at least, the following assumptions:

- If we have the ability to ask a complex question, the hearer has the ability to process it.
- If the hearer does not understand something we have said, he or she will tell us so – and why, in some cases.
- If we ask someone what happened he or she can tell us – if he or she knows.

However, for many people, and certainly for children, these assumptions are not necessarily true and therefore we must phrase our questions taking into full consideration the knowledge of the listener. It is paramount then that interviewers have information about children's ability to answer questions. As noted by Walker & Warren (1995), if adults want clear, reliable answers to their questions, then they must rid themselves of the assumption that if they can ask a complex question, children can answer it. As noted by Walker (1994: 2): "children of all ages can tell us what they know if we ask them the right questions in the right way" and thus it is the responsibility of the interviewer to ask age-appropriate questions. If interviewers are to achieve this then they need to know what can be reasonably expected of children. As Westcott (1992a: 78) notes: "training, especially on questioning techniques, has been identified as an essential requirement if the interviews are to succeed". Unfortunately, although this remark was made some years ago, the need for training remains (a point which a number of inter-viewing professionals made in response to our survey (Aldridge & Wood 1997a)).

## THE PURPOSE OF THE QUESTIONING PHASE

As discussed in the previous chapters it is important that interviewers adhere to two of the principles laid down in the MOGP (1992: 6) namely, "listen to the child, rather than directly question him or her" and "never stop a child who is freely recalling significant events". However, there invariably comes a point in the interview when the child struggles to recount his story and it is necessary to ask questions. The interview then enters phase three, questioning, which is a substantial part of the inter-view process. Indeed, in an analysis of children's initial video interviews, Davies et al (1995) reported that the questioning phase is generally the largest part of such interviews, lasting an average of 18 minutes. This questioning phase is a particularly vulnerable time in the interview as it is potentially easy to lead the child through questioning, thereby making the recording inadmissible in court. It is therefore very important that the questions asked are phrased appropriately and follow information given by the witness. According to the Memorandum there are four stages to this phase and we will briefly summarize these in turn without commenting, at this stage, on the accuracy of the advice given.

## Open-ended Questions

This stage involves open-ended questions which ask the child to provide more information in a way that does not lead the child or put him under pressure. The interviewer is reminded to reassure the child that it is acceptable to say, "I can't remember"/I don't know or admit to not understanding the question. It is suggested that a question such as, "Are there some things you are not very happy about?" might be tried if the child has offered little information during the free narrative phase or, with a slightly more forthcoming child, a question of the form, "Could you please tell me more about . . ." (picking up on something the child has already said) might re-open the child's account. We are reminded here to use simple sentence constructions and to avoid potentially confusing forms of language such as double negatives. It is also suggested that we avoid why-questions as they may be perceived by the children as attributing blame or guilt to them. It is also suggested that the same question should not be asked repeatedly as this will encourage the child to respond with the answer he thinks the interviewer wants rather than what he believes to be the truth. Finally we are advised not to seek clarification for what the child has just said but rather to return to the point at a later date.

## Specific yet Non-leading Questions

This next stage, according to the Memorandum, allows for extension and clarification of previously provided information both from the free narrative and the open question phase in an evidentially sound manner. The aim here is to obtain greater details about the events and people already mentioned and to iron out any inconsistencies which may have occurred during the interview thus far. We are reminded that questions which require a *yes* or *no* answer or ones which allow only one of two possible responses should not be asked.

## Closed Questions

Next, if further information needs to be obtained, it may be necessary to try closed questions which give the child a limited number of alternative responses. The example given in the Memorandum is, "Was the man's scarf you mentioned blue or yellow or another colour or can't you remember?". Such questions can be admissible in court but if the answer given to a limited response question concerns a fact to be disputed in court, the question may then be considered to be leading.

## Leading Questions

Ultimately it may be necessary to ask a leading question which implies the answer or assumes facts which are likely to be in dispute. We are reminded that such questions should be used with the greatest of care as it is likely that information gleaned through this mode of questioning will be excluded from court.

Having summarized the guidelines set in the Memorandum for questioning children, let us now review, in more detail, the main types of questions that can be used to elicit information.

# TYPES OF QUESTION

There are a variety of different question types that we can use to gain information. The more common types include:

- Direct *yes* or *no* questions: e.g. "Shall we invite mummy along?". These require a *yes* or *no* answer.
- Echo questions: e.g. "We shall invite whom?". These require a repetition and/or clarification of something just said.
- Wh-questions: e.g. "Who shall we invite?". These require a different phrasal response depending on the wh-word asked, e.g.

    "What shall we invite?" requires a non-human noun phrase, i.e. a *teddy bear*.
    "Who shall we invite?" requires a human noun phrase, i.e. *Mummy*.
    "Where shall we invite her?" requires a location response (a locative such as *there* or a prepositional phrase such as to my house).
    "When shall we invite her?" requires a time response, i.e. *tomorrow*.
    "How shall we invite her?" requires a response indicating manner, i.e. *by letter*.
    "Why shall we invite her?" requires a clausal response, i.e. because I love her.

- Indirect questions such as "I wonder whether we shall invite mummy?" require a *yes* or *no* answer to clarify the speaker's thoughts.
- "I wonder whom we shall invite?" requires a human noun phrase to clarify the speaker's thoughts.

- Positive tag-questions such as "We shall invite mummy, shall we?" require a *yes* or *no* answer but the listener is biased towards *yes*.
- Negative tag-questions such as "We shall invite mummy, shall we not?" requires a *yes* or *no* response but the question biases the answer.

Clearly, then, there are a whole variety of question types for children to master and intuitively some seem more complex than others. For example, it is naturally easier to answer *yes* or *no* to a question like, "Shall we invite mummy?" than it is to work out an answer for the question, "How shall we invite mummy?". And yet, the interviewer must be aware, as noted by Richardson (1993: 161) that wh-questions are considered to have higher validity in comparison with *yes* or *no* questions because in asking a *yes* or *no* question such as, "Did this happen on Saturday?" the interviewer is providing information (a possible timing of the event) and the child has a limited choice of responses. In contrast if the interviewer asks a wh-question such as, "When did this happen?" she is providing no information about possible timings of events and she does not limit the child's range of responses.

In addition, within the range of wh-questions some seem more straight-forward than others. For example, a question like, "Who shall we invite?" strikes us as easier to answer than a question like, "Why shall we invite mummy?". It is to be expected then that children will find some question types easier to master than others and thus blanket statements such as the following (contained in a training handbook for solicitors who represent young children): "The best questions usually start with *how, what, where, when* and *who*" (King & Young, 1992: 29) is at best misleading and at worst damaging advice as it fails to acknowledge a number of factors. First, there is an order of development in children's acquisition of comprehension of wh-question words (e.g. Ervin-Tripp 1970, Savic 1978, Parnell, Patterson & Harding 1984). Second, children are: "significantly less successful in giving appropriate and accurate responses when the question refers to objects, persons or actions not represented in the immediate setting" (Parnell, Patterson and Harding 1984: 297). Of course, this is precisely the situation which exists in the evidentiary setting. Third, the quote (from King & Young 1992: 29) fails to acknowledge that children adopt strategies to cope with wh-questions that they don't understand.

We now examine each of these points further by summarizing findings from the research literature in relation to presumed non-abused chil-dren's ability to understand different question types.

## PUBLISHED RESEARCH: CHILDREN'S
## UNDERSTANDING OF QUESTIONS

Here, we look at the most common types of questions addressed to children in the initial interview, namely yes/no questions, wh-questions and tag-questions and we report on presumed non-abused children's ability to cope with such questions in a neutral environment. In later sections we look at the relevant research literature concerned with the evidentiary setting and then at our own transcript data.

## Children's Understanding of Yes/No Questions

Research has suggested (e.g. Choi 1991) that children master the understanding of yes/no questions in stages. More specifically, at stage one (around 17 months) children are aware of the conversational requirement of yes/no questions. That is to say they understand that a yes/no question requires an answer and they give a verbal response. However, although they can fulfil the conversational requirement of answering a question (by taking their turn), they will not, initially, respond to the semantic content (meaning) of the question and may well give an inappropriate answer. Moreover, there is some suggestion that in the early stages they will persevere with one answer form. So if they answer one question with *yes*, they may well persevere with *yes* and answer all questions with that form. Choi suggests that *no* in English is the form most often used. At stage two (around 20–22 months) children acquire the affirmative question answering system, that is to say, they answer appropriately questions such as, "Was mummy at home when it happened?" but not its negative counterpart, "Wasn't mummy at home when it happened?". The ability to answer the negative question occurs at stage three (around 30 months). While these children may well be younger than those in the interview situation it is worth remembering that those aspects acquired late remain the most difficult for the child to process so that at any childhood age (and indeed even into adulthood) the affirmative answering system will be easier to respond to than the negative answering system.

## Children's Understanding of Wh-questions

Since the 1970s linguistic researchers have argued that there is an order of development in children's ability to understand wh-words (e.g. Ervin-

Tripp 1970, Tyack & Ingram 1977, Cairns & Hsu 1978, Savic 1978, Parnell, Patterson & Harding 1984, Aldridge, Timmins & Wood 1996). Taken overall, findings from these studies suggest that particular wh-question words are understood before others, namely *what, where* and *who* are easier to understand and are earlier acquired than *how, why* and *when*. Moreover, it is reported (Parnell, Patterson & Harding 1984) that the question forms which are the easiest for 3-year-old children to answer remain the easiest across all age groups, and, similarly, for the question forms that were the most difficult. Thus, it is worth remembering that *how, when* and *why* questions may be problematic for all children and certainly more so than *what, where* and *who* questions. In brief, research would suggest that children are at least 8 years of age before they can consistently cope with all types of wh-questions and children may be even older before they fully master *why*-questions.

## Ability to Answer Questions about Events and People not Present

Not surprisingly, it has been reported (e.g. Parnell, Patterson & Harding 1984) that children between the ages of 3 and 7 years experience more difficulty in providing the information required by the questioner when the person, object or event referred to by the question is not immediately present. This finding has been supported in our own experimental work (Aldridge, Timmins & Wood 1996). We examined children's ability (in the age range 2–8 years) to answer wh-questions in a language game where the referents were in front of them and then compared these findings to children's ability to answer yes/no questions in our transcript data in which, of course, they are talking about a past event without the referents being present. While there are other differences between the two scenarios other than presense/absence of the referent to affect the children's performance, recall was significantly higher in the language game. In our opinion, it is certainly the case that a delay in questioning is likely to weaken children's responses to questions and the interview should take place as soon as possible after the disclosure.

Moreover, the increased ability in children's performance to answer questions when the referent is present suggests that professionals need to explore ways of facilitating children's responses in answering wh-questions by giving them the opportunity to demonstrate their answer. Dolls (present referents), for example, might be used to demonstrate or explain how something happened rather than the child trying to describe absent referents. We have examples in our transcript data of situations where dolls have helped the child's description as the following excerpt illustrates:

(14)   From an interview with a 7-year-old boy:

      C:      He was rocking me in bed.

      I:      How was he rocking you?

      C:      He got on me and went like that [child rocks from side to side in seat].

      I:      I tell you what, shall we use two of these dolls [ordinary rag dolls, not anatomically correct]. Could you show us with those?

      C:      He was lying down like that and he just tumbled me over like that and put me like that and started going like that [demonstrates with dolls].

In this case, it seems that by combining the use of dolls with a verbal account the child is better equipped to give a clear description of his abusive experience. This example might suggest that the use of props may be advantageous when interviewing young children. We are fully aware that this is a controversial issue and the pros and cons of using dolls when interviewing young children is outside the scope of this chapter (we refer the reader to some further discussion of this issue in Chapters 3 and 6).

# Strategies used when Answering Wh-questions

It is well reported (e.g. Ervin-Tripp 1970, Savic 1978) that when children cannot answer the question asked they will often compensate by adopting a response strategy (a strategy we mentioned earlier in connection with the 3-year-old girl who responded to a question about shape by answering as if the interviewer had asked about colour). Typical strategies which occur in young children's speech are listed below.

- Strategy One: If you don't understand a particular question, respond as if it's in a form you do understand (Ervin-Tripp 1970, Savic 1978). For example, if asked, "When did this happen?" and you don't understand *when*, answer as if this were a where-question. For example by responding, "In my bedroom".

- Strategy Two: If you only understand part of a question, answer that part and ignore or repeat the rest (Savic 1978). For example, if asked, "How and why did you go to his house?" and you only understand *how* not *why*, ignore *why* and just answer the *how* aspect of the question. For example, answer, "Mummy and me go to his house by car".

- Strategy Three: If you don't understand the question, give a stereotypical response. For example, answer, "Where do you go to school?" with, "Home" and rely on the same answer if asked, "Where does nanny live?". That is, respond to this question with, "Home" too.

In addition, it is reported (e.g. Savic, cited in Waterson & Snow 1978: 224) that the use of response strategies is particularly common with the late acquired wh-question words (i.e. *how*, *why* and *when*). It is obvious that such communicative techniques may well have important implications for the interview situation and may account for some of the apparent inconsistencies found in children's evidence. Clearly, interviewers must be aware, for example, that a young child might respond to a when-question as if it was a what-question and she must be prepared to overcome such linguistic immaturities. A point we will return to later.

## Children's Understanding of Tag-questions

Researchers have suggested (e.g. Ervin-Tripp 1970, Horgan 1978) that children tend to respond to yes/no questions first, followed by tag-questions and finally they master wh-questions. Generally, children treat tag-questions like yes/no questions and learn to respond with a yes or no answer. Children are known to be suggestible to tag-questions, in the sense that they are more likely to answer *yes* than *no* to a positive tag-question such as, "You did that, did you?" and to a negative contracted tag-question such as, "Mummy's coming, isn't she?". In addition, children are more likely to respond *no* to a full negative tag-question such as, "Mummy's coming, is she not?".

## General Points

While a general order of acquisition has been established for children's understanding of wh-questions and while a set of compensatory strategies which children use when they don't understand, has been identified, it must be remembered that variation among children in overall performance and in the particular linguistic strategies employed is to be expected (e.g. Ervin-Tripp 1970, cited in Cairns & Hsu 1978: 478, and Parnell & Amerman, 1983). For example, Gullo (1981: 740) maintained that: "an important implication of the findings of wh-question studies is that the order of acquisition of wh-words may be different for middle and low socioeconomic status children and that different answering strategies may be employed by these two groups of children".

It must further be remembered when considering academic findings (such as those discussed here) that these results have been achieved by presumed non-abused children questioned in a comfortable environment to a large extent about neutral topics based on present referents. It is thus possible and, indeed, highly likely that the performance of these children will be better than the performance of those children who are being interviewed about an emotive topic, in an unfamiliar environment, about an event which happened some time ago. We turn now then to findings in relation, specifically, to the evidentiary setting.

## CHILDREN'S LINGUISTIC ABILITY IN THE EVIDENTIARY SETTING

### Open Questions

As discussed earlier the questioning phase begins with the interviewer asking the child open questions such as, "Could you please tell me more about . . ." or "What happened next?". Open questions are necessary because although the child may have given an accurate narrative account of what happened, it is very likely that he or she will have missed out crucial bits. In the previous chapter we looked, in detail, at different ways of triggering more information from children during the free narrative phase and the pros and cons of different types of open questions so we won't dwell too long on the matter here. We would, however, emphasize the value of cue questions along the lines suggested by Steller & Boychuk (1992: 50). If, for example, a child replies, "In the bedroom" when asked, "Where did something happen?", the interviewer should follow up with another general question such as, "Tell me as much as you can remember about what happened in the bedroom!". This type of question helps to provide a framework for the child's response along the lines of those outlined in the previous chapter. We turn now to more specific types of questioning.

# Specific Questions

## *Yes/no questions*

Reported findings on children's ability to cope with yes/no questions in the evidentiary setting are sparse but the overriding feeling is that yes/ no questions are not a good idea for a variety of reasons. First, children tend to be vulnerable to the pressures of turn-taking, second, they can tend to persevere with one particular response form and, third, yes/no questions have low validity. To take these points in turn, it is reported that children will often feel the need to answer a question and fulfil their turn-taking obligations even when they don't understand what is being asked of them. For example, Hughes & Grieve (1980) have shown that even when an authority figure asks a nonsense question such as, "Is milk bigger than water?" children are likely to answer *yes* or *no* rather than seek clarification. Similarly, Walker & Warren (1995) have noted that when children are asked complex questions containing more than one proposition (in effect, two questions in one) children will again answer *yes* without making it clear which part of the question they are responding to.

Perseveration is another possible trap. Some researchers have noted (e.g. Bull 1992) that some witnesses and in particular young children may be more willing to respond to yes/no questions with a *yes* response and thus, having begun with yes, will answer all questions with yes. As noted by Flavell et al (1981) young children do not routinely ask for clarification, nor do they recognize or announce when adult questions are defective. We must remember, then, that when we interview young children they will give us few explicit cues as to whether or not they understand us. Instead they will go ahead and respond to an adult question or statement with an answer or action, whether or not the adult intended the child to respond. As noted by Walker & Warren (1995) children lack the resources to listen, speak and monitor simultaneously; they talk to us with the assumption that adults are always right and they won't naturally seek clarification because generally parents are looking out for situations where the child has failed to understand and thus it is assumed that the adult and not the child is monitoring the conversation.

Finally, of course, is the point made earlier that, in court, yes/no questions have low validity as the child doesn't have to provide any new information but simply has to respond to the facts given.

## Tag-questions

Little has been written about children's ability to answer tag-questions. That which has been written supports Walker's (1994) suggestion that tag-questions should be avoided.

## Wh-questions

It has been noted by Wade & Westcott (1997) that many children depicted their interview as dominated by questions from the interviewer, and that the whole interview experience was actually a search for specific detail which the children experienced difficulty in providing. Wade & Westcott go so far as to urge interviewers to resist asking too many questions but rather to save these for the primary purposes of amplification and/or clarification. Clearly, most interviewers will have to ask questions and thus many other researchers (e.g. Boggs & Eyberg 1990) have been more conservative in suggesting simply that why-questions should be avoided. This is, indeed, the advice given in the MOGP. It is suggested generally that why-questions should be avoided because they are perceived by children as requiring them to account for or justify behaviour rather than simply to describe what led up to the behaviour. It is argued that why-questions typically result in feelings of defensiveness and perhaps hostility toward the interviewer and thus weaken the momentum of the interview. Little has been said about the use of other forms of wh-questions and it is therefore hoped that later sections will be particularly informative.

## Closed questions

After specific questions, the interviewer may need to ask closed, choice questions such as the example given in the MOGP, "Was the man's scarf you mentioned blue or yellow or can't you remember?". This type of question is fraught with problems. For example, as noted by King & Yuille (1987), if you ask an adult a question about whether a person had blonde, brown or black hair, the adult will try to remember but is unlikely to feel pressurized by the question. In contrast, if you ask a child the same question, he or she is likely to feel that because hair colour is being focused on, it must be important and thus that it is information the child should be able to provide. Thus, while an adult may resist this implicit demand, a younger child may misinterpret the interviewer's intentions and end up providing what he or she feels is an appropriate answer.

Another problem associated with choice questions as noted by White (1990) is that we must be sure that the child knows all the words in the multiple-choice question. It is possible, of course, that from a list of possible options, the child only recognizes one of the words and thus answers on the basis of familiarity rather than on what actually happened.

## Leading questions

Leading questions, by their very nature, suggest the answer that is expected. It is acknowledged in the literature that while the use of such questions fulfils a therapeutic role in the interview, their occurrence causes problems for the status of the interview should it be put forward as evidence (Vizard 1987). More specifically, the forensic needs of the interview require that only objective questions are used to elicit the details of the suspected abuse, and thus the use of leading questions significantly weakens the evidentiary value of the video-recording. Indeed, as Pigot (Home Office 1989) notes, excessive use of suggestive questioning will continue to prevent interviews being admissible in court.

The use of leading questions is a problem in all interview arenas but their occurrence is a particular problem when interviewing young children because, as many have reported (e.g. Warren, Hulse-Trotter & Tubbs 1991), younger children are more likely to acquiesce to leading questions than are older children or adults. This finding seems to be particularly true in situations where peripheral and poorly retained information rather than salient, memorable information is being discussed and/or when the questioner is of a relatively high status (Goodman & Helgeson 1988) as intimidation can add to an individual's suggestibility and younger children are more easily intimidated.

## Children's use of "don't know"

We said earlier that adults assume that if the hearer does not understand something we have said, he or she will tell us so – and why, in some cases. However, this assumption does not always hold when children are the hearers. As noted by Flin et al (in Dent & Flin 1992) children being interviewed by a stranger in a formal and highly unusual situation may be reluctant to say that they have not understood a question or to contradict the interviewer. In their study (of court situations) children rarely said that they did not understand a question, although

occasionally it would transpire during the examination that the child
had not in fact understood a previous question. It was found that 40% of
the children did answer, "I don't know" to at least some of the questions. However, as children sometimes give this response when they do
know but are not prepared to say (for example to sensitive questions)
the frequency with which children in court respond, "I don't know"
when they genuinely do not know the answer could not be estimated
from the data. However, only 6% expressed uncertainty in the context of
their answers. This reiterates the point that the interviewer must watch
the child constantly in an attempt to monitor his level of understanding.

## PUBLISHED RESEARCH: ADVICE FOR PROFESSIONALS

There already exists a great deal of research literature on different
aspects of interviewing children in the evidentiary setting. The main
points are summarized here.

*Make sure that the child is reassured that she can say, "I don't know/I can't
remember" to any questions asked*
We are reminded (e.g. Geiselman & Padilla 1988) that all questions used
must be phrased in a way which implies that an inability to remember is
quite acceptable. Indeed, it should be made explicit to the child that she
should say things such as, "I can't remember" and "I don't know" if she
does not understand what is being asked. In brief, the child should be
urged to indicate if she doesn't understand a question (a point which
was discussed in Chapter 2).

*Remind the child that the interviewer doesn't know everything and that the
child must tell the whole story*
Children may need to be reminded that the interviewer really does not
know exactly what has happened to them. Remember the point made
earlier that very young children may assume that because one adult (the
perpetrator) knows what took place, other adults must already know
(Toglia, Ross & Ceci 1992). Moreover, recent research has demonstrated
that when children are presented with misleading information by
someone who appears to be knowledgeable about the event, they are
more likely to succumb to the suggestions (Toglia, Ross & Ceci 1992). In
contrast, children are less likely to be misled when the interviewer
makes it clear in advance that he or she has no knowledge of the event
or appears to be less knowledgeable (Ceci, Ross & Toglia 1987). Thus
interviewers should begin by stating explicitly that they are uninformed
about the events in question and that they will be relying on the child's

memory (McGough & Warren 1994). This point was referred to in Chapter 3 in the context of maximizing children's free narrative accounts.

*Avoid repeating the question as this will confuse the child*
The research literature is unanimous in suggesting that quick repetition of the question should be avoided since this can be interpreted by children as a critisism of their original response. Siegal, Waters & Dinwiddy (1988), for example, have pointed out that close repetition of a question may cause the child to change his answer to one he then thinks the interviewer wants to hear. Similarly, Poole & White (1991) have reported that when a question is repeated children tend to assume that their original answer must have been incorrect and so they may therefore change their answer when the question is posed again. The same point is, of course, made in the MOGP. It is suggested (e.g. McGough & Warren 1994) that if repetition really is necessary, the child should be reassured by explicit comments from the interviewer that she is attempting to clarify understanding of an earlier answer rather than seeking a different one.

*Be prepared to reflect on the forensic value of the interview*
The forensic value of the videotape depends on precise details being elicited from the child such as the date, time and place of the abuse and the unequivocal identification of the suspect as the abuser. Interviewers need to make an assessment of whether the child is sufficiently aware of such details to be able to provide them for evidentiary purposes, if not there is no point continuing such questioning as it is not crucial to any therapeutic assessment.

## CURRENT PRACTICE: OUR TRANSCRIPT DATA

In order to illustrate some of the points raised in the preceding sections of this chapter, we turn now to an analysis of our own video interview data and we consider the following:

• How well did the children cope with the questions asked?
• To what extent did the interviewers use published advice (such as that outlined above)?

# How Well did the Children Cope with the Questions Asked?

We refer the reader to Chapter 3 for our discussion of children's responses to open questions and we focus here on responses to specific questions.

## *Yes/no questions*

Our transcript data suggest that even young children have no difficulty in knowing that a yes/no response is called for as the following extract shows:

(15)   From an interview with a 3-year-old girl:

|     |                                     |
|-----|-------------------------------------|
| I:  | Do you know what shape it is?       |
| C:  | Yeah.                               |
| I:  | Can you see them?                   |
| C:  | No.                                 |
| I:  | Do you know what colour that one is?|
| C:  | Yeah.                               |
| I:  | Have you got toys like that?        |
| C:  | No.                                 |

This excerpt shows clearly that the child senses that it is her responsibility to participate in the turn-taking role of a conversation and she does this by responding to every question. However, while there is no occurrence of perseveration in this excerpt (both *yes* and *no* forms are freely used), there is a feeling that the girl isn't really absorbed in the conversation but rather is responding for the sake of it. We see clearly that the yes/no answers do not lead to any expansion by the child and the questions are easy to dismiss. In the transcript data we repeatedly see children responding to the turn-taking obligation without any real attempt to offer any new information. The following examples illustrate this point further:

(16)   From an interview with a 6-year-old boy:

|     |                                |
|-----|--------------------------------|
| I:  | Can you remember my name?      |
| C:  | Yeah.                          |
| I:  | What is it? What's my name?    |
| C:  | [Silence].                     |

(17)  From an interview with a 5-year-old boy:

I:     Do you know where you live?
C:     Yes.
I:     Where?
C:     [Silence].

(18)  From an interview with a 5-year-old girl:

I:     Do you know why you're here today?
C:     Yes.
I:     You tell me why.
C:     [Silence].
I:     Can you tell me?

In brief, questions requiring a yes/no response do not show the child in a good light. They tend to encourage a rather apathetic response and because the child doesn't really need to concentrate, it is very easy for inconsistencies to creep in as the following examples illustrate:

(19)  From an interview with a 6-year-old girl:

I:     Was your dad in the bathroom when you had your bath?
C:     No.
I:     So who did you tell me before washes you when you're in the bath?
C:     My dad, sometimes my sister, sometimes my mum.
I:     Who did the washing last night?
C:     My dad.

(20)  From an interview with a 6-year-old boy:

I:     Did you take your underpants down?
C:     No.

Later in the same interview:

C:     He said take your undies down.
I:     And did you?
C:     Yeah.

In addition to the inconsistencies exemplified by the above, we also note that when additional questions are asked the child is often jolted back into the conversation but is unaware of the substance of the question and thus, simply repeats part of the question. The following examples illustrate this trend:

(21)  From an interview with a 5-year-old boy:

I:        Was it a good thing that he did?
C:       No, yeah, it was a good thing.

(22)  From an interview with a 6-year-old boy:

I:        Are you happy?
C:       Yeah.
I:        Are you ever unhappy, are you ever sad?
C:       Sad now.

As these examples illustrate, yes/no questions can be problematic in a variety of ways.

## Wh-questions

An analysis of our transcript data (Aldridge, Timmins & Wood 1996) suggests that many more what-questions are asked than any other forms of questions. The next most frequent types are who-, where- and how-questions. Followed by far fewer why- and when-questions. The number of why-questions, however, is not insignificant. Indeed in our data, there are only two transcripts which do not contain at least one why-question and thus, it seems that interviewers are generally not heeding the warning in published literature (such as the MOGP) to avoid why-questions.

Turning now to children's responses to wh-questions, it is firstly important to note that we observe a great deal of individual differences amongst children. Even within a given age group there is a great range of abilities. We can perhaps, then, be best guided by trends and patterns of ability rather than by making assumptions about what, for example, a 5-year-old child would understand.

As a trend, then, and in keeping with past research, we do notice that children perform better with questions of the forms *what, where* and *who* than they do with *how, when* and *why*. The children certainly seem to be struggling with *why* and, to a lesser extent, *how*. Furthermore, our analysis (Aldridge, Timmins & Wood 1996) suggests that children are at least 6 years of age before 100% correct scores occur with any regularity. Such figures illustrate nicely that acquisition of language is not an all or nothing process but rather is protracted and a number of months, even years may pass from the point when a child begins to use and/or understand a particular language form and has complete mastery of its usage. Thus, we can draw the following conclusions from our analysis:

- What-questions are the most common in our transcripts but we find significant numbers of all types of wh-questions including *why* forms.
- Children seem to have particular problems coping with *how* and *why* forms.
- There seems to be a developmental change with children responding more accurately to questions from around 6 years onwards.
- There is a lack of 100% correct responses across all age groups, illustrating that language acquisition is a protracted process and just because a child may answer a certain question form in one context, he may not be able to do so in another situation.
- When-, how- and why-questions are not only the last acquired but remain the hardest for children of all ages to respond to. This point is illustrated below in a series of extracts from the same interview.

(23)   From an interview with an 8-year-old girl:

*What*

| I: | What parts of your body does it [swimming costume] cover? |
| C: | Back. |
| I: | What did you used to wear for going to school? |
| C: | Uniform. |
| I: | What were you wearing? |
| C: | Clothes. |

*Where*

| I: | Where did he tickle you? |
| C: | Down there on my private. |
| I: | Where did you live? |
| C: | [Gives address]. |

*Who*

| I: | Who have we said is allowed to touch you there and have a look if something is wrong? |
| C: | Mum. |
| I: | Who's that then? |
| C: | Dad. |

*When*

| I: | When did he tickle you there? |
| C: | [Silence]. |
| I: | Do you remember when it would happen? |

C:      [Silence].
I:      Do you remember when she told you?
C:      [Silence].

*How*

I:      Do you remember how many times it happened?
C:      [Shakes head].

*Why*

I:      Can you think of a reason why it might cover those parts
        of your body?
C:      [Shakes head].
I:      Why did [name of alleged abuser] do this?
C:      Don't know.

As these examples show, for the question types *what*, *where*, and *who* the child produced 100% appropriate responses. That is, the two where-questions met (appropriately) with responses of either a location or a prepositional phrase. For the two who-questions there were two (appropriate) animate noun responses and for the three what-questions there were three (appropriate) inanimate noun responses. In contrast, there were no correct responses for the how-, why- and when-questions.

## Evidence of Strategies

Next we consider to what extent we see evidence for the strategies mentioned by researchers such as Ervin-Tripp (1970) and Savic (1978). From our analysis (Aldridge, Timmins & Wood 1996), it is interesting to note that although the children rarely achieved a 100% success rate for what-, where- and who-questions, their incorrect responses were either silences or, "I don't know", or "I can't remember". We find no instances in our sample where these question forms were answered as if they were another type of wh-question. This is not, however, our finding for the forms *when*, *how* and *why* where we do see evidence of children using Savic's strategies of answering a question as if it was another form, of repeating part of the question and of giving a stereotypical response.

Although children did on occasions remain silent to when-, how- and why-questions or gave a "don't know/can't remember" answer, we also found examples of children replying as if the question was in another form. The following examples illustrate and in (24) and (25), we see how-questions answered as if they were why-questions:

(24)  From an interview with a 3-year-old girl:

> I:      How did he do that?
> C:      He did it on purpose.

(25)  From an interview with a 4-year-old girl:

> I:      How can people hurt you then?
> C:      'Coz they are being nasty.

In (26), (27) and (28) we see how-questions answered as if they were when-questions:

(26)  From an interview with a 5-year-old girl:

> I:      How did he do it?
> C:      Years ago.

(27)  From an interview with a 5-year-old boy:

> I:      How many times has this happened?
> C:      Yesterday ago.

(28)  From an interview with a 5-year-old boy:

> I:      Can you tell me how he did that?
> C:      When I had my jeans on.

Similarly, we see when-questions answered as if they were a different form. For example, in the following exchange, the child answers a when-question as if it were a where-question:

(29)  From an interview with a 4-year-old girl:

> I:      And when is that? When does that happen?
> C:      In the bath.

Why-questions are vulnerable to this strategy too as the following example illustrates. In this case the child answers the why-question as if it were a where-question:

(30)  From an interview with a 3-year-old girl:

> I:      Why does grandad smack you?
> C:      Here [points].

Why-questions are also vulnerable to answers along the lines of "because they do" or "because it is". Hence we see examples such as the following:

(31)   From an interview with a 4-year-old girl:

I:      Why do boys wear trunks?
C:      Because they do and the girls wear costumes because they
        do.

Further strategies which were also outlined earlier are also apparent in
our interview data as the following examples illustrate. The child
repeats part of the question:

(32)   From an interview with a 6-year-old girl:

I:      How did your dad manage to put his fingers in?
C:      He put his fingers in.

The child gives a stereotypical answer. As the following example
illustrates, when in doubt about how to respond to a where-question,
this child relies upon a stereotypical response, "In Sainsbury's":

(33)   From an interview with a 3-year-old girl.

I:      Have you seen any of these before? Any of these people?
C:      Yeah.
I:      Where's that?
C:      In Sainsbury's.
I:      Is there anywhere else you play apart from at home?
C:      Yeah.
I:      Where else do you play?
C:      In Sainsbury's.

Similarly, the child in the following example relies upon the stereotypical response, "Yesterday":

(34)   From an interview with a 4-year-old boy:

I:      When do you think this happened?
C:      Yesterday.
I:      Yesterday?
C:      I think it was yesterday but I don't know when it was.

The implication of these response strategies when interviewing children
for evidential purposes is clear. Such responses, on the surface, give
an impression of incompetence and make the child appear to be an
unreliable witness. And yet, experimental linguistic evidence with presumed non-abused children indicates that the reason for these responses

is a developmental one. It is the child's limited language ability to answer all question forms which results in these responses rather than the child's actual understanding of the situation or his inability to remember what happened. The message is clear: interviewers must ask the right types of questions if the child is to have a chance of recounting the events. Interviewers must use *when, how* and *why* with caution and evaluate the child's linguistic ability before asking more difficult questions. There is enormous individual variation within language development and it is difficult to predict how children will perform. Some 10-year-olds will struggle with certain wh-questions while some 5-year-olds cope with them admirably as the following illustrates:

(35)   From an interview with a 5-year-old boy:

I:       *Who* else have you told about what happened?
C:      Mum.
I:       And *when* did you tell your mum?
C:      When my bum was hurting.
I:       OK, *why* was your bum hurting?
C:      'Coz it's where dad put his fingers there.

But, with other children, the interviewer might need to tease the information from the child using a choice question in support of the wh-question as in the following example:

(36)   From an interview with a 6-year-old girl:

I:       How many other boys and girls are there in your class?
C:      I don't know.
I:       Is there five or 10, or more?
C:      Well, there's 10 girls and seven boys.

As we discuss in a later section, choice questions can be helpful when interviewing some children but they need to be used with care.

## Tag-questions

In our transcript data we find only positive tag-questions and contracted negative tag-questions, full negative forms of the kind, "You did that, did you not?" are absent from our corpus. This finding is not surprising as full negative tag-questions are infrequent in everyday speech. They are, however, a characteristic of court speech but court language is outside the scope of the present discussion. When we look at the tag-questions in our transcript data, a random selection of which is listed below, it is striking that we find a *yes* response on every occasion:

(37)  From an interview with a 5-year-old boy:

  I:    I think you went to hospital, didn't you?
  C:    Yeah.

(38)  From an interview with a 5-year-old boy:

  I:    Now you saw the camera and the TV before, didn't you?
  C:    Yeah.

(39)  From an interview with a 5-year-old boy:

  I:    Would I be telling a lie, do you think?
  C:    Yes.

(40)  From an interview with a 5-year-old girl:

  I:    You've just moved, have you?
  C:    Yeah.
  I:    You share a bedroom together, do you?
  C:    Yeah.

(41)  From an interview with a 7-year-old boy:

  I:    You know this room because you've been here before, haven't you?
  C:    Yeah.

It is clear that the child is likely to respond with *yes* to a tag-question and thus, the interviewer would be well advised to avoid tag-questions as much as possible for fear of being accused of leading the child.

## Closed questions

If specific questions fail to elicit all the information from the child then the interviewer is likely to move on to closed questions where the child is given a choice of responses and he has to pick one of the options. Remember, for instance, the example given in the MOGP: "Was the man's scarf you mentioned blue or yellow or another colour or can't you remember?". We find many examples of closed questions in our transcript data and we will now discuss a random selection of these beginning with data from children under 6 years of age:

(42) From an interview with a 3-year-old girl:

I:    Do you think it's yellow or orange?
C:    Orange.

(43) From an interview with a 4-year-old girl:

I:    When you put your pyjamas on, do you normally do it before tea or after tea?
C:    After tea.

(44) From an interview with a 4-year-old boy:

I:    Is that older than you or younger than you?
C:    Younger than you.
I:    Was it big or was it small?
C:    Big.
I:    Which toilet was she in, upstairs or downstairs?
C:    Upstairs.

(45) From an interview with a 5-year-old girl:

I:    On your clothes or under your clothes?
C:    Under your clothes.

(46) From an interview with a 5-year-old boy:

I:    Was it light outside or was it dark outside?
C:    Dark.

(47) From an interview with a 5-year-old girl:

I:    What's truth, is it a good thing or a bad thing?
C:    A good thing.
I:    What about a lie? A good thing or a bad thing?
C:    A bad thing.
I:    Is it good or naughty to tell lies?
C:    Naughty.

In these examples, the child most frequently gives the last option as the reply. This is a very serious finding because clearly it is likely that the child is recalling the last bit of the question rather than necessarily answering with the truth. Clearly, with such question forms, the interviewer could be accused of leading the child and thus, closed choice questions must be used with extreme care. If we look at the data from slightly older children:

(48)  From an interview with a 6-year-old boy:

I:      Is she bigger than you or smaller?
C:      Smaller.
I:      Did he bang his head at the bottom of the bed or at the top?
C:      Not at the top but in the middle and top bit.

(49)  From an interview with a 6-year-old girl:

I:      Is that good or bad?
C:      Good.
I:      Is the bathroom upstairs or downstairs?
C:      Upstairs.

(50)  From an interview with a 7-year-old girl:

I:      So which area do you call [name], the front or the back?
C:      The front.
I:      Was that on your skin or on your knickers?
C:      On the skin.

(51)  From an interview with an 8-year-old girl:

I:      Was it before or after Christmas?
C:      After Christmas.
I:      Were you wearing daytime clothes or were you wearing night-time clothes?
C:      Daytime clothes.

From these examples we see far fewer occurrences of the last option being recalled and thus, again we see a developmental change in children's ability around 6 years of age as these children are less vulnerable to repeating the last part of the question. Thus, with older children choice questions might be an option.

## Leading questions

When all else fails, the interviewer can be tempted into using leading questions. Of course, their occurrence significantly weakens the chance of the video being considered as suitable for the child's evidence-in-chief and thus, leading questions should be used with great caution. Considering our own interview data, it is interesting to note that a leading question often occurs in the form of a tag-question, where we know, from previous discussion, that the child is likely to give a *yes* answer, as the following examples show:

(52)   From an interview with a 6-year-old boy:

      ([name] has not previously been mentioned and he is an
      adult)
I:    Who's [name], 'coz I don't know him, is a he a little boy?
C:    Boy, yeah.

(53)   From an interview with a 5-year-old girl:

      (No friends of mummy have been mentioned)
I:    I thought mummy had a friend as well, a man friend, is
      that right?
C:    Yes.

(54)   From an interview with a 5-year-old girl:

      (The child hasn't mentioned daddy hurting her)
I:    I thought that you told [name] that daddy had put his
      finger inside you and hurt you, is that right?
C:    [Nods] yes.

From these examples, we might suggest that if the interviewer avoids
tag-questions she might in the process ask fewer leading questions. If
leading questions must be used they should be reserved until the final
stages of the interview. By delaying leading questions it is hoped that
the child will have volunteered details of the abuse spontaneously or in
response to objective, non-leading questions.

### Children's use of "don't know"

An analysis of our transcript data (Aldridge, Timmins & Wood 1996)
suggests that children sometimes use a "don't know" response as a
blocking strategy to prevent further questioning. The interviewer thus,
must be sensitive to the child's responses and try to re-motivate the
child if substantial numbers of "don't know" responses are noticed.

## INTERVIEWER'S USE OF PUBLISHED ADVICE

Earlier in this chapter we summarized the published advice for interviewers on questioning strategies and we evaluate below the extent to
which interviewers, in our transcript data, utilized this advice. Taking
each of the pieces of advice in turn, we note the following:

*Make sure that the child is reassured that he can say, "I don't know" or "I can't remember" to any questions asked*

In our corpus, we do find examples where the interviewer tells the child that it is acceptable to say, "I don't know". For example, there are examples of interviewers doing this in Chapter 2. However, this advice was not issued in all the interviews we have seen and we would therefore emphasize its importance.

*Remind the child that the interviewer does not know everything and that the child must tell the whole story*

In our corpus, there are examples where the interviewer tells the child that she doesn't know what has happened, a strategy which can be seen in the following examples:

(55)    From an interview with a 5-year-old boy:

    I:      Can you tell me your full name 'cos I don't know it properly.

    I:      I don't know much about you, so . . .

    I:      Tell me who [name] is because I don't know him.

    I:      Can you tell me what a winkie is because I'm not too sure.

(56)    From an interview with a 5-year-old girl:

    I:      Now, I don't know much about you at all so I'm going to ask you some questions and you tell me all about yourself.

    I:      Now, I don't know anything else about you, so can you tell me who lives in your house?

(57)    From an interview with a 7-year-old girl:

    I:      I want to ask you some questions while you're here today, OK? . . . I don't know much about you, all I know is that I met you this morning all right and we had a little chat in here, but I don't know much about you.

However, in some of our interviews this claim was not explicitly made and we would remind interviewers that it is good practice to do so. This was a point which was made in connection with the elicitation of free narrative accounts in Chapter 3.

*Avoid repeating the questions as this will confuse the child*

On the whole, in our corpus, interviewers are careful to avoid repetition of the question and this is a very positive finding. On a few occasions where repetition does occur, we can clearly see how it confuses the child as the following examples illustrate:

(58)   From an interview with a 3-year-old girl:

I:      Your nanny. What does she have to put cream on you for?
C:      I got a poorly bum.
I:      Have you? Why?
C:      I have.
I:      Why is your bum poorly?
C:      It is.
I:      What do you mean by poorly? What's it like?
C:      It's poorly.
I:      Does it hurt?
C:      No.
I:      Why's it poorly then?
C:      It isn't poorly.
I:      It isn't poorly?
C:      No. Let's do some more now jigsaws.

Clearly here the child has got confused and irritated by the repetition and changes her answer and the focus of the conversation. However, when the interviewer returns to the issue a few minutes later she gets the answer she needs:

(59)   I:      Has anybody ever done anything to make your bum hurt?
        C:      My grandad.

Other examples of situations where the child is clearly fed up with question repetition are given below:

(60)   From an interview with a 4-year-old girl:

I:      When you go with mummy visiting and you go with [name] who do you go to visit?
C:      I told you once.

(61)   From an interview with a 5-year-old boy:

I:      How did he touch you then?
C:      With his hand. I told you!

It seems that if repetition is really necessary the interviewer must explain why she's going over the same point again as the following interviewer does with a 4-year-old boy:

(62)  I:    Can you please tell me again because I didn't quite hear everything.

*Be prepared to reflect on the forensic value of the interview*
The interviewer must get precise details from the child of the incident and it is clear from our transcript data that interviewers are acutely aware of this need. It is, however, a problem to know when it is best to obtain the precise details and in our corpus there are examples where the need to obtain the facts actually adversely affects the child's evidence. Below is one example to illustrate the point. This girl spontaneously offers to describe what happened to her:

(63)  From an interview with a 5-year-old girl:

        C:    We went over there to show him our picture and he said do you want to see my willy and I said yeah. Then he said if you do and he wanted us to open it and he got his finger and put his hand in there.
        I:    OK, so you told us a bit about what happened.
        C:    [Nods].
        I:    When did it happen?
        C:    The day before yesterday.
        I:    The day before yesterday.
        C:    [Nods].
        I:    OK, so you and [name] took over a picture that you'd done?
        C:    Yeah.
        I:    What time was that? Do you know?
        C:    No.

In this case, we see that in a search for specific details about time the interviewer inadvertently silences the child. We see that the child changes from being animated and prepared to give relevant details to becoming rather withdrawn and monosyllabic. The child has clearly been put off by the interviewer's need to obtain specific details. Such examples illustrate that the child must be given the space to recount the event in her own way and the interviewer must feel confident to delay questions about specific details until much later in the interview (a point which was emphasized in Chapter 3).

The need to obtain clear forensic details from the child is a real problem for interviewers because topics such as conventional systems of measuring are acquired gradually over the school years. Children can be at least aged 7, for example, before they can tell the time and thus it is not surprising that many questions searching for specific details fail and make the child appear an incompetent witness, as the following examples show:

(64)   From an interview with a 4-year-old girl:

I:      How long have you been staying at [name of foster carer]'s for then? Do you know?
C:      No.
I:      Do you know how many miles it was?
C:      Three miles, no 30 miles.

(65)   From an interview with a 5-year-old girl:

I:      When did it happen?
C:      On Friday.
I:      What day are we on today?
C:      Monday.
I:      We're on Thursday, aren't we?
C:      Yes.

(66)   From an interview with a 6-year-old boy:

I:      Now, today is Tuesday, isn't it?
C:      Yeah.
I:      So what day do you normally start school?
C:      I don't know, I don't know the days.

(67)   From an interview with a 6-year-old girl:

I:      How long had you been in the bath for then before you got out?
C:      I think it was two minutes, I don't know.
I:      You don't know, was it a long time or a short time.
C:      I don't know.

Children under 7 years are going to struggle with questions concerning measurements and thus it is crucial that the interviewer makes use of other strategies for pinning down details of time, etc. such as linking the question to food time, television programmes and special events. From the age of 7 onwards children are much more able to cope with specific questions as the following illustrate:

(68)   From an interview with a 7-year-old boy:

  I:      Right, and how many times did that happen?
  C:      Quite a few.
  I:      And what's quite a few?
  C:      Every time I slept there.

(69)   From an interview with a 7-year-old girl:

  I:      Can you tell me the days of the week?
  C:      [Recites all seven].
  I:      Can you tell me what days you go to school?
  C:      [Recites Monday through to Friday].
  I:      Right and what are the other two days?
  C:      Days off.
  I:      And what are they called?
  C:      Saturday and Sunday.

Having discussed all the types of questions the interviewer might ask
the child, we must also emphasize that the child should be given an
opportunity to ask questions as well as answer them. This opportunity
can be provided in the closure phase. At this time, some children will be
keen to ask what is likely to happen now that the interview is complete.
Thus, this is a time for reassuring the child. The interviewer might say,
for example: "Well, I don't have any more questions I'd like to ask you
but, have you got any questions you would like to ask me?" Once the
child has asked any of his own questions, the interviewer might say that
she can be contacted at any time after the interview if there is anything
that the child needs to know. The interviewer should also take this
opportunity to thank the child for his participation in the interview. By
reassuring and thanking the child, the interviewer can help to leave the
child with a positive view of his interview experience. The closure phase
should never, therefore, be omitted.

We end this chapter with a summary of guidelines for questioning
children and a self-assessment sheet.

# GUIDELINES

* Avoid yes/no questions.
* How-, why- and when-questions should be used with care with
  younger children.
* Use non-leading ways of helping the child to demonstrate what has
  happened.

- Be aware that the child may answer a wh-question as if it were another form.
- Be aware that the child may repeat part of the question if she doesn't understand it.
- Be aware that the child may give a stereotypical response to a question she doesn't understand.
- Avoid tag-questions.
- Avoid choice questions with children under 6 years of age.
- Pay attention to how children are using "don't know".
- Remember to tell the child that it's OK for her to say, "I don't know" or "I can't remember".
- Remember to tell the child that you do not know what has happened.
- Avoid repeating the question.
- Avoid asking specific questions of time to children under 7 years of age.

## SELF-ASSESSMENT SHEET

(1) Was your interviewee willing to answer questions? If not, why do you think this was?

(2) Did you tell the child that it was OK to answer "don't know", "can't remember"?

(3) Did you tell the child that you didn't know the answers to all the questions?

(4) Did you manage to avoid yes/no questions? If no, did you notice whether the child tended to answer yes or no to this question type?

(5) Did you avoid why-questions? If not, did your interviewee answer why-questions appropriately?

(6) Did you sense that in choice questions the child was favouring the first or second option more?

(7) Can you remember asking any leading questions? Write them down. How might they have been rephrased in a non-leading fashion?

(8) Were you aware of repeating any questions? Did the repetition force the child to change his answer?

(9) What was your most successful open question in the interview?

(10) What was your least successful question in the interview?

(11) Any other comments?

# INTERVIEWING OBSERVED: CHILD LANGUAGE AND DEVELOPMENT

The last three chapters have focused on three key stages of the investi-gatory interview (the rapport phase, the free narrative phase and the questioning phase) and aspects of language use which may be prob-lematic in each of these phases have been considered. This chapter examines an aspect of language use which can be problematic across any, or all, of the interview phases; namely the vocabulary (henceforth words) used.

In general terms, the words used within the investigatory interview can be problematic in a number of different ways and these are considered below. The discussion then turns to specific types of words that can be problematic within the interview setting (namely, legal and body part terminology, emotion descriptive words, pronouns and prepositions). First of all though, what general difficulties are encountered in relation to the words used in the interview setting?

## USING A WORD THE CHILD DOESN'T KNOW OR UNDERSTAND

An obvious difficulty with the words used within the interview setting is where the interviewer uses a word the child does not understand. In the following example, the interviewer uses the word *anorak*, and gets no response from the child. In contrast, the child's mother asks the same question but replaces the word *anorak* with the word *coat* and succeeds in obtaining a correct response from the child:

(1)    From an interview with a 4-year-old girl:

I:        And what colour's your mum's anorak?
C:       [Silence].
M:       What colour's my coat?
C:       Green.

There are two general points to be made in connection with this example. First of all, we should always be aware that even apparently simple or "everyday" words such as *anorak* can sometimes be difficult for children to understand. Second, child language research (e.g. Clark 1993) makes clear that children learn general words (in this case *coat*) before they learn more specific words (in this case *anorak*: a particular type of coat). This trend recurs in the specific types of words discussed later in this chapter.

When a child does not understand a word used by the interviewer this often becomes apparent in one of two ways. Either the child is silent (as in the example above) or the child admits that he does not understand the word used, as in the example below:

(2)    From an interview with a 6-year-old boy:

I:        Do you know what "subjects" means?
C:       What?
I:        What "subjects" are?
C:       No.
I:        Well, they're the lessons that you do in school like, em, drawing and painting.
C:       I didn't know that.

Of course, in cases such as these the interviewer is aware of a problem and is able to use an alternative word (in the example above, for instance, the interviewer replaced the word *subjects* with the word *lessons* which the child knew). More dangerous in the interview setting are cases such as the following.

## SAME WORD: DIFFERENT MEANINGS

In some cases, the interviewer and the child may use the same word but may mean different things by it. In the example below, for instance, the child and the interviewer do not have in mind the same thing when the word *video* is used:

(3)    From an interview with a 5-year-old boy:

I:      Well, perhaps I'd better explain a bit. Have you got any
        videos at home?
C:      Yeah, one.
I:      One and what's on it?
C:      Numbers.

Here, the interviewer is referring, in her initial question to videotapes or
films. The child, on the other hand, interprets *video* as referring to a
video-recorder or machine and says that his family has one of these. In
her second question, the interviewer asks, "What's on it?" meaning what
film or programme is on the videotape. The child though still interprets
*video* as referring to the machine and says it has numbers on it (presumably a reference to the video's control panel). Instances such as this
where the child and interviewer are operating at cross purposes may go
unnoticed and this may lead to a dangerous misunderstanding of the
child's account.

## KNOWING THE RIGHT WORD

Throughout our lives, we acquire more and more words and thus
children's knowledge of words is not as extensive as adults' and there
are therefore bound to be occasions when the child does not have a
word(s) to express what he wants to say. An example of this can be seen
in the following:

(4)    From an interview with a 7-year-old boy:

I:      And have you got anything on your bed?
C:      No.
S/W:    Well, isn't it a bit cold when you go to bed at night?
C:      Oh! I got covers on it.
S/W:    Yeah?
C:      Or, sometimes, in the winter, I have a different thing
        which is em . . ., er. . . ., em.
S/W:    Oh that word!
C:      Big things like that and they go under your bed and you
        press this button and it warms your bed up.
S/W:    An electric blanket yeah?
C:      [Shakes head].

In this example, it is not clear whether or not the child is trying to describe an electric blanket as the social worker suggests. What is clear, however, is the fact that the child does not have a word or words to name the item he is trying so hard to describe. The result of this deficit is, of course, that, on the one hand the child has a more difficult task in telling his story and, on the other hand the interviewer has a more difficult task in interpreting what the child is trying to describe. Absence of the necessary word also makes the child vulnerable to suggestion. On this occasion, the child disagrees with the word (electric blanket) that the social worker suggests in a non-crucial area, but what would have happened if the topic had been part of central information and the child had gone along with the word the social worker suggested? The interviewer can easily lead in such cases thereby weakening the case.

These difficulties with the words used can apply throughout the course of the interview. There are also a number of specific types of words which are likely to occur in the interview and which may be problematic. These include:

- Legal terms: words such as *police-officer, social worker, arrest* and *court*.
- Body part terms: words such as those used to describe the genitalia and sexual acts.
- Expressions of emotion: words such as *angry* and *frightened*.
- Pronouns: words such as *it* and *that*.
- Prepositions and temporal terms: words such as *in* and *on*, *before* and *after*.

We discuss each of these types of words, in turn, below:

## LEGAL TERMS

A number of research studies (e.g. those by Aldridge, Timmins & Wood 1997, Flin, Stephenson & Davies 1989, Saywitz & Jaenicke 1987 and Warren-Leubecker et al 1988) have shown that legal terminology including words such as *police-officer, social worker, judge, arrest* and *witness* may be misunderstood or not understood at all by some children.

## Police-officer and Social Worker

Of particular concern within the initial interview setting is the fact that video interview and research data suggest that children may not fully understand the role of those who are interviewing them (i.e. police-officers and social workers). General anxieties about the role of police interviewers can be seen in a number of interviews. Examples include the following:

(5)    From an interview with a 4-year-old girl:

I:     You know when I talk to children, they tell me about all kinds of things but, do you know what I like them to tell me?
C:     Yeah.
I:     Only about things that have really happened. Do you know what that means?
C:     If you're naughty.
I:     Oh right but you've not been naughty have you? That's not why you're here today.
C:     Are you a police?
I:     Yes I am.
C:     Do you know what my brother does that's naughty? He spits his bottle out.

Later in the same interview:

I:     OK so, you said you do painting and gluing. Where do you do that?
C:     I not telling you.
I:     Why aren't you telling me?
C:     'Coz I don't like telling people.
I:     Why don't you like telling people?
C:     'Coz I don't, just don't.
I:     Oh right, why? What happened?
C:     Nothing.
I:     Is it a secret?
C:     Are you a police?
I:     I am yes.
C:     Police girl?
I:     Police girl, yes.
C:     Whose dress is that?
I:     I haven't got a uniform have I?
C:     I thought you did.
I:     Why did you think that?
C:     I just did.
I:     Right.

It is clear, from these extracts, that the child has a number of anxieties. First of all, she seems unable to reconcile the fact that police-officers, in her experience, wear a uniform whereas this interviewing officer is wearing plain clothes. Second, the child appears unwilling to talk about "secrets" or "being naughty" when she is talking to a police-officer. Similar anxieties arise in another interview:

(6)   From an interview with a 4-year-old girl:

    I:      Are you worried that I might tell you off for telling something to me?
    C:     [Nods].
    I:      You are? What are you worried about?
    C:     Because you got that skirt on.
    I:      A skirt on?
    C:     It looks like just a skirt not a police skirt it doesn't look like.
    I:      Yeah so, 'coz I've got a skirt on you think . . .
    C:     It's not a police skirt.
    I:      No, it's not is it? It's my skirt isn't it?
    C:     Yeah.
    I:      But, I'm still a police lady aren't I?

Later in the same interview:

    C:     I saw your police car.
    I:      Did you? I didn't come in a police car.
    C:     I saw your police car.
    I:      Was that here or somewhere else?
    C:     Here.

Again, the child seems to have anxieties about the interviewer arising from an inability to reconcile her previous experience of policewomen in uniform driving police cars with the plain clothes interviewer driving an unmarked car.

Clues as to why these two children may be anxious about being interviewed by police women can be found in extracts from interviews with other children. There are some children, for example, who have direct experience of what going to a police station means and who because of this may have a limited view of the role of police-officers as the following exchange illustrates:

(7)    From an interview with a 5-year-old girl:

    I:      I understand that you sometimes call [name of alleged
            abuser] daddy?
    C:      [Nods].
    I:      Does he still live with you?
    C:      [Shakes head] Gone to the police station.
    I:      He's gone to the police station?
    C:      [Nods].
    I:      And why's he gone to the police station then?
    C:      'Coz he's naughty.
    I:      Right.
    C:      He's taken the video and a telly.

Clearly, this child thinks that you go to a police station if you've been
naughty. Another child holds similar views as the exchange below
illustrates:

(8)    From an interview with a 5-year-old girl:

    I:      Do you know what my job is?
    C:      No.
    I:      I'm a police lady.
    C:      [Silence].
    I:      Do you know what a police lady does?
    C:      Yeah.
    I:      What does she do?
    C:      Er, gets people in prison.
    I:      Right, yeah and what else does a police lady do?
    C:      Er, the ones that are killed they bring them to the
            ambulance.

Again, the child thinks that police-officers only either put people in
prison or deal with those who've been killed. Of even greater concern
are those children who appear to think that they themselves might be
arrested. The extract below illustrates this:

(9)    From an interview with a 6-year-old boy:

    C:      Who broke that? [a reference to one of the toys].
    I:      I don't know, perhaps some other children who have been
            here.
    C:      Broke it? Did you arrest them?
    I:      Oh no! I don't arrest children.

S/W:    Wouldn't do that.
C:      No, they go to a naughty boys' home.

And later in the same interview:

I:      I see, is there anyone else that's naughty?
C:      Sometimes I am.
I:      Right, what sort of things do you do that's naughty?
C:      Don't arrest me!
I:      I won't arrest you, no. I've told you I don't arrest children.
C:      You only arrest big people.
I:      Yes, big people who do something wrong. I don't think
        you've done anything wrong have you?
C:      No.
I:      Well then, I won't arrest you today in that case!

Children who think that police-officers simply arrest those who are
naughty may be particularly anxious for a number of reasons. First, they
may mistakenly think that they themselves have been naughty and thus
that they are at risk of being arrested. The extract below illustrates this
possibility:

(10)   From an interview with a 4-year-old girl:

I:      Right and what were you doing when it happened?
C:      Sitting on his knee. It's OK to sit on his knee?
I:      Yeah.

Apparently, this child thinks that she may have been at fault for sitting
on the alleged abuser's knee. Thus some children may think that they
have been naughty and that they are to be interviewed by the police
because of this (this issue was addressed in Chapter 2 and ways of
explaining to the child that he has done nothing wrong were suggested).
Second, the abuser may have threatened the child in some way thus
reinforcing or introducing the possibility that the child may be in trouble
with the police. An example of this can be found in the following
interview exchange:

(11)   From an interview with a 7-year-old boy:

C:      And then he shouted me back up and said to me, "If I tell
        mum I'll go in jail".
I:      Who would go in jail?
C:      I would.

I:        You would?
C:        [Nods].

Clearly then, children may have good cause to think that they might be in trouble if they disclose. It is also possible that children may be afraid of the consequences of disclosure on those who they make allegations against. The following extract illustrates this point:

(12)   From an interview with a 6-year-old boy:

I:        In this room, we can talk about anything like that can't we [name of social worker]?
S/W:    Yes, it's OK.
C:        But about if grown-ups then you arrest them don't you?
I:        Well, it depends.

Of course, if these kind of anxieties become apparent within the interview then the child can be reassured about the role of the interviewing officer. This reassurance could be along the following lines:

(13)   From an interview with a 6-year-old boy:

I:        Have you ever seen a police lady before?
C:        Arresting [name].
I:        Arresting [name] oh well, have you ever seen a police lady out in [place name] at all in uniform, wearing a hat and a skirt and a shirt?
C:        [Shakes head].
I:        Well, my job means that I talk to lots of children so there's nothing to worry about.

In the above interview, it becomes apparent that the child has a limited but vivid experience of the role of a police-officer and the interviewer is able to offer reassurance that her job means she talks to lots of children and that the child has nothing to worry about. It may be the case, in other interviews, though, that the child's anxieties do not become apparent in this way. It is still possible, however, that these anxieties exist even if they are not voiced. It is therefore important that in all interviews the child is reassured about the role of the interviewing officer.

In some interviews, of course, the interviewer may be a social worker rather than a police officer. Our interview data suggest that children are often totally unaware of the role of a social worker. In the following interview extract, for example, the social worker asks the child about the job of a social worker:

(14)   From an interview with a 7-year-old boy:

   S/W:   Do you know what I do?
   C:     No.
   S/W:   I'm a social worker, that's my job. Have you heard of one of those before?
   C:     No.
   S/W:   Well, it's a special kind of job. A bit like [name of WPC]'s really.

In this instance, the child not only admits that he doesn't know what the social worker's job is, he also concedes that he's never heard of a social worker before. Further data, from a language game with assumed non-abused children (Aldridge, Timmins & Wood 1997) also suggests that whereas a limited understanding is likely to be apparent in relation to the role of a police-officer, the role of a social worker is more likely not to be understood at all. Only at 10 years of age do we see children able accurately to describe the role of a social worker. For example, one 10-year-old told us that a social worker is, "somebody who works helping the police". Another child (again a 10-year-old) said that, "she [a social worker] talks to you and she explains things to you if you don't know something or if you're scared or something like that". A lack of understanding of the role of a social worker interviewer on the part of the child is likely to be as frightening for him as the limited understanding we report in relation to the role of police-officers. On the basis of these findings, we suggest that it should be standard practice for the interviewer (whether she is a police-officer or social worker) to explain her role to the child before the interview commences.

## Other Legal Terms

What about other legal terminology that the child might encounter? In recent research (Aldridge, Timmins & Wood 1997), we report on findings from a language game presented to 32 assumed non-abused children. Within this game, the children were presented with a doll who was unable to understand a variety of legal terms (including *arrest*, *judge*, *court* and *witness*). The children were then asked to explain, to the doll, what these terms meant.

**Table 2**   Legal terms acquired* by each age group

| Age 5 | Age 7 | Age 8 | Age 10 |
|---|---|---|---|
| burglary | burglary | burglary | burglary |
| police-officer | police-officer | police-officer | police-officer |
| criminal | criminal | criminal | criminal |
| | arrest | arrest | arrest |
| | judge | judge | judge |
| | | guilty | guilty |
| | | crime | crime |
| | | court | court |
| | | law | law |
| | | | innocent |
| | | | social worker |
| | | | police constable |
| | | | witness |
| | | | jury |
| | | | accused |
| Total 3 terms | Total 5 terms | Total 9 terms | Total 15 terms |

* Our criteria for suggesting that a term is acquired by a given age group is that 50% or more of the children in a given age group were able to provide some correct description of a given term.

In terms of the age at which children are able to define these words, it was noted that at the age of 5 years only 15% of the terms presented to the children could be considered to be acquired (i.e. were defined with some correct description by more than half the children in that age group). In contrast, 79% of the terms were acquired (by the same criteria) at the age of 10 years. Table 2 provides a summary of the findings. From Table 2, it is clear that children have a limited understanding of various legal terms including *arrest* (not acquired until the age of 7), *guilty* (not acquired until the age of 8) and *witness* (not acquired until the age of 10). In addition, the terms *custody*, *magistrate* and *probation* are not acquired (by our criteria) until after the age of 10 years. Perhaps more worrying than children's inability to define some of these terms is the nature of their misunderstandings. We have the following examples in our data:

- A 5-year-old suggests that a court is a sort of jail.
- A 7-year-old thinks that witnesses whip people when they're naughty.
- Another 7-year-old, when asked to define the term *witness* claims that the police think that witnesses have done something naughty.
- Another 7-year-old suggests that prosecution is when you die, you get hanged or something awful like that.

- One 7-year-old suggests that judges get money at pet shows.
- A further 7-year-old thinks that a judge judges people, like when you go to jail and you have to tell the judge what you've done.
- An 8-year-old suggests that when you're arrested, a policeman will come along and put you in chains.
- Another 8-year-old similarly thinks that court is like a jail, it's like when they're in chains and there's bars stopping them from getting out.

If children harbour these kinds of misunderstandings about aspects of the legal process it is hardly surprising that they are often reticent in recounting details of abusive events. The only way to counter these misunderstandings is to confront them. Thus if legal terminology such as *arrest* or *court* is used within the course of the interview then the interviewer should ensure that the child has a realistic understanding of these terms. Just because the child appears to be using a word appropriately does not mean that he has an adult-like understanding of that word. In fact, as the above examples show, the child may have a dangerous misunderstanding of the word. Potential misunderstandings need to be identified and clarified. If they are not then the child may well be frightened to tell his story if he thinks that he has been naughty and may be arrested which in turn means being put in chains! We turn now to an aspect of vocabulary which is often central to the investigation of child sexual abuse; namely body part and sexual terminology.

## BODY PART AND SEXUAL TERMINOLOGY

As we discussed earlier, another difficulty with the use of words arises when the child does not have the word(s) to name what he wants to describe. Body part and sexual terminology is one area where the child's limited word stock becomes obvious. Intuitively, we might think that names for different parts of the body are everyday words that children are likely to be well aware of. We might think that such words occur regularly in day-to-day settings; when a child has a bath or gets (un)dressed, for example. However, our research findings suggest that children are not as aware, even of non-sexual body part terminology, as we might expect them to be.

In a recent experimental study (Aldridge & Wood 1996), we conducted a language game with 90 assumed non-abused children aged 2–6 years of age. Within this study, we examined children's ability to:

- Name the non-sexual parts of a doll which we pointed to and
- Point to the non-sexual parts of a doll which we named.

Our findings suggest that the number of body part words both understood and named increases with age. It also appears that a pattern exists
in that words for parts of the face (e.g. eyes, ears, nose) are acquired
before words for the extremities (e.g. arms) which, in turn, are acquired
before words relating to the torso (e.g. tummy). Some words (e.g. ankles
and elbows) are not fully acquired until after six 6 years of age (see also
Anderson 1978 and MacWhinney, Cermak & Fisher 1987). This
highlights the fact that we should not assume that even non-sexual
body part words are easy or "everyday" words which the child is likely
to have acquired.

In line with the general trend in the knowledge of words which we
highlighted earlier, we also see that general body part words (e.g. eyes
and legs) are acquired before more specific words (e.g. eyebrows and
ankles). This finding has clear implications for children's ability to name
sexual body parts in the interview (e.g. children often use the general
word *bum* in preference to more specific words identifying the genitals).
We return to the significance of this point later.

A further finding, from our language game, is also significant to the
interview setting. This is that children's ability to point to the body parts
which we named was often greater than their ability to name the parts to
which we pointed. For example, all our 4-year-olds were able to point to
the doll's lips when we named them. In contrast, only 72% of the 4-year-
olds could produce the word *lips* when we pointed to this part of the
doll. The significance of this finding for the interview setting is that it
may suggest that the child should be given an opportunity to show the
interviewer what happened or to point to parts of the body if they
appear unable to name them (see also the discussion about dolls in
Chapter 3).

It is clear therefore that some children may not have the words to describe
sexual body parts. The following extract illustrates this possibility:

(15)  From an interview with a 3-year-old girl:

      I:    Do you know where you do a wee-wee from?
      C:    Yeah.
      I:    Do you know where that is?
      C:    Yeah.
      I:    Can you point to me and show me?
      C:    Toilet.

I:      Toilet?
C:      Yeah.
I:      Can you show me where on you, where you do a wee-wee
        from?
C:      Don't know.
I:      You don't know?
C:      I can't find a toilet.

A similar exchange occurs with a 5-year-old boy:

(16)  I:      If you were having a wee, where would that come from on
              you? Which bit?
      C:      Em, a toilet.

It seems that both these children are oblivious to the fact that a particular part of the body is used when they urinate. Certainly, neither child has a word to name these parts (or, if they have, it is one that the interviewer is unable to elicit).

More common than instances where the child has no name for his genitals are instances where the child is simply reticent in disclosing the word(s) that he uses. An example of this occurs in the following interview extract which also highlights a number of strategies which the interviewer can use in order to help the child overcome his reticence:

(17)  From an interview with a 7-year-old girl:

      I:      Right so, what I'd like you to do, is to tell me a little bit
              more.
      C:      Can't.
      I:      Well, you said he touched you somewhere on your body
              that he shouldn't have touched you. Is that right?
      C:      Yeah.
      I:      OK. So, what part of your body are we talking about?
      C:      I don't want to tell you 'coz it'll embarrass me, that's why.
      F:      Well, I tell you what, say it really quickly.
      C:      No!
      I:      What about if I do it another way. Do you go swimming?
      C:      [Nods].
      I:      Right, what do you wear when you go swimming?
      C:      A cossie.
      I:      Right. On your body, where does a cossie cover? Which
              parts of you?

C:      All from here.
I:      And what does [name of child's brother] wear when he goes swimming?
C:      Some trunks.
I:      And what parts of his body do the trunks cover?
C:      From here to here.
I:      Right so why is it different on you to [name of child's brother]?
C:      'Coz it's covering this part [chest].
I:      And why is it different?
C:      'Coz he's a boy.
I:      So, if I went swimming, what parts of me would I cover?
C:      Here to here.
I:      Right so you know all about that. All we've got to do now is decide names for those parts of the body isn't it?
C:      [Nods].
I:      Right so what part of my body is this called?
C:      An arm.
I:      Right, so it's all right to say that?
C:      Yeah.
I:      And what's this part?
C:      A leg.
I:      A leg, so those words are OK to say. It's maybe the other ones that are a bit harder to say?
C:      No, more embarrassing to say.
I:      Right, well the thing is, you see, I don't know what you might call certain parts of your body 'coz some children call things, they have funny little names for them. Now, there's a difference there now between boys and girls isn't there?
C:      [Nods].
I:      What's on a boy then?
C:      A long thing.
I:      A long thing. Right, what's that long thing? What do you call it at home?
C:      I don't want to say.
I:      You don't want to say. OK, what does [name of child's brother] call it?
C:      Sometimes a jimmy.
I:      OK and what else?
C:      I don't want to say that.
I:      OK, what's it used for?
C:      What do you mean?

| | |
|---|---|
| I: | What's a jimmy used for? |
| C: | To wee out of. |
| I: | To wee out of. OK, right so what does daddy call it? |
| C: | The same. |
| I: | A jimmy? Is that right? |
| C: | Well, he calls it a different name. |
| I: | He calls it a different name. What's that? |
| C: | Which is spelt W.E.L.Y. |
| I: | Is that, if I say it, welly? |
| C: | No. |
| I: | What is it then? |
| C: | W. I .L., two Ls, yeah. W.I.L.L.Y. |
| I: | Right, is that willy? Is that the word you don't want to say? |
| C: | [Nods]. |

There are three points to highlight in connection with this extract. First, it shows just how reticent some children can be in naming sexual body parts when they are embarrassed to do so. Second, we see that persuading the child that it is all right to name these parts can be a protracted process. And third, we see that there are a variety of strategies that interviewers can use in order to help children overcome their reticence in naming these parts. These strategies include:

*Suggesting that the child says the word quickly*
Earlier on in the above interview, this strategy was successfully employed as follows:

(18)   From an interview with a 7-year-old girl:

| | |
|---|---|
| C: | Can I say it quickly? |
| I: | Yeah. |
| C: | [Unintelligible]. |
| I: | So can you say it quickly but so that we can understand it 'coz that was a bit too quick. |
| C: | He touched a part of my body. |

In this case, the child felt more comfortable saying what she felt embarrassed about quickly. A similar strategy, used in some interviews, is for the child to whisper to the interviewer any words which he does not wish to say aloud.

*Talking about the parts of the body the child's swimming costume/trunks covers*
As the above transcript shows, if the child can be persuaded to indicate which parts of the body his swimwear covers then this can serve to isolate the relevant "private" body parts from other parts of the body. Once the relevant parts are isolated in this way then the child may feel less nervous about naming them than he would about naming these parts spontaneously.

*Talking about the parts swimwear covers on other people*
The child may feel less embarrassed to label the genitals if he feels that it is not only his own body that is the focus of the conversation. Thus, if the interviewer asks about what parts of the body swimwear covers on herself, on parents, or on siblings then this may well help the child to feel less self-conscious.

*Talking about non-sexual body part terms*
If the child can be encouraged to label non-sexual body part terms then he may proceed to name the sexual body parts. In some cases, this will be a natural progression from naming the non-sexual parts and in other cases, the child may need to be encouraged to make the transition from naming non-sexual to naming sexual parts. As in the above exchange, this transition can be encouraged by the interviewer by emphasizing that if it is all right to name non-sexual parts then it is equally all right to name sexual parts. The child can be encouraged that he is in a special room where it is all right to use words even though these words might be considered rude in other contexts. It may also be helpful if the child is reassured that his parents will not mind if he uses these words in the interview.

*Referring the child to the similar difficulties experienced by other children*
In the above exchange (17), the interviewer points out that all children have different names for parts of the body and that some children have "funny little names" for some parts. Such a statement reminds the child that the interviewer has to talk to lots of children in the course of her work and this offers reassurance that the child is not alone in having to name parts of his body which he is embarrassed about. Also, such a statement reassures the child that other children might use idiosyncratic words to label parts of the body and this may allay the child's fears that his word isn't the "proper" or correct word. It is similarly helpful if the interviewer can tell the child that any words the child uses are "what lots of children call that part" or that the word the child uses is the one she uses too.

*What does mum/dad/sibling call these body parts?*
If the child is uncertain about the validity of his words for sexual body parts then he may feel more confident to tell the interviewer what his parents and/or siblings call the relevant parts of the body. Asking the child what words other family members use also serves as a reminder that other people use these words and this may reassure the child that it is all right for him to use these words in the interview.

*What is this part used for?*
A discussion of the function of body parts, as in (17) above, may also be useful in that it removes one type of information that the child may feel uncomfortable about discussing. Thus, some of the burden of "taboo" topics is lifted.

*Can you spell the word for me?*
Spelling out the body part words that she is embarrassed to say is the strategy that worked for the child in the interview extract above. A similar strategy that works with some children is to allow the child to write down those words which he is reticent to say aloud. Clearly, of course, this strategy is age-dependent in that younger interviewees will not be capable of spelling or writing words they may not wish to say.

Finally, there are two further possible strategies for eliciting body part words: the first is to allow the child to talk into a toy telephone and the second is to allow the child to tell one of the toys in the room and for the toy to tell the interviewer with the child's help. Both these strategies can be successful in taking the spotlight away from the child.

There are, then, a variety of strategies which interviewers can use to help children overcome their reticence in naming sexual body parts. When children do name sexual body parts though, what words are they likely to use?

## Terms for Sexual Body Parts

In our experience, children use a variety of terms to label the genitals. Examples can be seen in Table 3. A common problem when children use the body part words in Table 3 is where they offer a general word and it is not clear exactly what is being referred to. This is in line with our earlier report that children in our language game could produce general body part words (e.g. eye) before more specific words (e.g. eyebrow). Similarly, children in the interview context may use the general word

**Table 3**   Terms commonly used for sexual body parts

| Male genitals | Female genitals |
| --- | --- |
| Dick, jimmy, long thing, privates, tap, willy, willy wonka, winkie, wobbly bits | Bum, fairy, fanny, flower, mary, peach, privates, that hole, tuppence, tutty |

*bum* in preference to more specific words which identify the genitals. The following extract illustrates this:

(19)   From an interview with a 7-year-old girl:

I:      Right and would you be able to tell me, in a bit more detail, about what it was that she did that was naughty?
C:     She stuck something up my bum.

In this case, the child uses the general word *bum* and it is not clear whether this is used to refer to the vagina or anus. How can this be clarified? Well, perhaps the clearest strategy in this case is to ask the child the function of the part she is referring to. We see this strategy successfully employed in the following example where the child's use of the word *private* needs to be clarified:

(20)   From an interview with a 9-year-old girl:

I:      OK, so what do we use a private for?
C:     Wee.
I:      I see and when you go for a poo, what do you call that part?
C:     Your bum.

In this case, the strategy works well and it is clear that the child uses the word *private* to refer to her genitals. This strategy is similarly successful in the following exchange:

(21)   From an interview with a 4-year-old girl:

I:      Right, so I know where your bum is. Where's your bum?
C:     [Points].
I:      Right and what do you use your bum for?
C:     Pooing.
I:      For pooing, and what's your tutty?
C:     For my wee.

Again, by focusing on the function of the named body parts, the interviewer is able to clarify what the child refers to when she says *tutty*.

Unfortunately, some children may be confused about the function of different parts of the body and thus the strategy employed above may not always be successful. This can be seen in the following example:

(22) From an interview with a 5-year-old boy:

    I:     What do you do with your winkie?
    C:    Have wee-wee and poo in the toilet.
    I:     Have wee-wee and poo in the toilet. OK.

In this case, the child reveals some confusion about the function of his winkie. It becomes clear via a drawing produced by the child later in the interview that he, in fact, uses the word *winkie* to refer to his penis. Allowing the child to draw a picture of the relevant part of the body may then help to clarify what the child is referring to. Another strategy is to ask the child to point to the body part he has mentioned. This strategy is successfully employed in the following example:

(23) From an interview with a 4-year-old girl:

    I:     Have you hurt anywhere else on your body recently?
    C:    Yeah [name of alleged abuser] put his fingers in my private.
    I:     I see and when you say your private, could you show me on your body which part do you mean?
    C:    There [points to groin].

In many cases, asking the child to point to where he means will be successful in differentiating between the parts at the back and front of the body. Interviewers should be aware though that some children may be uncomfortable about showing which part of the body they are referring to. This is demonstrated by the following extract:

(24) From an interview with a 4-year-old girl:

    I:     So, show me where does he touch you?
    C:    [Points and whispers] On my tutty.
    I:     So, stand up and show me, where's that then?
    C:    [Points but looks up nervously at the camera].

The child indicates that she is nervous about pointing to her tutty in two ways. First, she whispers in response to the interviewer's initial request and then when asked to point a second time she looks nervously up at the camera. A strategy of pointing to body parts which may be less uncomfortable for the child is to ask him to point to the parts on a doll. We are not advocating the use of anatomically correct dolls here; ordinary rag dolls can be used to enable the child to point to different parts of the body (see also the discussion about the use of dolls in Chapter 3).

A strategy where the child can point to or show the interviewer relevant parts of the body can also be advocated on the basis of findings from our language game (Aldridge & Wood 1996), mentioned earlier. That is, the 2–6-year-olds who took part in our language game were better at pointing to the parts of the doll we named than they were at naming the parts we pointed to. That children's language comprehension is ahead of their language production is a common finding in language acquisition research and it may therefore be the case that where a child cannot name a body part, he may be able to understand that body part name if the interviewer says it, or points to the body part if given an opportunity to do so.

Of course, if the child is to give a full account of a sexually abusive incident then he will need to be able to do more than just name the body parts involved. There are a variety of sexual acts which children may need to describe. However, in our experience children are often unable to describe sexual acts and this frequently appears to be because they do not have an adult-like understanding of the significance of these acts. For example, the child in the following interview exchange is clearly unaware of the penis's sexual function:

(25)    From an interview with a 5-year-old girl:

    I:      You know when boys have willy wonkas?
    C:      Yeah.
    I:      What are their willy wonkas for?
    C:      For doing a wee.
    I:      For doing a wee. Can they do anything else with a willy
            wonka?
    C:      No. Don't know.

Some of the sexual information children often struggle to convey is discussed below.

*Penetration*
In many accounts that young girls give of sexually abusive incidents, it is unclear whether or not any sort of penetration has taken place. This is often a result of the fact that girls tend to use a general term to label their genitals and do not have a specific label for the vagina. This difficulty can be seen in the following interview extract:

(26)   From an interview with a 5-year-old girl:

I:      Whereabouts on your peach did the cream go?
C:      On top.
I:      On top?
C:      Yeah.
I:      Did it go inside?
C:      Yeah, I think so, yeah it did.

In this account, the child's term, *peach*, is not sufficiently specific to indicate exactly where the cream was applied. A similar problem arises in the following interview where the child discloses that she has been touched on her *tuppence*. The following extract, from this interview, shows one way in which the interviewer might establish whether or not (digital) penetration has taken place:

(27)   From an interview with a 7-year-old girl:

I:      Right. Now, your tuppence is a part of your body that's used to do what?
C:      Wee.
I:      Wee. Right and where does the wee come from?
C:      A little hole.
I:      Right, OK, what about that little hole then?
C:      [Silence].
I:      Where did the finger go?
C:      Like that [drawing an imaginary line across the chair seat with her finger].
I:      Right.
C:      It was sliding like that.
I:      Sliding along. Right and where was the little hole?
C:      Here [pointing to the middle of the imaginary line just drawn on the seat of the chair].
I:      So, the hole was here?
C:      Yeah.

I:      So, that's the hole and that's your tuppence and this is the finger that [name of alleged abuser] touched you with. Show me how the finger went.

C:      Like that [running her finger along the line and across the top of the hole].

In this case, the child was aware of her vagina and although she did not have the precise word to label it, she could refer to the "little hole" and was able to both show the interviewer (and later describe to her) that digital penetration did not occur. Younger children may be less aware of their bodies and thus may not be able to express this distinction.

*Stimulation/masturbation*

Again, due to lack of awareness of sexual acts, some children fail to understand the significance of questions which try to establish whether stimulation/masturbation has taken place. In the following interview, for example, the interviewer tries to establish what the alleged abuser did with his hand when he touched the girl's genitals. Unfortunately, the child answers the question by explaining in which direction the alleged abuser's hand moved rather than describing how his hand moved:

(28)    From an interview with a 9-year-old girl:

I:      And what about his hand, what did he do with his hand?

C:      Moved it.

I:      Can you tell me in what way he was moving it?

C:      That way.

In another interview, this time with a 9-year-old boy, the interviewer struggles to establish whether the boy witnessed his father urinating or masturbating. In his initial account the boy has alleged that his father put a "sweet wrapper on his willy and then weed into it" and that "the wee was going everywhere". In an attempt to secure a more detailed account, the interviewer pursues the following line of questioning:

(29)    From an interview with a 9-year-old boy:

I:      Was he doing anything when he was having a wee?

C:      No, that's it.

Later:

I:      Now, when dad went for a wee, was he doing anything else with his willy?

C:    No, that's just it.
I:    Where were his hands?
C:    On the sweet wrapper.
I:    And what were they doing?
C:    Well, my dad was holding the sweet wrapper with two hands and then when he'd done the wee it went all over the toilet seat and on the floor.
I:    OK, was your dad doing anything else with his hands?
C:    Just holding it and then when he let go he just squeezed my willy.

It seems unlikely, in this case, that the child understands the significance of the interviewer's repeated questions. Even in cases where children are able to give some indication of masturbation taking place they do not have the words to give a precise account. The girl in the following interview, for example, describes her grandad's sexually abusive behaviour:

(30)   From an interview with a 9-year-old girl:

I:    Tell me a little bit more about that.
C:    He was, er, rubbing my leg and bouncing his willy.

The child's description of the abuser "bouncing his willy" is about the best that can be expected from a child whose sexual understanding and word knowledge is limited.

*Ejaculation*
Prior to the following interview exchange, the child has described the alleged abuser "touching his willy". The interview then continues as follows:

(31)   From an interview with a 9-year-old girl:

I:    OK and did anything happened to his willy after he was touching it?
C:    All white thing was coming out.

Although the child gives a clear indication of the presence of semen, she later shows that she is unaware of the significance of this:

I:    And did he say anything to you?
C:    He said "let me come", he said it twice.
I:    And do you know what that means?
C:    Don't know.

Other children may be similarly unaware (e.g. the 9-year-old boy mentioned earlier who said his father "weed" into a sweet wrapper) and thus unable to understand the significance of associated questioning strategies. In the interview with a 9-year-old boy mentioned earlier, the interviewer tries to establish whether what the child describes as *wee* is, in fact, urine or whether it is semen:

(32)   From an interview with a 9-year-old boy:

     I:      And what was his wee like?
     C:     Yellow.
     I:      Was it?
     C:     Yeah.
     I:      And did you see the wee on the toilet seat?
     C:     Yeah.
     I:      And did you see what colour it was on the toilet seat?
     C:     No, it was white on the toilet seat.
     I:      I see, when you say it was white, what do you mean when you say white? Was it a colour or?
     C:     It wasn't a colour.
     I:      OK, did it look like ordinary wee?
     C:     Yeah.

In cases such as this, the interviewer can ask the child for a description of the wee or can ask the child to make a comparison – was what the child describes as wee like ordinary wee or was there anything different about it?

In cases like this, the interviewer should also keep in mind that children often employ language overgeneralization strategies. That is, if they do not have a word for something they will label it by using the word for something similar that they do have a label for. Thus we see examples in our language game (Aldridge & Wood 1996) where children do not know the word *ankles* and so instead overgeneralize and label the ankles as *legs* or *feet*. In a similar way, it is quite likely that a child who does not know the word *semen* will describe this as *wee* instead.

*Erection*
A further aspect of some children's accounts which is often difficult to clarify is whether or not the abuser experienced an erection. In fact, a number of interviewers in our survey (Aldridge & Wood 1997a) noted that this is one of the most difficult aspects of the child's account to establish. This difficulty is illustrated by the following exchange:

(33)   From an interview with a 9-year-old boy:

    I:      I see, what did his willy look like?
    C:    Yellow.
    I:      Right, what shape was it, his willy?
    C:    It was, em, like one of them circle shapes.
    I:      Em, I don't know what you mean, can you perhaps draw it in the air for me, what sort of shape you mean, what was it like?
    C:    It was a circle one.
    I:      I see.
    C:    It was like that [draws circle in the air].

Later:

    I:      I'm just wondering what his willy looked like.
    C:    It was a circle one.
    I:      Right. OK, would you say it was pointing.
    C:    Up, forwards.
    I:      OK now, what's a willy like normally?
    C:    Sometimes I have a wee and it's all yellow.
    I:      OK, what shape is it normally?
    C:    Yellow, a circle one.
    I:      I'm just wondering if it was pointing? Which way was it pointing?
    C:    Forwards.
    I:      And what did it look like? Did it look soft or hard?
    C:    It was soft.
    I:      I'm just wondering whether it looked straight or floppy?
    C:    I'm not quite sure.

Beyond the questioning strategies employed already, there is little the interviewer can do to establish the desired information. Not only does the child lack the vocabulary to describe what he saw, he also lacks the sexual knowledge which would enable him to understand the significance of the questions he is being asked. In cases such as this, the only other possibility is to ask the child to draw what he has seen.

*Condoms*
In a number of children's accounts (e.g. the account where the child mentions a "sweet wrapper"), it appears that condoms have been used during abusive incidents. However, it is only with one 9-year-old girl that we have seen evidence that young children can label this item. In

other interviews, we have seen condoms described as *balloons, plastic bags* and *sweet wrappers*. This again illustrates that when children do not have the necessary word to label an item they will overgeneralize and choose a word for another item which is in some way similar (usually in appearance) to the item for which they lack the word.

We turn now to a further aspect of children's knowledge of words which may be limited, that is emotion descriptive vocabulary.

## EMOTION DESCRIPTIVE VOCABULARY

One strategy which interviewers often employ in order to give the child an opportunity to strengthen his account of abusive events is to ask the child about how he felt about the abuse and/or abuser. Our interview and research data (from a language game with assumed non-abused children – Aldridge & Wood 1997b), however, suggest that this may be unsuccessful with many children. From our interview data we see examples such as the following:

(34)   From an interview with a 5-year-old boy:

   I:       How did your winkie feel?
   C:      [Name of alleged abuser] squeezed my winkie in.
   I:       He squeezed your winkie in and what did you think about that?
   C:      Don't know.

In this case, the child has alleged that the abuser put a *balloon* (condom) on his (the child's) *winkie*. As we see, when given an opportunity to say how this felt, he is only able to respond with a factual reply. He seems unable to explain how this felt. Similarly, older interviewees appear to find questions about feelings difficult to respond to. We see the following example, from an interview with a 14-year-old girl:

(35)   I:     How did you feel when he did that? [penetration].
       C:    I felt, em, hurt and, er, terrible.
       I:     How did you feel inside?
       C:    Em, I don't know, it's sort of hard to say.

These interview data suggest that feelings, both physical and emotional, can be difficult for children to describe. Our data from a language game with 56 assumed non-abused children supports this view. The game involved a set of plastic toy play people and a playground scene. A series of scenarios were described to the children in an attempt to elicit emotion descriptive vocabulary. Details of the findings can be found in Aldridge & Wood (1997b). However, a number of findings are particularly relevant to the interview setting and we highlight those here. Of the eight scenarios described in Aldridge & Wood 1997b, four are referred to here.

In the first of these scenarios, we described and enacted a situation where one of the play people falls off a slide and hits his head. The aim of this scenario was to get the children to respond to the question, "How do you think he feels about that?" in an attempt to elicit words describing hurt or pain.

In a second scenario, we again wished to elicit words to describe hurt or pain. This time, however, we described and enacted a situation where this was deliberately inflicted and thus more reflective of the abusive situation (in the first scenario, described above, the pain had an accidental cause). The scenario describing deliberate pain consisted of one of the play people pulling the hair of one of the other toys. Again, we asked the children, "How do you think she feels about that?". This time, our intention was to elicit words describing anger as well as pain.

In a third scenario, we described and enacted a situation where one of the play people climbs to the top of a climbing frame and gets stuck. The aim of this was to elicit words describing fear and again we posed the question, "How do you think he feels about that?".

In the fourth scenario we described and enacted a situation where one of the play people felt unwell and thus did not want to go on the roundabout. Ignoring his protests, his friends drag him onto the roundabout against his will. The aim of this scenario was to elicit words to describe coercion.

The findings suggest a variety of limitations to children's knowledge of words describing emotions.

## Extent of Emotion Descriptive Vocabulary

The earliest emotions that the children expressed verbally, in our language game, were happiness (expressed by 87.5% of our 5-year-olds), sadness (expressed by 62.5% of our 5-year-olds) and pain or hurt (expressed by 37.5% of our 5-year-olds). This finding highlights, once again, the way that children acquire general words before more specific words. In our language game, the children tended to rely on *happy* to express any positive emotion and *sad* to express any negative emotion. There are examples of this in our interview data too:

(36)   From an interview with a 5-year-old girl:

      I:      What do you think of [name of alleged abuser] now?
      C:     He's gone to the police station.
      I:      Yeah, but what do you think about him?
      C:     Sad.
      I:      Just sad are you?

In this interview, we see that the child is unable to explain what she thinks about the alleged abuser in response to the interviewer's first question. Then, in response to the interviewer's second question, the child relies on the general negative word *sad*. Similarly, children may resort to a general word such as OK when their knowledge of words is limited. An example of this can be seen below:

(37)   From an interview with a 4-year-old girl:

      I:      And what did it feel like when he did that? [an abusive act].
      C:     OK.

In fact, far from feeling OK, the act may have been painful and/or frightening for the child. However, it may be the case that the child simply didn't have the necessary words to explain this. In our language game, for example, only 37.5% of 5-year-olds could express hurt or pain and no 5-year-old could express fear. Instead, they were forced to rely on general words such as *happy* and *sad*. Similarly, OK and *all right* may be general terms which children rely on in place of more specific words beyond their reach. At what age, then, are more specific words available?

*Anger*
None of the 5-year-olds in our language game produced words such as *cross* or *angry* or any other words to describe any kind of anger. By 6 years of age, 25% of children could produce words to express anger and this rose to 37.5% and 60% of 7- and 8-year-olds, respectively. Thus it is only at 8 years of age and above that we see a reasonable level of acquisition of these kinds of words.

*Fear*
Words such as *frightened* and *scared* which describe fear were not used by any of the 5-year-olds in our language game. In addition, only 12.5% of each of our 6- and 7-year-olds produced these types of words and it is only at 8 years of age that we see 62.5% of the children able to produce these kinds of words. Again then, 8 years of age appears to be the point at which the majority of children become fluent in their ability to express more specific emotions.

*Coercion*
None of the children in the language game produced any words to describe coercion. Thus we would suggest that such words are acquired after the age of 11 years. The implication of these findings for the interview setting is clear. That is, children under the age of 8 years may respond poorly to questions which ask them to describe how they felt about the abuse and/or abuser.

In addition, the language game findings suggest that when children overcome their struggle to describe emotions, the range of words that they are able to draw upon is restricted. The 5-year-olds were limited to only five words (happy, all right, hurted, unhappy and sad). In contrast, adults who took part in the language game had 28 words. Thus it appears that children have both limited ability to express emotion concepts and limited variety of expression within these concepts.

*Conflicting emotions*
A further finding of concern in relation to the interview setting relates to the age at which children are able to express conflicting emotions. Other researchers (e.g. Harter & Whitesell 1989) have suggested that children may have to be at least 10 years of age before they are able to appreciate the existence of opposing emotions in relation to a single target. Our language game data supports this view in that it is only at the age of 11 years that we see the response, "happy but upset" provoked by the same target. If the abuser (a single target) is someone close to the child then it may well be very difficult for the child to express mixed feelings about this person. We see evidence of this in our interview data:

(38)   From an interview with an 8-year-old girl:

    I:     Do you like daddy?
    C:     Yeah.

In this case, the child has made allegations of sexual abuse against her father. Given the fact that we know how difficult it is for children to understand and voice mixed emotions about a single target we should not take the child's response, in the above exchange, at face value. The child may well have negative feelings towards her father but, if her feelings are confused, she may not be able to express them. As one child in a research study illustrates, mixed feelings are difficult for children to comprehend: "I couldn't feel happy and scared at the same time; I would have to be two people at once!" (Harter & Whitesell in Saarni & Harris 1989: 85).

There are two further points to be made in connection with these findings. First of all, the children who took part in our language game were assumed to be non-abused. Findings from other researchers (e.g. Beeghly & Cicchetti 1994) suggest that abused children are even less able to express their emotions than are non-abused children. Thus the findings from our language game with non-abused children may indicate a greater ability than would be apparent with abused children in the interview setting.

Second, the language game we played was conducted in a neutral setting and was focused on neutral topics. Other researchers have noted that children may perform at their best in such circumstances and "lose their social competence when they are angry or upset" (Dunn & Brown 1994: 121). Again then our findings from a language game with assumed non-abused children in a neutral setting may indicate a better performance than we could expect from abused children in an emotive setting discussing an emotive topic. We turn now to a further type of words which can be problematic for the interview setting; namely, pronouns.

## PRONOUNS

Pronouns are words such as *she, he, it* and *that* which are used to refer to something without repeating its name. Most often they are used to refer back to something already mentioned. Thus, in the following example, *he* can be used to refer back to John: when John got home, he took a shower. On occasion, we might use a pronoun such as *he* to refer forward in a conversation. Thus, we could also say the following where *he* can again refer to John: when he got home, John took a shower. However, in both these cases *he* doesn't necessarily refer to John. In the first case, we could mean that when John got home someone else took a shower and in the second case, we could mean that when someone else got home John took a shower. It is these alternative interpretations for pronouns which can cause problems in an interview. We see this in the example below:

(39)   From an interview with a 9-year-old girl:

    I:    Do you have rules in school?
    C:    Yeah.
    I:    What are the rules in school?
    C:    No swearing, no spitting, no kicking, no fighting.
    I:    OK, is *that* a good thing?
    C:    No.

In this example, *that* could refer to one of two different things (referents). First of all, *that* could refer back to "having rules" (the interpretation that the interviewer intended). Alternatively, *that* could refer back to one of the banned activities (e.g. fighting). This second interpretation is the one that the child has. Thus, by the interviewer's interpretation, the child appears to say that having rules is a bad thing. In fact, the child is not answering the question the interviewer intended. We see a similar example below:

(40)   From an interview with a 5-year-old girl:

    C:    My mum doesn't let me have felt pens.
    I:    No?
    C:    Yeah, don't tell my mum.
    I:    So, if we don't tell mum that you've got a felt pen in your room, what sort of thing is *that*?
    C:    A black pen.

In this case, the interviewer intends *that* to refer to not telling the child's mother about the felt pen. Therefore, the expected answer is that *that* is a secret. In contrast, the child interprets *that* as referring back to the pen and says that *that* is a black pen. A similar exchange occurs with the use of he in the following interview with another 5-year-old girl:

(41)   S/W:   Did you say that daddy locks [name of child's brother] up?
    C:    Yeah.
    S/W:    Where does he lock him up?
    C:    In the bedroom.
    I:    Was he locked up when he put the cream on your peach?
    C:    Yeah.

In this example, it is the use of he in the interviewer's question which is problematic. When the interviewer asks, "Was he locked up when he put the cream on your peach?", the second *he* could refer to one of two

people. The first possibility is that the second *he* refers back to the first
*he* which in turn refers back to the child's brother. The second possibility
is that the second *he* refers back to the child's father who the child
earlier alleged put cream on her peach. Because there are two possible
interpretations for this question, it is unclear which of the two interpretations the child's answer relates to (i.e. was her brother locked up when
her brother put cream on her peach or, was her brother locked up when
her dad put cream on her peach). This example also highlights another
difficulty with pronouns. That is, they do not necessarily refer back to an
object or person mentioned immediately prior to the pronoun. In the
above example, for instance, the pronoun can refer back to something
mentioned far earlier in the conversation. To add to the confusion, it is
also possible for there to be an intervening alternative referent for the
pronoun. Taking the above example for instance, the second *he* could
refer back to the first *he* (the most recently mentioned possibility).
Alternatively, the second *he* could refer back to *daddy*, an earlier mentioned possibility. If the latter is the intended interpretation then we see
that this may be obscured by the intervening possibility that the first *he* in
the interviewer's question could be the intended referent for the second
*he*. We see that the distance between the pronoun and its referent is
problematic in the following examples from an interview with a 4-year-
old girl:

(42)  I:     So you know you said you fell over before and you cut
             your lip and it hurt. Did you have any hurts on your
             private after that?
      C:     No.

In this case, the interviewer intends *that* to refer back to a previously
mentioned allegation of digital penetration. In contrast, the child
interprets that as referring back to falling over and cutting her lip. Thus,
the child's reply is not that she didn't have any hurts on her private at
the time of the abusive incident but that she didn't have any hurts on
her private when she fell over and cut her lip. Similarly, we see the
following exchange later in the interview:

(43)  S/W:   You know what colour blood is and you had a bleed from
             your lip but when you said it hurt there was nothing.
      C:     [Shakes head].

In this exchange, the social worker intends *it* to refer to the abusive
incident that had been discussed earlier. An alternative is that *it* refers to

the cut lip. Thus, again, it is unclear which of these possibilities the child replies to. Similar confusions arise in the following exchange:

(44) From an interview with a 5-year-old girl:

I:    What happened to his willie wonka when he put the cream on?

C:    He didn't put any cream on it.

I:    He didn't put it on his willie wonka?

C:    No.

I:    He put it on your peach didn't he?

C:    Yeah.

I:    And what was he doing when he put it on your peach?

C:    Nothing.

There are a whole range of possible interpretations for the pronouns in this exchange and consequently a whole range of potential misunderstandings. Let's take this exchange line by line and examine the use of pronouns:

I:    What happened to his willie wonka when he put the cream on?

This type of sentence is understood by reading it as if there is something after *on*. The problem in this case is that there are two possibilities. We can read this sentence as meaning either:

I:    What happened to his willie wonka when he put the cream on (his willie wonka), or

I:    What happened to his willie wonka when he put the cream on (the child's peach).

The interviewer intended the second interpretation. However, the child takes the first interpretation and replies:

C:    He didn't put any cream on it.

Another problem arises here in that *it* can refer back to either the willie wonka or the child's peach. The interviewer assumes (based on the child's previous disclosure) that the child means *it* to refer to the willie wonka and says:

I:    He didn't put it on his willie wonka?

the child replies:

C:     No.

The interviewer seeks further clarification and says:

I:     He put it on your peach didn't he?

The interviewer intends *it* to refer to the cream here. Unfortunately, *it* here has an alternative interpretation. That is, *it* could refer back to the more recently mentioned *willie wonka*. Because of these two possibilities, it is unclear what the child means when she answers:

C:     Yes.

She could be confirming that the cream was put on her peach (as the interviewer intended). Alternatively, if she's taken *it* to refer back to the willie wonka, she could be making a new disclosure that the abuser put his willie wonka on her peach.

It is not only the child's understanding of the interviewer's use of pronouns which can lead to misunderstanding. The child's use of pronouns may also be unclear. The following example illustrates this possibility:

(45)   From an interview with a 5-year-old girl:

C:     When daddy finished, he was hitting me and he said go on, get to bed.

In this statement, it is unclear who the child is referring to when she uses *he*. The most obvious interpretation is that both uses of *he* refer back to daddy. In fact, this isn't the case as we see when the interviewer seeks clarification:

(46)   I:     Who was hitting you?
       C:     My brother.

Another problem with children's pronoun use is that they may reverse the pronouns they use and, for example, use *you* for *I* or vice versa. We see an example of this in the following exchange:

(47)   From an interview with a 5-year-old boy:

I:     How did he manage to do what he did?
C:     He put my fingers in.

I:    He put your fingers in?
C:    No, dad's.

In this example, the child has used *my* instead of *his*. Fortunately, the interviewer's follow-up question allows the child to correct his mistake.

What all these examples show is that interviewers need to be very aware both of their own and children's use of pronouns. If two (or more) possible interpretations for a given pronoun are possible, then the interviewer should ask a follow-up question to clarify that she and the child are responding on the basis of the same interpretation. We move on now to consider another class of words which can be problematic in the interview situation, namely prepositions.

## PREPOSITIONS

Prepositions are words such as *in, on, under, by,* and *near*. As we are aware, the interviewer has to elicit very specific details about the alleged incident and therefore tends to make a great deal of use of prepositions as the following examples taken from our transcript data illustrate (prepositions are marked in italics).

I:    When it happened who were you at home *with*?
I:    What else can you remember *about* him?
I:    Did your mum work *in* the daytime or *at* night time?
I:    Shall we turn away *while* you tell us?
I:    Did you have anything on *under* your nightie?
I:    Do you know how long he did it *for*?
I:    Has he done anything like that *before*?
I:    Does he smack you *on* your clothes or *under* your clothes?

Considering, for example, the last sentence, it is clear, as noted by Shuy (1993: 193), that "prepositions are a subtle but very important grammatical construction". For example, it will make a substantial difference to the child witness' account whether he replies *on* or *under*. More specifically, we can sense immediately that the nature of his allegation is potentially more serious if he claims that he smacked him *under* his clothes rather than *on* them.

However, because prepositions such as *on, with, by* and *to* are short and easy to pronounce it is not surprising that professionals assume that children will find them easy to understand and hence they are freely

used in questions to elicit specific information. However, while understandable, this assumption is misguided because understanding prepositional use is actually more complicated than it first appears as
prepositions can carry more than one meaning. For example, *by* can be
used to indicate location such as "the man by the chair" (its locative
use), or to indicate the agent of the action such as "the toy bought by the
man" (its agentive use).

So, to understand prepositions, the child not only has to have the lexical
item in his vocabulary but he also needs to understand the word in all
its meanings. Research (e.g. Bremner & Idowu 1987, Durkin 1981,
Tomasello 1987, Shuy 1993, Aldridge & Timmins (unpublished)) has
suggested that children acquire prepositional use in a certain order as
we illustrate using Shuy's (1993) categorization:

- Locative prepositions are acquired first. These locate items in
  dimensional space, e.g. the doll is *in* the pram, please go *to* daddy.
- Next children acquire connective prepositions. These show the relationship of people/things to each other, e.g. put it *with* the dollies, I
  had *on* pyjamas.
- Children next acquire temporal prepositions. These show the relationship of things/people in time, e.g. did he do that *before* or *after*
  tea?
- Then children acquire attributive prepositions. These carry the
  meaning of attribution, e.g. what's this a picture *of*?, are you ready
  *for* your bath?
- Finally, agentive prepositions are acquired. These carry the meaning
  of an agent of an action, e.g. he did that *to* you?, show me *with* the
  dolls.

As noted by Shuy (1993) the fact that attributive and agentive prepositions are acquired late has clear implications in the interview setting
since the need to establish who did something and how it was done will
involve frequent use of prepositions in these types of use. The following
excerpt from our transcript data illustrates the problem children can
experience with agentives:

(48)    From an interview with a 4-year-old girl:

    I:     What I was wanting to ask you about was I thought
           something had happened to you.
    C:    I haven't had any happen.

A little further into the interview, the question is rephrased and achieves
a response.

I:      Can you tell me what somebody did to you?
C:      A boy got my hood and pulled me up and down.

From our transcript data and the results of a study (Aldridge &
Timmins, unpublished) involving a language game with 120 presumed
non-abused children in the age range 3–8 years, the following conclusions about children's understanding of prepositions can be made:

- Children aged 3 years and under are unable to answer questions
  containing prepositions unless they are in their locative form.
- Children aged 4 years and above can understand prepositions in
  their locative, connective and attributive use.
- Children under 6 years have difficulty understanding prepositions
  in their agentive use. For example, given a question such as, "What
  does the man push the pram with?" children under 6 years are likely
  to give a connective reply, "A baby" rather than an agentive reply,
  "His hands". It is therefore suggested that questions containing
  agentive *with* should be avoided with children under 6 years of age
  and questions such as, "What did he do that with?" might be
  rephrased as, "What did he use to do that?".
- Children of all ages find agentless questions such as, "What
  happened to you?" much more difficult to understand than a direct
  agentive question such as, "What did somebody do to you?". In
  agentless questions children are likely to respond as if the question
  is phrased, "What are you doing?".
- Temporal prepositions are acquired late and children will acquire
  *after* earlier than *before*. When using temporal prepositions it is
  advisable to link them to specific reference points in the child's daily
  routine.

We have illustrated here that advising the use of short, simple words is
not always accurate because prepositions, although short, can carry
complex meanings which children find difficult to interpret. It is
suggested here that the agentive use of prepositions should be avoided
with young children as should agentless questions and that where
possible the use of prepositions should be linked with real-life events.

## SUMMARY

In this chapter, we have looked at various aspects of children's knowledge of words which may lead to diffficulties within the interview

setting. A number of problems that occur in relation to the words used in an interview have been highlighted:

- Children may not know a word the interviewer uses. Examples include the interviewer referring to school *subjects* when the child knows the word *lessons* instead.
- The child and the interviewer may use the same word to refer to different things. Examples include the interviewer using the word *video* to refer to videotapes whilst the child took this word to mean the video machine or recorder.
- Children may not have the words to label what they want to describe. Examples include children's difficulties in labelling some body parts.

This chapter has also highlighted general features of children's word knowledge including:

- Children acquire general words before more specific ones, examples include *coat* before *anorak*, *eye* before *eyebrow*.
- Children may overgeneralize: if they don't have a word for something then they may well choose to use a word for something similar that they do have a word for. Examples include *balloon* instead of *condom*.

We conclude this chapter with a checklist of dos and don'ts, based on the findings reported in this chapter, and a self-assessment sheet.

| AREA OF VOCABULARY | DOs | DON'Ts |
|---|---|---|
| GENERAL | Be aware of the limitations listed on the left Accommodate these by checking that the child understands the words you're using Check that you're both talking about the same thing Be wary of overgeneralizations: the child is likely to resort to these if he hasn't got a word for something | Don't assume that the child: Knows the word you're using Is thinking of the same thing as you when you use a word Has got a word for the thing he is trying to describe |

| AREA OF VOCABULARY | DOs | DON'Ts |
|---|---|---|
| LEGAL TERMS | Do: Explain the role of the social worker interviewer Explain that the police-officer interviewer has a much wider role than arresting people. Make clear that the child is not in any trouble and that the interviewer is not going to be arresting the child Check that the child's understanding of legal terms is realistic. The child may use the word *court* but harbour the belief that this is some sort of jail | Don't assume that the child: Knows what a social worker does Has a full understanding of the role of a police-officer (i.e. something beyond knowledge of the police's role in arresting criminals) Understands legal terms such as *court* in an adult-like way. An apparently accurate use of such words may hide a misunderstanding |
| BODY PART and SEXUAL TERMS | Do: Give the child a chance to use non-verbal means to identify parts of the body; drawing, pointing (on self or doll) To elicit body part terms: use strategies such as saying a word quickly, spelling a word, writing a word down, talking about parts of the body that swimwear covers Be aware of overgeneralization strategies | Don't: Assume that the child has a word for every part of the body Overlook children's reticence in using some body part terms Overlook the possibility that children may overgeneralize if they don't have a word for something (e.g. a *condom* could be referred to as a *balloon*) |
| EMOTION DESCRIPTIVE WORDS | Do: Remember that the child may use terms (e.g. *sad, all right*) and over-generalize these to indicate a distinction between negative and positive emotions Give the child an opportunity to express all the feelings he may have about an abuser by distinguishing, in your questions, between different attitudes towards the abuse and/or abuser (e.g. ask the | Don't: Assume that if a child uses a general term like *sad, all right* or *OK* that this is how the child really feels about an abuse and/or abuser. It may simply be that these are the only emotion descriptive words a child has Assume that the child will be able to explain mixed feelings (e.g. about an abuser who is a close relative) |

| AREA OF VOCABULARY | DOs | DON'Ts |
|---|---|---|
| | child to focus separately on how he feels about the abuser in connection with abusive versus non-abusive situations) | |
| PRONOUNS | Do<br>Check what the child means when his answer to a question contains a potentially problematic pronoun (i.e. one with more than one interpretation) | Don't<br>Overlook the possibility that pronouns can be interpreted as referring to more than one thing. You and the child may have different interpretations for a given pronoun |
| PREPOSITIONS | Do<br>Remember that children will acquire prepositional use at differing rates, e.g. locative *to* will be acquired before agentive *to*<br>Remember that, "What happened to you?" is harder for the child to understand than, "What did someone do to you?"<br>Link questions to real-time events, e.g. before bedtime | Don't<br>Assume that all prepositions are easy for the child to understand just because they are short<br>Use agentless questions<br>Assume the child will have a concept of time |

## SELF-ASSESSMENT SHEET

(1)  Did you use any words which you know the child didn't understand? If so, what were these?

(2)  Were there any instances where the child couldn't find the word he needed? If so, make a list of these.

(3)  Did you broach the subject of the roles of police and social worker interviewers? How did the child respond?

(4)  Were any other legal terms (e.g. *arrest* or *court*) used during the interview? Did you try and find out what the child's understanding of these words was?

(5)  How did the child cope in terms of naming sexual body parts? If he struggled, did you give him a chance to point to these parts on himself or a doll?

(6)   How did the child cope in terms of describing sexual acts? If there were any problems, what were these?

(7)   What facilitative techniques (if any) did you use (e.g. drawing) to elicit information about sexual acts? If you used any facilitative techniques, how well did they work?

(8)   Was the child able to tell you how he felt about the abuse and/or abuser? If so, what sort of words did he use (general words like *sad* or more specific ones like *frightened*)?

(9)   Did any misunderstandings arise in terms of pronoun use? For example, were you always sure what the child was referring to when he used pronouns such as *he* and *it*?

(10)  How did the child cope with prepositions such as *before* and *after*?

# 6

# INTERVIEWING CHILDREN WITH SPECIAL NEEDS

In this chapter, attention turns to interviewing children with a variety of special needs. Given that our professional background is a linguistic one, we have concentrated our attention on special needs in relation, specifically, to children's language skills. However, even with this narrow focus, there are many groups of children who could be considered to have special needs in relation to language. Twins, for example, may develop language in a different way to non-twins and socioeconomic factors may also influence language development. Cultural, racial and religious factors, too, may be influential. Differences may exist, for instance, in terms of attitudes towards sex and sex education (see Renvoize 1993 for a number of relevant case studies). Such differences may well need to be accommodated within the investigatory process. As Nadira Osmany (manager of the Tower Hamlets' ethnic minorities child protection team) notes in Bond (1996): "Child abuse is a problem in all communities but it needs to be communicated in ways which are accessible and culturally appropriate for particular communities". Unfortunately, constraints of space mean that cultural, racial and religious factors are beyond the scope of this chapter (although we do address the associated issue of second language use). We therefore refer the interested reader to Gupta (1997) and Phillips (1993) for a discussion of issues of race and culture in investigative interviewing.

The focus of this chapter, then, will be on two groups of children. First, we consider issues relating to the abuse of disabled children and second, we consider the needs of bilingual children and those children who speak a minority language (in the UK a language other than English) – who may also be considered as special in linguistic terms. This chapter is therefore divided into two sections. In Section 1, we discuss the following issues in relation to the abuse of disabled children:

- Vulnerability to abuse and access to justice for disabled populations.
- Professionals' experience of interviewing disabled children.

- The Memorandum and disabled children.
- Disabled children's linguistic skills.
- Interviewing disabled children.

In Section 2, we turn to a discussion of the needs of bilingual children and minority language speakers and we address the following issues:

- Professionals' experience of interviewing bilingual children and minority language speakers.
- Linguistic factors in interviewing bilingual children and minority language speakers.

## SECTION 1: DISABLED CHILDREN

### Vulnerability to Abuse and Access to Justice for Disabled Populations

A variety of previous studies have noted that disabled children are particularly vulnerable to abuse (see Westcott 1991 in particular and also 1993 for a detailed review as well as relevant chapters in Westcott & Jones 1997). This increased vulnerability has been attributed to a number of factors including increased exposure to multiple caretakers and to care outside the home as well as increased reliance on others for personal care. A further factor which many researchers (e.g. Turk & Brown 1992) suggest increases the vulnerability of disabled children to abuse is communication problems. That is, children who are likely to experience difficulty in telling of their abuse may be seen as "easy targets" by abusers.

This difficulty in telling may arise from a variety of sources. Some children (for example those who have been hospitalized for long periods and have undergone frequent medical examinations or those who are reliant on caretakers for personal care) may find difficulty in distinguishing, definitively, between appropriate and inappropriate touching (see, for example, some of the accounts in Westcott 1993 and Westcott and Cross 1996). Other children may not have the linguistic means to tell. For example, Westcott and Cross (1996: 84) note:

"Children who cannot communicate easily with others may be 'ideal' for abusers to target, since they will face extreme difficulties in trying to tell someone – by whatever means – of their experiences. Further, they may not even have been given the necessary vocabulary (and by implication, permission) to describe abusive activities or private body parts".

Given their increased vulnerability to abuse and their increased difficulty in telling, it is especially important that facilities and practices are in place which enable disabled children to report their abuse (we turn to further discussion of issues involved in the reporting of abuse later in this chapter). It is also vital that the criminal justice system accommodates the needs of disabled children so that, once abuse has been reported, cases may proceed to trial and justice be obtained. There are a variety of indications that this accommodation is not currently in place. Firstly, as Pam Cooke – the coordinator of the National Association for the Protection from Sexual Abuse of Children with Learning Disabilities (NAPSAC) – notes in Bond (1997: 23):

> "We know that most abused children don't get proper justice or the therapeutic services they need so there's even less likelihood that children with communication difficulties and disabilities are receiving these services."

In other words, if the needs of non-disabled children are not being fully met then it is unlikely that those of disabled children are being met. This is because, as Kennedy & Kelly (1992: 149) note, there has been a tendency for policy makers to say "let me sort out the *normal* child first".

Additionally, Westcott (1992b, reported in Bull 1993) notes that evidence from children with special needs has rarely been used in court (even though a variety of reports suggest that such children are at heightened risk of abuse). This suggests that facilitative procedures are not in place to allow abused disabled children access to criminal justice. This reflects Marchant & Page's (1997: 77) comment that:

> "more far-reaching changes are needed in the criminal justice system if disabled children are to demonstrate their competency and credibility as witnesses within courts".

Lastly, the experiences of adults with disabilities within the criminal justice system indicate how difficult it is likely to be for disabled children within, essentially, the same system. As witnesses, disabled children have the dual difficulties of their youth and disability to counter and the adult disabled experience provides some indication of the difficulties that disability alone presents.

The "fair hearing" campaign currently being pursued to improve the criminal justice system for people with learning difficulties (*Community Care* 1998) is a reflection of the extent of the difficulties involved in pursuing justice in cases involving those with learning difficulties and other disabilities. Individual cases are also indicative of the difficulties faced by adult disabled populations, particularly in cases of sexual assault. The following cases, reported in the media, reflect these concerns.

Prime-time television (*Here and Now* BBC 1997) has reported on the case of a woman with multiple sclerosis who communicates via a communication board. This woman's evidence was not heard – apparently because of judicial doubts about her communication skills. On the same programme, a further case involving two Down's syndrome women (whose case had failed to reach court) was reported. Similarly illustrative is the experience of a 27-year-old man with cerebral palsy and learning difficulties (reported in Fisher 1997). In this case, the man was the (alleged) victim of a sexual assault but was not called to give evidence and the defendant was found not guilty. Fisher (1997: 25) maintains:

> "John [not the man's real name] has communication difficulties but he could still have given evidence in person with the right support. It would have been possible if he had been allowed an interpreter in the courtroom or the support of his advocate."

Also particularly illuminating is one adult's description of his concerns about getting involved in the justice process:

> "I am a deaf black man with learning difficulties. If I had to report a crime I would feel very uncomfortable . . . I'd be worried the police would ask questions I didn't know the answers to . . . I think the words they use would be too difficult to understand" (Quote taken from West 1997: 23).

As well as highlighting the difficulties faced by adult disabled populations in getting access to justice – difficulties likely to be compounded by the youth of disabled children, these quotes also highlight the fact that communication is a key concern. As the cases above illustrate, it is often doubts about the communication skills of disabled witnesses which result in cases not reaching court or evidence not being presented. As Marchant & Page (1997: 78) note:

> "The scales of justice are tipped against all child victims when the main evidence is their oral testimony and they are undoubtedly tipped even further for children whose impairments affect their communication."

More specifically, these quotes highlight a number of different aspects of communication which may be problematic. First, the issue of non-verbal communication and the use of augmentative communication systems (in the case of the woman with multiple sclerosis) is raised. Second, the issue of the use of interpreters (in the case of the man with cerebral palsy) is highlighted and third, the quote from the deaf man with learning difficulties raises concerns about the interviewee's ability to understand what the interviewer is asking. Of course, such difficulties can be overcome if processes are flexible and individual needs accommodated. Such accommodation can only take place, however, if the interviewing professionals are well informed. Results from a recent survey (Aldridge and Wood 1997a) indicate that, unfortunately, many professionals currently lack information on the needs of disabled children and we report on these findings below.

## Professionals' Experience of Interviewing Disabled Children

In a recent survey of 41 interviewing police-officers in Wales (Aldridge and Wood 1997a) we asked a variety of questions about the interviewing of disabled children. First of all, in order to obtain a picture of the extent to which children with disabilities are becoming involved in the initial stages of the legal process, we asked whether the interviewers had any experience of interviewing disabled children. Of the interviewers in our survey 50% had some experience of interviewing disabled children and 50% had no such experience. At least some of the 50% who had experience of interviewing disabled children indicated that these experiences were not unusual or one-off experiences. Illustrative quotes include the following: "On several occasions I have been involved in investigations where I have interviewed children with special needs", and similarly, "I've conducted many interviews with children with learning difficulties".

Furthermore, our survey findings suggest that this interviewing experience extends to disabled children with a variety of different needs. When asked to elaborate on the type of experience of interviewing disabled children they had, the following details were among those which became apparent:

- 71% of those interviewing officers who had interviewed a child with a disability had interviewed a child with learning difficulties.
- 46% had interviewed a deaf child.
- 25% had interviewed a Down's syndrome child.
- 15% had interviewed a child with cerebral palsy.

In stark contrast to the amount and range of interviewing experience with disabled children are our findings in relation to training. When asked if they had had any specific training regarding the interviewing of children with special needs, all the interviewing officers said that they had none. Quotes such as the following are typical of interviewing officers' comments on training for interviewing disabled children:

- "There are no 'special facilities' in being at the unit to deal with children who have these impairments. As police-officers, we are not specifically trained to cater for these needs."
- "We have no real training in dealing with these needs and the prosecution do not understand the difficulties."
- "I've interviewed children with learning disabilities but I've had no real training in dealing with their needs."

More detailed questions within our survey further exposed the lack of training. We asked how the needs of children with (a) hearing impairment, (b) visual impairment and (c) learning difficulties would be catered for. The interviewing officers' responses revealed that:

- 12% didn't know how they would cater for the needs of a hearing impaired child.
- 32% didn't know how they would cater for the needs of a child with a visual impairment.
- 25% said they didn't know how they would cater for the needs of a child with learning difficulties.

Perhaps even more revealing than the above figures are the following quotes. These comments were made in response to our question about catering for the needs of visually impaired, hearing impaired and learning disabled children:

- "I have no immediate answers but it has made me stop and think, if placed in that position, what would I do?"

In response to the same question one interviewing officer answered simply that she would interview children with the specified disabilities:

- "With great difficulty!"

Furthermore, an analysis of the responses of those officers who did know something of how they would cater for the needs of children with the specified disabilities reveals clear limitations to the extent of knowledge. Most of those who did know how they would cater for disabled children replied (perfectly correctly) that they would ensure greater pre-interview planning, consult widely and call in a relevant expert or qualified personnel (e.g. a social worker for the deaf or a sign language interpreter), where necessary. There were few specific comments, however, about the conduct of the interview. For example, only 2% of interviewers mentioned that the process of familiarizing the child with the facilities of the interview suite (e.g. the camera and technical equipment) would have to be modified in the case of a child with a visual impairment. Only 5% mentioned that props might be useful for interviewing a child with learning difficulties and only 10% suggested that visual aids would be useful when interviewing a child with a hearing impairment.

Significantly, however, a number of the interviewers indicated that they would welcome further information and training on the needs of disabled children. For example, we have the following comments from our survey:

- "I need a more in-depth understanding of special needs."
- "I feel that specific training about disability would be advantageous."

Although the scope of this chapter is limited, we would like to provide some information, particularly from a linguistic perspective, on interviewing disabled children. We begin by providing a review of the advice already available for interviewing officers within the Memorandum.

## The MOGP and Disabled Children

As others have noted (e.g. Bull 1993 and Westcott 1992b), the MOGP makes only limited reference to the needs of disabled children. Practitioners have also expressed concern in our survey and elsewhere (e.g. reports of social service departments' reservations reported in Bond 1995) about the limited amount of information provided in the MOGP. We outline below the guidelines that the MOGP does offer. In terms of witness' competence, the MOGP (1992: 11; their emphasis) offers the following advice:

"It is not possible to predict precisely how the courts will treat the question of competence, if it is raised, in cases involving child witnesses following the 1991 Act. For the present, and in view of Parliament's clear intentions in reforming the law, it is suggested that *joint investigating teams should assume that the courts will be willing to listen to the evidence of any child who is able to communicate about the alleged offence in a way which the team as a whole can understand."*

On the surface this seems to be a positive position; if the investigating team can understand the child's evidence, the courts will listen to that evidence. However, experience suggests that decisions about witness' competence are not always this straightforward. Certainly, difficulty arises when the investigating team's understanding is facilitated in any way by a third party. For example, Spencer (1992) notes that, in criminal proceedings, the contribution of an expert known to the child is limited so that no comments on the significance of a child's drawings may be made even where the child is only able to communicate via such drawing.

Adults with disabilities have faced similar difficulties in relation to assessments of competence. The woman with multiple sclerosis whose case we referred to earlier (*Here and Now* BBC 1997) was precluded from giving evidence because of the facilitative role her partner plays in her use of a communication board. Similarly, Fisher (1997) comments that a man with cerebral palsy (again, a case we referred to earlier) was perfectly capable of giving evidence if supported by an interpreter or advocate. But he was precluded from doing so. It seems, then, that further consideration is needed in terms of what, realistically, constitutes witness' competence particularly in those cases where non-verbal communication systems are used and/or where third party facilitation of communication is needed.

In terms of the accommodation of the physical needs of disabled children, the MOGP (1992: 7) observes that: "Some children will require wheelchair access to the interview room and other facilities, and those with a hearing disability may require an induction loop. (The needs of the disabled should be taken into account when setting up any new facilities)". This is clearly a sound recommendation in as far as it goes. However, as we shall see in our later discussion of the needs of individual disabled populations, wheelchair access and induction loop facilities are the tip of the iceberg in terms of providing appropriate facilities; the toys and props present, the arrangement of the furniture and the role of audio and video equipment are also key issues when considering the physical needs of a number of disabled populations.

The Memorandum also makes a number of recommendations on how interviews with disabled children should be conducted. These include:

"If the child has any disabilities, for example, a speech or hearing impedi-
ment, or learning difficulties, particular care should be taken to develop
effective strategies for the interview to minimize the effect of such disabilities. The use of dolls and other 'props' as communication aids should
be considered . . . In some cases it may be necessary for communication to
pass through an appropriately skilled third party, for example, a person
who can use sign language. In others, it might be necessary to consider
asking such people to conduct the interview . . . As when any other
language is used, a translation will need to be made available to the court".

This statement reflects the MOGP's concentration on three key issues in
relation to interviews with disabled children. First, props can be particularly useful when interviewing disabled children. This is demonstrated in the extract above and also in the following:

"'Props' including dolls, drawings, dolls' houses and small figures which
can serve as potentially very useful communication aids in interviews
carried out for the purposes of this Memorandum. Young children and
those with communication difficulties, may be able to provide clearer
accounts when such props are used, compared with purely verbal
approaches" (MOGP 1992: 24).

The value of props in assisting disabled children to recount events is
not in doubt. For example, in the recent case (July 1995) where mother
and daughter Lin and Megan Russell were murdered and another
daughter (Josie Russell) critically injured, props have proved invaluable
to the investigation. They have helped Josie Russell (the sole survivor of
the incident) recount vital details of the attack. In the early part of the
investigation, Josie's speech was severely impaired and specially made
props were introduced. These included model figures of the children
and their mother in a replica outdoor scene with a figure matching
Josie's description of the attacker and a model of the hammer used in the
attack. One of the investigating officers described how the props were
used:

"The models are bendable and Josie picks them up and puts them into
position. She wants everything to be perfect on the model board . . . one of
the first times we used the board, she was trying to tell us something. We
didn't know what it was, but she went around her home and found a
house made of china and put it on to the board because in real life there is
a house there, at that particular point" (Reported in McGowan 1996).

Overall then, props can clearly be very useful for disabled children.
However, it should be added that different props are suitable for
different disabled populations. This is a point that the Memorandum

does not mention and one which requires further discussion (we return to the issue of props later in this chapter).

Another issue which the MOGP highlights is the possibility of using an interpreter (e.g. a sign language interpreter). Again, this can be seen in the extract from the MOGP presented above. However, for interviews using an interpreter to proceed smoothly, much more detailed advice is needed. This is particularly important when we consider reports of cases where the role of an interpreter has apparently been brought into question (see, for example, the case referred to earlier where a man with cerebral palsy was precluded from giving evidence even though he could have done so through an interpreter).

Additionally, as the above quote shows, the MOGP recognizes that, for some disabled children, it may be appropriate for a signer or someone well known to the child to conduct the interview. Hence we see the following recommendation (MOGP 1992: 13):

"Exceptionally, it may be in the interests of the child to be interviewed by an adult in who he or she has already put confidence but who is not a member of the investigating team. Provided that such a person is not a party to the proceedings, is prepared to co-operate with appropriately trained interviewers and can accept adequate briefing this possibility should not be precluded".

The MOGP also observes that disabled children may need to be accommodated in terms of the types of questions used. For example, the MOGP (1992: 27; their emphasis) notes:

"[In some cases] the courts accept that . . . it is *impractical to ban leading questions.* . . it may be because the witness does not understand what he or she is expected to tell the court without some prompting, as in the case of a young child or a child with a learning difficulty."

The MOGP (1992: 27; their emphasis) continues:

"As the courts become more aware of the difficulties of obtaining evidence from witnesses who are very young or who have a learning difficulty . . . a sympathetic attitude may be taken towards *necessary* leading questions."

Clearly, recognition of the possible need to modify questioning strategies is a positive step. However, the quote above implies that practitioners need to "wait and see" and hope that the courts acquire a more sympathetic attitude and an understanding of the difficulties involved in obtaining evidence from children with disabilities. In fact, greater judicial understanding is far more likely to be facilitated by specific advice on what can and cannot be expected of disabled children rather than by a rather vague "wait and see" strategy. Again then the MOGP advice does not go far enough.

Unfortunately, outside of the MOGP, there are few specific resources for professionals to turn to for advice on how to conduct investigatory interviews with disabled children. Useful resources which are available include:

*   The ABCD (ABuse and Children who are Disabled) training and resource pack (available from the NSPCC training group whose address appears at the end of this chapter).
*   Publications by Ruth Marchant and Marcus Page (1993, 1997).
*   *Child Abuse Review* special issue (1992).

Given the limited amount of information currently available, it is impossible to "plug all the gaps" within the confines of a single chapter. What is provided, however, is a review of two aspects of interviewing disabled children.

First, we provide a review of key linguistic factors to consider when interviewing disabled children. We have chosen to present this information for two reasons: (a) our professional background is a linguistic one and linguistic factors have received limited specific attention and (b) we think it is important to emphasize that disabled children are a far from homogeneous group – different types of disability are characterized by different linguistic needs and it is important to address these needs separately.

Second, we review, by way of summary, general factors to consider when interviewing disabled children by going through details of the MOGP interview stage-by-stage.

## Disabled Children's Linguistic Skills

Clearly, there are many disabilities which impact on language and we do not have space (or expertise) to comment on all of these. However, we can offer advice on those disabilities which professionals in our survey reported were those most frequently encountered. We will therefore offer advice on the linguistic skills of children with learning disabilities, cerebral palsy, Down's syndrome and sensory impairment (hearing and visual impairment).

## Children with learning disabilities

The term *learning disabilities* covers a wide spectrum of difficulties. Individual children with learning disabilities will have widely varying abilities and the following advice is therefore highly generalized. Essentially, learning disabilities are cognitive in nature and will therefore impact (to differing extents) on the child's ability to understand. In general terms, then, we would refer the reader to the recommendations contained within Chapters 2–4. This is because, often, a successful strategy in interviewing a child with learning disabilities is to pitch questions at a linguistic level which would be appropriate with a younger child who has no learning disability. In addition, we should note that, often, children with learning disabilities will have particular difficulties with certain aspects of the interview. Details such as times and dates may be beyond their understanding. Therefore questions about these matters will need to be framed in terms of their relationship to aspects of the child's routine. Again, this is a technique we advocated for use with younger children.

A further area of limited understanding may be sexual knowledge (Marchant & Page 1993). Our own data from an interview with a 16-year-old with a learning disability illustrates this point:

(1)    Interviewer:   What happened between you and [name of cousin]?
       Interviewee:   We had like a, like an affair but he didn't go in me. I'm not pregnant I can remember that bit from the doctor.

In this case we see that the interviewee has no concept of what her later descriptions reveal is sexual abuse over a prolonged period of time. Instead she refers to this as, "like an affair". Also, although she states that her cousin "didn't go in" her, her conclusion that she is not pregnant is not derived from this evidence but instead from her limited memory of what the doctor has told her. Interviewers need to be aware that those with learning disabilities may well have limited sexual knowledge which does not match what we would expect for their age.

## Children with cerebral palsy

Cogher, Savage & Smith (1992: 3) note that: "Cerebral palsy refers to a group of conditions which share the features of a central motor deficit . . . acquired in early life". As such, children with different sub-types of cerebral palsy may experience different areas of disability. For example, the following sub-types have differing characteristics as described, briefly, below. (Sub-type categorization and characteristics taken from Cogher, Savage & Smith 1992.)

- Ataxia: This condition leads to diminished muscle control and thus head control may be affected. This may mean that the child's signals of "yes" and "no" are affected and these signals may have to be clearly established at the outset of the interview.
- Spastic hemiplegia: Here, there may be associated learning difficulties. Hence linguistic understanding may be affected.
- Quadriplegia or total body involvement: In these conditions, there may be oral and facial difficulty. Hence language production may well be affected. In some cases this will mean that pronunciation is laboured and, perhaps, unclear. In others augmentative communication systems may be used. In some cases, these oral and facial problems will coexist with learning difficulties and in these instances, language understanding as well as production will be affected.
- Diplegia: In this type of cerebral palsy, the major clinical signs are in the lower limbs (Cogher, Savage & Smith 1992). Hence there is no linguistic impact. However, in the interview context other physical needs will have to be considered (e.g. wheelchair access).

### Down's syndrome children

Cognitive deficit is the most striking feature of Down's syndrome. However, Burns & Gunn (1993) note that those with Down's syndrome, although sharing some common characteristics, may well be very different. Therefore, a detailed examination of the cognitive effects of Down's syndrome is beyond the scope of this chapter and we refer the interested reader to Cicchetti & Beeghly (1990) for a detailed discussion of these issues.

In terms of language skills, there are also individual differences. Some children with Down's syndrome also have coexisting conditions which impact on language. For example, hearing impairment is common in Down's syndrome. In these cases, sign language systems such as Paget Gorman or Makaton might be used (see our later section on hearing impairment for further information about these systems). Others may use augmentative communication systems (which we discuss in a later section of this chapter).

Centrally though there are a variety of characteristics which typically feature in Down's syndrome. First, a variety of studies have shown that

Down's syndrome may affect memory skills (e.g. Marcell & Weeks 1988). Second, articulation (production of speech) may be affected (e.g. Bleile & Schwartz 1984). Third, the grammatical development of those with Down's syndrome may be limited (e.g. Fowler, Gelman & Gleitman 1994).

Interviewers can accommodate these possible linguistic difficulties in a variety of ways. First, if articulation is poor then technicians should be consulted about how well audio equipment is likely to cope with this. If it is likely that microphones will fail to pick up some of what a Down's syndrome child has to say then simultaneous note taking should be considered. Second, because cognitive deficits may be coupled with grammatical limitations, interviewers should take extra care to ask only a single question at a time (Burns & Gunn 1993). The techniques we outlined in earlier chapters (e.g. facilitating explanations of truth and lies and facilitating free narrative accounts) will be particularly applicable to Down's syndrome children.

## Hearing impaired children

The language systems employed by hearing impaired children vary considerably according to individual needs (e.g. the presence or absence of other disabilities and the extent of hearing loss). Social and personal choice may also influence the language system used. Traditionally, some deaf children have been forced (unsuccessfully) to try and acquire spoken language (see Kyle & Woll 1984 for a historical review). However, a more common approach, today, is for a variety of communication methods to be employed in combination. This may well mean that the child uses sign supported English (SSE). This is a signing system which relies on spoken English word order. Lip reading may also be utilized (organizations such as the NDCS and RNID – whose addresses appear at the end of this chapter – produce materials which describe how lip reading can be facilitated). Alternatively, the child may have acquired British Sign Language (BSL) which is a sign language which is fully recognized as being a language just like English, French or Welsh. In these cases, an appropriately skilled person will be needed to conduct (or act as an interpreter at) the interview.

Other children with hearing impairments (especially those who have an additional cognitive deficit, e.g. in some cases of Down's syndrome) may use a simpler sign system such as Makaton or Paget Gorman. In these cases, the systems are limited to only a few hundred signs. These are not fully-fledged languages and children who use these systems may have difficulty in expressing all they want to tell due to limitations of the system. Again, qualified personnel will be needed to conduct (or act as an interpreter at) the interview.

Alternatively, some deaf children may have had a cochlear implant fitted (details of this procedure are beyond the scope of this chapter and we refer the interested reader to the organizations listed at the end of this chapter who represent deaf children and to Rose, Vernon & Pool 1996). Where cochlear implants have been successful (and this is not always the case), the child will be able to speak but the language acquisition process is likely to be delayed. Therefore interviewers need to be aware of this and pitch their questions accordingly.

## Visually impaired children

In our survey of interviewing professionals (Aldridge & Wood 1997a), we found that 15% of interviewing officers felt there would be no problem in catering for the needs of a visually impaired child in that, in terms of the interview, a visually impaired child would be no different to a sighted child. Such a view is clearly misguided. Visually impaired children will have different physical needs to sighted children and there may be linguistic differences too. For example, visually impaired children may experience delayed language skills as a result of limited experience of certain aspects of life that sighted children (and adults) take for granted. For example, visual aspects of life such as colour are beyond the experience of children with visual impairments. Similarly, much of our ability quickly to acquire names for objects is based on our ability to visualize them. For example, if we think of words such as *apple*, *cat* and *piano* our recognition of what these refer to is, to a great extent, visual – we see the objects in our "mind's eye". Visually impaired children have to acquire object labels by utilizing non-visual means. Therefore, there may well be language delay as this is a more arduous process.

## Children using augmentative communication systems

Augmentative communication systems are many and varied and are used to allow communication to take place non-verbally. Augmentative communication systems can be based on boards, computers or communication frames and can involve symbols, photographs, pictures and/or words. For a detailed review of these systems we refer the reader to Kennedy (1992) and the Disability Information Trust (1995).

Both these publications include clear pictorial representations and/or photographs of the different systems. What is important to note, however, is that these systems vary in terms of their levels of sophistication (and as such they vary in terms of how much they allow a child to communicate). For example, one simple pictorial system is the Pictures Please! language which employs 1232 pictures. The Mayer–Johnson Communication system is a similar type of system but, in contrast to Pictures Please! language, it employs in excess of 3000 picture symbols. The increased number of symbols allows a wider range of topics to be represented and thus increases the communicative potential.

Rebus symbols and Makaton symbols are slightly more sophisticated systems in that they include some symbols which are arbitrary (that is not simply pictorial representations). A much more sophisticated symbol system, however, is Blissymbolics. This system can be used on boards or charts and is suitable for pointing using either the hands or eyes. It has a constantly updated vocabulary and allows for sophisticated communication. For example, it is possible to build sentences and to create new expressions by using symbols in combination. Also, words appear alongside symbols which facilitates communication with those unfamiliar with the system.

Obviously, the more sophisticated systems (like Blissymbolics) are used by those who have greater cognitive skills. These systems have the advantage of allowing their users to communicate more detailed information. In contrast, those with lesser cognitive skills may use a less sophisticated system such as Rebus or Makaton symbols. However, these two systems are more limiting in terms of what they allow their users to communicate. Specialist knowledge will be needed for interviews to be conducted using any of these systems.

Having considered some of the key linguistic features of a variety of disabilities, we turn now to how we might apply this information within an MOGP interview.

# Interviewing Disabled Children

## Planning the interview

As the interviewing professionals who responded to our survey (Aldridge & Wood 1997a) note, extensive pre-interview planning is vital for interviews with disabled children. This is a point which is also emphasized elsewhere (e.g. Marchant & Page 1997). This pre-interview planning may involve consultation and discussion with a range of professionals. Specialist social workers (e.g. social workers for the deaf) or professionals with knowledge of the needs of individual children may, for example, need to be consulted. During this consultation and planning, a number of factors will need to be considered.

First, the timing and location of any interview will need to be considered carefully. In Chapter 2, we noted that, in terms of the timing of an interview, it is vital to take full account of the child's routine. For disabled children, there may be an increased number of elements of routine to consider. Disabled children cared for outside the home may, for example, be used to living by a far less flexible routine than children living at home. Others may be governed by medical appointments (for example with physiotherapists). It is important to take account of these factors so that the child is not unduly disorientated by the interview timing.

Second, the location for an interview to take place is an important consideration. Marchant & Page (1993), for example, have discussed the need to weigh the benefits of a technically superior but unfamiliar setting with the benefits of a technically inferior (because of the limitations of mobile equipment) familiar setting. The balance will, of course, be tipped in favour of the familiar setting if the standard interview accommodation is, in any way, unsuitable for a particular child. Most obviously, in some cases, ground floor facilities will be needed and in our experience interview suites are often located on upper floors. Not only is it impractical for an interview with, for example, a child in a wheelchair to take place in such a suite but also it may send out a negative message to the child. That is, as Marchant & Page (1993) note, if the child has to be carried up to first floor facilities this may send out a message to the child that this building is not for him and that he doesn't belong there.

Other "special" facilities may also be necessary. Toilet facilities, for example, need to be appropriate. Also, in some cases, the arrangement of the furniture within the interview suite will need to be considered. For example, in cases where an interpreter or accompanying adult (or both) are to be present, it will be necessary to arrange the furniture so that all these are within view of the camera. This is important because the MOGP (1992: 13) notes that: "The court, in considering whether to admit the recording, may wish to be assured that the witness was not prompted or discouraged during the interview". As the MOGP (1992: 13) continues, achieving visual evidence that the child has not been prompted or discouraged is not always easy: "To provide a comprehensive record of the words and gestures of more than two persons can be technically demanding". The greater the number of people to be included in the camera shot, the greater the technical demands, and careful planning of the layout of furniture in the room can facilitate this process. It may also be advisable to consult an audiovisual technician to optimize the equipment available. Other aspects of the technical facilities available may also need to be considered. For example, it is useful to keep in mind the following MOGP recommendations:

- "A good clear picture of the child's face may help the court determine what is being said" (MOGP 1992: 49).
- "The video recording should capture the child's responses directly as the interviewer's description of the child's response is itself hearsay. For example, if a child is asked where she was touched by an abuser and in response she points to her genitals, that action should be captured by the camera. It will not be enough for the interviewer to say 'she is pointing to her genitals' as this is a statement of the interviewer, not the child. Once this is understood, it should be relatively easy to ensure that the relevant evidence comes from the child" (MOGP 1992: 29).

In the case of children who communicate via augmentative communication systems, these are particularly relevant points and it is important to be true to the essence of the above recommendations. That is, a good, clear picture of the child's use of any communication board or frame should be maintained so that the camera shot shows any pictures, symbols or words to which the child points.

Also, some speech impairments mean that children's pronunciations are unclear (as we noted earlier, this may well be the case for some Down's syndrome children) and it should be considered, in advance, how well the audio equipment will cope with this. As the MOGP (1992: 49; their emphasis) notes: "The evidential value of the video recorded interview will depend very much on the court being able to discern clearly what was said, both by the interviewer and by the child witness". If, after consultation, it is considered unlikely that all of what the child says will be discernable from the video recording then the use of simultaneous note taking should be considered. In addition, it may be advisable to modify the following MOGP (1992: 32) recommendation:

"It is recommended that a brief index to the tape is prepared at this stage, in liaison with the interviewer, so that the most relevant passages regarding the alleged offence can be readily located later on . . . The index is not a full transcript of the tape but it should serve similar purposes, enhanced by the video recording itself."

That is, a written record more detailed than the usual brief index may well be useful.

A further technical aspect to consider, in some cases, is lighting. The MOGP (1992: 49) notes that "modern video equipment does not normally require special additional lighting". For children who lip read, however, lighting will be an important consideration. Lighting should be directed towards the interviewer in these cases.

Finally, in terms of technical matters, the availability of an induction loop facility for those with a hearing impairment should be considered. This is a system which works in conjunction with some hearing-aids and allows the hearing-aid user to focus on just what he wants to hear without background noise interference. Having considered issues of timing and location, a further significant part of pre-interview planning is to consider who should be present at the interview. In Chapter 2 we considered the advantages and disadvantages of an "attached" adult presence (i.e. the presence of an adult well known to the child) and we concluded that such a presence can often be problematic for a number of reasons (e.g. the additional emotional burden for the child). However, for some disabled children, these disadvantages, although still applicable, may be outweighed by advantages which are not applicable to non-disabled children. For example, as Marchant & Page (1993) note, it is often the parents of disabled children with augmentative communication systems who are most familiar (and most at ease) with the child's communication system. If a parental presence is ill-advised (e.g. where the abuse is or, may be, familial) the same advantage may well apply to the presence of a key worker familiar to the child. Where abuse outside the family is suspected the reverse situation would, obviously, apply.

In addition to the presence of those who are not formally qualified to assist in communicating with the child it may also be necessary to involve an expert who is formally qualified. For example, it may be necessary to call in an interpreter (e.g. a sign language interpreter). In these instances, only a registered person should be contacted. It is also important to involve any interpreter in the pre-interview planning so that she or he is familiar with the process which is to take place. This is particularly important because it is rare to find a person who has a dual specialism both in child protection and interpreting. An additional part of the interpreter's preparation should be to meet with the child so that the interpreter has advance knowledge about the child's stage of language development (e.g. what signs the child is familiar with).

Finally, it will also be necessary to plan how the interview is going to proceed. For example, the issue of who is going to lead the interview will need to be considered. In some cases, it will be beneficial for the child protection specialist to lead. In others it might be necessary for someone whose specialism is in the child's language system to lead. If this person is unfamiliar with child protection procedures and the MOGP style of interview then she will require extensive briefing and time should be allowed for this to take place. Alternatively, if the interviewing police-officer or social worker is unfamiliar with the child's method of communication then time should be set aside for familiarization with this. Having emphasized (as others before us have done, e.g. Marchant & Page 1993, 1997) that pre-interview planning on a variety of issues is vital, we turn now to issues involved in the actual conduct of the interview.

## Conducting the interview

On the issue of duration of the interview, the MOGP (1992: 12) suggests that "as a rule of thumb, the team should plan the interview to last for less than an hour". The MOGP (1992: 12) then makes a statement which, in the case of many disabled children, contradicts the above suggestion. This potential contradiction is the recommendation that: "The basic rule is that the interview should go at the pace of the child and not of the adult". If the sound recommendation to proceed at the child's pace is to be fulfilled then the rule of thumb to complete the interview in less than an hour will often have to be broken in the case of disabled children (and also in non-disabled children). Marchant & Page (1993), for example, note that interviews using alternative communication systems are often very lengthy and the same authors (1997) report that, in their experience with disabled children, it is not unusual for rapport phases, alone, to take 30–40 minutes. Given the sometimes slow progression of interviews with some disabled children, a further recommendation of the MOGP may also need to be reconsidered. That is, the MOGP (1992: 12) states that: "It will be difficult to keep a proper record if the interview is spread over more than one day, and it is therefore strongly recommended that the interviews are conducted on one day if at all possible".

It is not only the slow progression of some interviews which may necessitate revision of this recommendation. It should also be considered that prolonged use of some alternative communication systems can be particularly tiring (some children will be used to using these systems for short periods rather than for prolonged question and answer sessions). Also, some disabled children may have associated health problems which mean that they can only be interviewed for short periods of time. These needs require accommodation and this might mean scheduling interviews to take place on more than one day or, certainly, allowing for more frequent breaks. We turn now to the specific phases of an MOGP interview.

As outlined earlier, the rapport phase of the interview has a variety of functions. We will address relevant features of each of these, in turn.

*Building an effective rapport*
The MOGP (1992: 16) notes that: "The rapport phase should be tailored to the needs and circumstances of the individual child. With younger children a rapport phase may involve some play with toys, drawing or colouring to help the child relax and/or interact with the interviewer". If the rapport phase is to be tailored to the needs and circumstances of the individual child as the MOGP suggests then a number of factors need to be considered. For example, suitable topics of conversation need to be identified. Various suitable topics for rapport building were suggested in Chapter 2.

One feature of rapport building that may require special attention in the case of disabled children is the use of toys and play. This is because, for some disabled children, some toys will be unsuitable. For example, those with visual impairments will benefit from toys which stimulate non-visual senses (e.g. touch). Additionally, in some cases (e.g. some types of cerebral palsy) there may be problems in terms of the ability to use the hands to manipulate toys. It is therefore important that there are suitable toys available which different children are able to manipulate succcessfully and that a situation whereby the child is confronted by a series of unsuitable toys is avoided. This is because such toys will be frustrating and may give the negative impression that the disabled child doesn't belong in the interview room.

*Supplementing developmental information*
As with non-disabled children, the rapport phase can be used to supplement information about the child's developmental stage. Therefore, many of the recommendations we made in Chapter 2 apply equally to interviews with disabled children. For example, the child's ability to provide a free narrative account of a neutral event is equally indicative of the ability to recount an abusive event for a disabled child as it is for a non-disabled child. See Chapter 2. Before moving on, however, it is

useful to note some additional information. In interviews with disabled children it may be particularly important to utilize the rapport phase to demonstrate the child's communicative competence. Such demonstration will help counter any assumption that a disabled witness is an incompetent witness. In particular, the rapport phase can be used to demonstrate the child's language skills. For example, it may be useful to show that a child with a communication board can communicate perfectly effectively. Marchant & Page (1993) report that often disabled children are keen to demonstrate their communication skills and that adult attention to, and interest in, how the child communicates can be flattering and therefore encouraging. Additionally, for example, where communication is taking place through an interpreter, the rapport phase can be an important "practice run" for all concerned.

*Explaining why the interview is taking place*
Explanations about the purpose of the interview may be of even greater importance for disabled children than for non-disabled children. This is because in some cases (for example if the child has a learning disability) he may not understand what the interview is and/or why it is taking place (Westcott & Cross 1996). It is therefore important that such matters are addressed at the outset. We suggest ways in which the function of the interview can be explained in Chapter 2.

*Reassurance that the child has done nothing wrong*
Again this is an issue which we addressed in Chapter 2 and the recommendations that we made there are equally applicable to disabled children. One point that must be emphasized though is that such reassurance may be of even greater importance with some disabled children. For example, Middleton (1992) and Westcott & Cross (1996) note that some children may believe that they have been abused because they are disabled and, by implication, they may be under the impression that the abuse is their own fault. Reassurance that this is not the case and that the child has done nothing wrong takes on an increased importance in these cases.

*The camera equipment*
A number of researchers (e.g. Cogher, Savage & Smith 1992) have noted that one of the difficulties associated with some disabilities is that they can lead to reduced life experience. For example, for many non-disabled children (and also some disabled children) video equipment (watching cartoon videos, etc.) is part of their everyday experience. As such, it can easily be explained and understood. However, for some disabled children (most obviously those with visual impairments) this will not be

the case. In these situations, careful attention will have to be paid to the explanation of the technical equipment.

*Explaining the need to tell the truth*
The establishment of the child's understanding of truth and lies is an issue to which we paid much attention in Chapter 2. Again, we refer the reader to the recommendations on this issue in that chapter. In addition, it should be noted that the truth/lies issue will not always be a straight-forward one to address with some disabled children (as we saw in Chapter 2, it is not always a straightforward issue with non-disabled children either). Marchant & Page (1993: 23), for example, report on their experience of an interview with a child with cerebral palsy and addi-tional learning difficulties. In this case, the interviewer was forewarned that the child "enjoyed joking with adults and would often give bizarre answers for humorous effect". Extra caution about the importance of truth telling is useful in such cases.

*Responding with, "I don't know" or "I don't understand"*
In Chapters 2 and 4 we outlined the importance of informing the child that it is OK to reply to interviewers' questions with "I don't know" or "I don't understand". The information we presented in those earlier chapters should be considered equally for disabled as for non-disabled children.

We turn now to the conduct of the free narrative phase. Having dedi-cated an entire chapter (Chapter 3) to issues relating to the free narrative phase we do not intend to repeat information already presented. In terms of the free narrative phase and disabled children there are, however, a few additional considerations to be taken into account.

First of all, there may be additional social constraints which make it more difficult for a disabled child to provide a free narrative account of an abusive event. For example, Westcott (1992b) and Westcott & Cross (1996) report cases where disabled children have been under increased pressure not to tell (e.g. through fear of institutional recriminations). Also, some disabled children are reported to be "protected" from issues of sexuality. This may lead to even greater difficulty in telling.

Furthermore, in some cases, disabled children are "protected" to such an extent that they do not have access to the language necessary to tell of sexually abusive experiences. For example:

> "Where children use artificial [communication] systems, their carers have absolute power over what vocabulary they may acquire and use. Thus

Cross was told of a 14-year-old boy who used Bliss symbols having the symbols for penis and vagina removed from this board by the physiotherapist who decided he did not need them yet" (Westcott and Cross 1996: 86).

Similar linguistic constraints are reported elsewhere, too. For example, Marchant & Page (1993: 7) note:

"The question of access to an appropriate vocabulary was most obvious for those children using communication boards . . . not one child had any words to describe their private body parts, even basic words like 'bottom'."

The same authors (1993: 19) report on one particular child who "did not have access to the necessary vocabulary to tell about abuse: the child did not have the words 'shut', 'smack' or 'hit' on her word board". Similar problems of restricted access to vocabulary may also arise for verbal communicators too. As Marchant & Page (1993: 19) note: "Even with those children able to speak, there were difficulties with vocabulary, especially when investigating possible sexual abuse".

It is not just in terms of access to the necessary vocabulary that some disabled children will experience difficulty in providing a free narrative account. For example, Marchant & Page (1997: 74) note that: "Impairments do not necessarily prevent a child from giving a spontaneous account, except possibly when a child is relying heavily on yes/no signalling, or using a restricted communication board". In these cases, linguistic constraints clearly preclude the provision of a free narrative account.

A further issue to consider in disabled children's provision of free narrative accounts is the potential facilitative effect of props. This is a point which the MOGP raises and one which we addressed, briefly, earlier in this chapter. See also Chapter 3 for a general discussion of the effectiveness of props in facilitating free narrative accounts. However, we would caution that there are certain additional factors to consider when using props with disabled children. That is, some props are not suitable for some disabled populations. For example, some props require good manual dexterity and thus some disabled children (e.g. those with certain types of cerebral palsy) might find it difficult to manipulate these because of poor hand control. As Marchant & Page (1993) note, it may also be difficult for some disabled children to identify with some dolls which are significantly different from themselves. Care must be taken then in ensuring that the use of props is appropriate with an individual disabled child.

We turn now to issues associated with the questioning phase. Chapter 4 is devoted to issues related to this phase and we therefore refer the reader to the discussion within that chapter. In addition, we emphasize the possible increased reliance on leading questions in interviews with disabled children (a point which the MOGP 1992 emphasizes). For example, Marchant & Page (1993: 26) report that, in their experience, some disabled children need to be asked some leading questions. The examples they provide involve children using augmentative communication systems which in day-to-day usage tend to rely on this type of question which needs just a *"yes"* or *"no"* answer. In order to increase the evidential validity of this question type, Marchant & Page (1993: 27) suggest that least likely alternatives are presented first. So, instead of asking, "Did that touch feel horrible?" they suggest that the child is first asked the least likely, "Did that touch feel nice?".

Finally, in terms of interviewing disabled children the closure phase has been identified as being particularly important. Marchant & Page (1993), for example, note that reassurance can be offered about any fears the child might have of repercussions if she has disclosed abuse.

Having considered various ways in which an MOGP interview could be used with disabled children, we turn now to issues of bilingualism and minority language use.

# SECTION 2: BILINGUAL CHILDREN AND MINORITY LANGUAGE SPEAKERS

In terms of linguistic surroundings, we are privileged to live and work in a bilingual community in North Wales. Within this community, Welsh and/or English speakers are well catered for by a police force which has speakers available to match the linguistic needs of the community it serves. In real terms, this means that a child (or adult) can be interviewed in either Welsh or English (often by a bilingual officer) as he chooses. However, our community is an unusual one within the UK in that the two languages (Welsh and English) coexist and the linguistic profile of the wider community is mirrored within the police force. Where a variety of minority languages are spoken (e.g. within some UK inner cities) these language communities are, at best, under-represented but, sometimes, not represented at all within the police and social services. This means that it is impossible for some children to be interviewed in their first language. For example, some children who speak English as a second language are interviewed in English by a monolingual English-speaking professional. The alternative being to interview through an interpreter.

Findings from our recent survey (Aldridge & Wood 1997a) reflect professionals' experiences of each of these situations. Our survey shows that 25% of interviewing officers in Wales have experience of interviewing a child with a different first language to themselves. It would be interesting to see how this figure compares with figures for police forces outside Wales. This is because our 25% figure may be untypically low in that many of the officers who responded to our survey are, themselves, bilingual. However, even within the 25% of officers who had interviewed a child with a different first language to themselves a number of different situations were reported.

Some of the (monolingual English-speaking) officers reported interviewing bilingual Welsh/English-speaking children. Hence we have comments such as the following from our survey:

- "I have interviewed a Welsh-speaking child in English but didn't encounter any problems." (Presumably, what this officer means is that she has interviewed a bilingual child whose first language is Welsh!)
- "The child's first language was Welsh. However, she had an excellent understanding of English and was happy to be interviewed using English."
- "The child's first language was Welsh but she spoke English fluently."

In these cases, the interviewers all emphasize that there were no problems encountered or that the child spoke fluent English. However, we would suggest that interviewing a bilingual child in his second language may not be an ideal situation. A point which we will return to later.

Interviewing officers in our survey also reported instances where they had interviewed children with languages other than Welsh and English. For example, the following situations were described:

- "I have interviewed a Somali youngster but with a good enough knowledge of English to conduct the interview through that medium."
- "I once interviewed an Asian child and involved a social worker in the interview who was conversant in the child's first language."
- "I have interviewed a French speaking child through an interpreter."

A clear concern arises in connection with the first of these reports. In this report, the interviewer states that the Somali youngster had a "good enough knowledge of English" for the interview to be conducted by a monolingual English-speaking interviewer. Whilst acknowledging the difficulties that arise in providing either a minority language interviewer or an interpreter, we would express concern about what constitutes a "good enough" knowledge of English. Given the often overwhelming linguistic demands that monolingual English-speaking children can face in interviews conducted by monolingual English-speaking interviewers (demands that we have devoted an entire book to outlining) we would be very concerned about the additional demands of being interviewed in a second language. Our concerns would be particularly acute in cases such as the one above where the assessment of "good enough" knowledge is clearly questionable. But, to a lesser extent our concerns also apply (as we noted above) to situations where a bilingual Welsh/English-speaking child is interviewed in English by a monolingual interviewer. This is because one of the linguistic characteristics of bilingual speakers is that they code-switch (i.e. interchange their languages) within conversations and this natural process would be restricted by the presence of a monolingual interviewer. This concern is supported by the following quote from one of the interviewing officers who responded to our survey: "I interviewed a child who disclosed part way through the interview that she would have preferred to have been interviewed in the Welsh language". Using bilingual interviewers for bilingual children wherever possible would reduce the risk of the above situation occurring and would allow bilingual children more flexible (and natural) use of their two languages.

We would also tentatively suggest that, for bilingual children, the language environment in which an abusive experience took place may also be significant. That is, it is often the case that bilingual people's languages are domain specific (e.g. they speak one language at home and another at school or, they speak one language with their father and a different language with their mother). If this is the case and a bilingual child was abused in an environment in which only one of his languages is spoken it might facilitate the child's recall of events if he was interviewed in that language. This would reflect research findings which suggest that reinstatement of context (e.g. mental reinstatement as in the cognitive interview protocol outlined in Chapter 3) can facilitate recall. Mirroring, in the interview, the language spoken at the time of the abusive event could, similarly, reinstate one aspect of the context. We do not have specific findings to support this possibility but it is certainly intuitively sound.

Of course, the language of the abusive event may not be the child's first language and this would mean that the facility for a bilingual interview could be helpful so that the child can rely most heavily on his first language but has the opportunity to use his second language as he recalls events. Imagine, for example, that the child is a bilingual speaker whose first language is English and second language Welsh. The child has been abused by her grandfather who speaks only Welsh. If the child is interviewed in English by a monolingual English speaker, this may increase the difficulty that the child faces in reporting events. Imagine, for example, that the interviewer asks the child what (if anything) her grandfather said to her – to answer the child would have to translate from Welsh (her grandfather's language) to English (the interviewer's language).

Finally, the third of the survey reports above (where a French-speaking child was interviewed by an interpreter) brings to our attention the issue of using interpreters to conduct interviews with children speaking languages outside the experience of the available interviewing professionals. Although all the interviewing officers who responded to our survey said that they would call in an appropriately qualified interpreter where necessary, there were also a number of concerns expressed about the use of interpreters. The greatest concern that interviewers expressed was that interpreters may not be MOGP trained. The following comment typifies this concern: "I would obtain the services of an interpreter but have reservations if this person is not MOGP trained".

Clearly, an ideal situation would be for any interpreter for any language to be MOGP trained. However, given the reality that this is an unusual combination of skills, a number of measures can be taken to try and alleviate potential problems. Clear pre-interview planning will be essential where the interpreter is not MOGP trained and sufficient time must be allowed for the interpreter to be briefed about relevant procedural matters and also about specific types of questions which will be asked. A further concern expressed by some interviewing officers was that the use of an interpreter threatens rapport building. A typical comment was: "It is my opinion that it is unlikely that an interview conducted through an interpreter or signer will succeed. There is no feeling of confidentiality or rapport. Without this confidence, many children will not communicate".

Clearly, it will be more difficult to establish an effective rapport (between all parties) when the interview is being conducted through an interpreter. However, if this potential problem is recognized prior to the interview then steps may be taken to minimize its effect. For example, it could be decided to allow extra time for neutral discussion where the interviewer and interpreter get to know the child. Joint play with toys may also be facilitative. It may also be useful for the interviewer to reveal something of her concerns to the child. For example, she might say that she wishes she spoke the child's language because she'd prefer to be able to talk to the child directly but that she's pleased that the interpreter is there to help both herself and the child.

In terms of confidentiality, reassurance may be offered. However, difficulties may remain. For example, cultural factors may be influential. If the child and interpreter have a shared culture (where sexual matters are taboo), the child may find it more difficult to reveal intimate details (for example, Westcott 1992b reports on a case where cultural constraints were reported as the reason for delayed disclosure). Again, reassurance needs to be offered and confidentiality assured.

In summary it is recommended that:

- Bilingual children should, where possible, be interviewed by bilingual interviewers.
- Assessments of children's skills in a second language should be carefully considered – what, for example, constitutes a "good enough" knowledge of a second language?
- Where interpreters are being used pre-interview planning should be extensive. This is especially true where the interpreter is not MOGP trained.

# CONTACT DETAILS

The following is a list of contact details for relevant organizations for disabled children.

**Disability and Child Protection Consultancy and Training**
5 Albion Works
Sigdon Road
Hackney
London E8 1AP
0171 249 1593

**Down's Syndrome Association**
155 Mitcham Road
London SW17 9PG
0181 682 4001

**NAPSAC** (National Association for the Protection from Sexual Abuse of Adults and Children with Learning Difficulties)
Department of Learning Disabilities
University of Nottingham Medical School
Queens Medical Centre
Nottingham NG7 2UH
0115 970 9987

**NDCS** (National Deaf Children's Society)
15 Dufferin Street
London EC1Y 8PD
0171 250 0123

**NSPCC** (National Society for the Prevention of Cruelty to Children)
42 Curtain Road
London EC2A 3NH
0171 825 2500

**RNIB** (Royal National Institute for the Blind)
224 Great Portland Street
London W1N 6AA
0171 388 1266

**RNID** (Royal National Institute for Deaf People)
19–23 Featherstone Street
London EC1Y 8SL
0171 296 8000

**SCOPE** (for people with Cerebral Palsy)
Freecall – Cerebral Palsy Helpline: 0800 626216

**VOICE UK** (A group which supports victims of abuse who have learning difficulties)
PO Box 238
Derby DE1 9JN
01332 519872

# BIBLIOGRAPHY

Aldridge, M. & Timmins, K. (1997). Children's understanding of preposition types (unpublished).

Aldridge, M., Timmins, K. & Wood, J. (1996). Children's understanding of wh-questions. (unpublished).

Aldridge, M., Timmins, K. & Wood, J. (1997). Children's understanding of legal terminology: Judges get money at pet shows, don't they? *Child Abuse Review, 6,* 141–146.

Aldridge, M. & Wood, J. (1996). Children's understanding and use of body part terminology: A guide for child witness interviewers. In J. Wood (Ed), *Research Papers in Linguistics, Volume 8* (pp. 1–14). Bangor: University of Wales.

Aldridge, M. & Wood, J. (1997a). A survey of police-officers' attitudes towards and knowledge of the guidelines set out in the Memorandum of Good Practice (unpublished).

Aldridge, M. & Wood, J. (1997b). Talking about feelings: Young children's ability to express emotions. *Child Abuse and Neglect, 21,* 1221–1233.

Aldridge, M. & Wood, J. (forthcoming). Children's free narrative accounts.

Anderson, E. (1978). Body part terminology. In J. Greenberg (Ed), *Universals of Human Language, Volume 3: Word Structure.* Stanford: Stanford University Press.

Applebee, A. (1978). *The Child's Concept of Story.* Chicago: Chicago University Press.

Baker-Ward, L., Gordon, B.N., Ornstein, P.A., Larus, D.M. & Clubb, P.A. (1993). Young children's long term retention of a pediatric examination. *Child Development, 64,* 1519–1533.

Bamberg, M. & Damrad-Frye, R. (1991). On the ability to provide evaluative comments: Further explorations of children's narrative competencies. *Journal of Child Language, 18,* 689–710.

Beeghly, M. & Cicchetti, D. (1994). Child maltreatment, attachment and the self system. Emergence of an internal state lexicon in toddlers at high social risk. *Development and Psychopathology, 6,* 5–30.

Berman, R.A. & Slobin, D.I. (1994). *Relating Events in Narrative: A Crosslinguistic Developmental Study.* Hillsdale, New Jersey: Lawrence Erlbaum Associates.

Bleile, K. & Schwartz, I. (1984). Three perspectives on the speech of children with Down's syndrome. *Journal of Communication Disorders, 17,* 87–94.

Boggs, S. & Eyberg, S. (1990). Interview techniques and establishing rapport. In A. La Greca (Ed), *Through the Eyes of the Child: Obtaining Self-reports from Children and Adolescents.* Boston: Allyn & Bacon.

Bond, H. (1995). Environmental care. *Community Care,* 7–13 September.

Bond, H. (1996). Audience participation. *Community Care,* 8–14 February.

Bond, H. (1997). Having someone to help. *Community Care*, 30 November–5 December.

Bremner, J. & Idowu, T. (1987). Constructing favourable conditions for measuring the young child's understanding of the terms in, on and under. *International Journal of Behavioural Development*, **10**, 89–98.

Brennan, M. (1994). The battle for credibility – themes in the cross examination of child victim witnesses. *International Journal for the Semiotics of Law*, **7**, 51–73.

Brownlow, J. & Waller, B. (1997). The Memorandum: A social services perspective. In H. Westcott & J. Jones (Eds), *Perspectives on the Memorandum Policy, Practice and Research in Investigative Interviews* (pp. 13–26). Aldershot, Hants: Arena.

Bull, R. (1992). Obtaining evidence expertly: The reliability of interviews with child witnesses. *Expert Evidence*, **1**, 5–12.

Bull, R. (1993). Innovative techniques for the questioning of child witnesses especially those who are young and those with learning disability. An invited paper for the Kent State University (DH10) Annual Kent Psychology Forum.

Bull, R. & Davies, G. (1996). The effect of child witness research on legislation in Great Britain. In G.S. Goodman & B.L. Bottoms (Eds), *International Perspectives on Child Abuse and Children's Testimony* (pp. 36–113). Sage, CA: Psychological Research, and Law.

Burns, Y. & Gunn, P. (Eds) (1993). *Down's Syndrome: Moving Through Life*. London: Chapman & Hall.

Bussey, K. (1992). Lying and truthfulness: Children's definitions, standards and evaluative reactions. *Child Development*, **63**, 129–137.

Butler, T. (1997). The Memorandum: The police view. In H. Westcott & J. Jones (Eds), *Perspectives on the Memorandum Policy, Practice and Research in Investigative Interviews* (pp. 27–38). Aldershot, Hants: Arena.

Cairns, H.S. & Hsu, J.R. (1978). Who, why, when and how: A developmental study. *Journal of Child Language*, **5**, 477–488.

Cassel, W.S. & Bjorklund, D.F. (1995). Developmental patterns of eyewitness memory and suggestibility: An ecologically based short term longitudinal study. *Law and Human Behaviour*, **19**, 507–532.

Ceci, S.J., Ross, D.F. & Toglia, M.P. (1987). Age differences in suggestibility: Narrowing the uncertainties. In S.J. Ceci, M.P. Toglia & D.F. Ross (Eds), *Children's Eyewitness Memory*. New York: Springer Verlag.

Child Abuse Review (1992). *Special Issue*, **1**, 145–210.

Choi, S. (1991). Children's answers to yes-no questions: A developmental study in English, French and Korean. *Developmental Psychology*, **27**, 407–420.

Cicchetti, D. & Beeghly, M. (Eds) (1990). *Children with Down Syndrome: A Developmental Perspective*. Cambridge, MA: Cambridge University Press.

Clark, E.V. (1993). *The Lexicon in Acquisition*. Cambridge, UK & New York: Cambridge University Press.

Clarke, C. (1994). The effect of police-officers' language when interviewing children. *Police Research Award Scheme*, London: Home Office.

Cogher, L., Savage, E. & Smith, M.F. (Eds) (1992). *Cerebral Palsy: The Child and Young Person*. London: Chapman & Hall Medical.

Cole, C.B. & Loftus, E.F. (1987). The memory of children. In S.J. Ceci, M.P. Toglia & D.F. Ross (Eds), *Children's Eyewitness Memory* (pp. 178–209). New York: Springer Verlag.

*Community Care* (1998). Thousands join justice campaign. *Community Care*, 29 January–4 February.

Coulborn-Faller, K. & Corwin, D.L. (1995). Children's interview statements and behaviours: Role in identifying sexually abused children. *Child Abuse and Neglect*, **19**, 71–82.

Davies, G. (1991). Children on trial? Psychology, videotechnology and the law. *Howard Journal of Criminal Justice*, **30**, 177–191.

Davies, G.M. & Noon, E. (1991). *An Evaluation of the Live Link for Child Witnesses*. London: Home Office.

Davies, G., Tarrant, A. & Flin, R. (1989). Close encounters of the witness kind: Children's memory for a simulated health inspection. *British Journal of Psychology*, **80**, 415–429.

Davies, G. & Wilson, C. (1997). Implementation of the Memorandum: An overview. In H.L. Westcott & J. Jones (Eds), *Perspectives on the Memorandum Policy, Practice and Research in Investigative Interviews* (pp. 1–12). Aldershot, Hants: Arena.

Davies, G., Wilson, C., Mitchell, R. & Milsom, J. (1995). *An Evaluation of the New Provision for Child Witnesses*. London: Home Office.

Dennet, J. & Bekerian, D. (1991). Interviewing abused children: A training initiative involving Cambridgeshire constabulary with other agencies. *Policing*, **7**, 355–360.

Dent, H. & Flin, R. (1992). *Children as Witnesses*. Chichester: Wiley.

Dent, H.R. & Stephenson, G.M. (1979). An experimental study of the effectiveness of different techniques of questioning child witnesses. *British Journal of Social and Clinical Psychology*, **18**, 41–51.

Department of Health (1994). *Social Services Inspectorate. The Child, the Court and the Video*. Heywood, Lancs: Health Publications Unit.

Disability Information Trust (1995). *Communication and Access to Computer Technology*. Oxford: Disability Information Trust.

Dunn, J. & Brown, J. (1994). Affect expression in the family, children's understanding of emotions and their interactions with others. *Merrill Palmer Quarterly*, **40**, 120–133.

Durkin, K. (1981). Aspects of late acquisition: School children's use and comprehension of prepositions. *First Language*, **2**, 47–59.

Ervin-Tripp, S. (1970). Discourse agreement: How children answer questions. In J. Hayes (Ed), *Cognition and the Development of Language* (pp. 79–109). New York: Wiley.

Evans, M.A. (1987). Discourse characteristics of reticent children. *Applied Psycholinguistics*, **8**, 171–184.

Fielding, N.G. & Conroy, S. (1992). Interviewing child victims: Police and social worker investigations of child sexual abuse. *Sociology*, **26**, 103–124.

Fisher, R. (1997). State of indifference. *Community Care*, 4–10 December.

Fivush, R. (1994). Young children's event recall: Are memories constructed through discourse? *Consciousness and Cognition*, **13**, 356–373.

Fivush, R. & Hamond, N.R. (1991). Memories of Mickey Mouse: Young children recount their trip to Disneyworld. *Cognitive Development*, **6**, 433–448.

Fivush, R., Gray, J.T. & Fromhoff, F.A. (1987). Two-year-olds talk about the past. *Cognitive Development*, **2**, 393–410.

Flavell, J.H., Speer, J.R., Green, F.L. & August, D.L. (1981). The development of comprehension monitoring and knowledge about communication. *Monographs of the Society for Research in Child Development*, **46**, 1–65.

Flin, R.H., Boon, J., Knox, A. & Bull, R. (1992). The effect of a five month delay on children's and adult's eye witness memory. *British Journal of Psychology*, **83**, 323–336.

Flin, R.H., Stephenson, Y. & Davies, G. (1989). Children's knowledge of court proceedings. *British Journal of Psychology*, **80**, 285–297.

Foster, S.H. (1990). *The Communicative Competence of Young Children*. London: Longman.

Fowler, A.E., Gelman, R. & Gleitman, L.R. (1994). The course of language learning in children with Down syndrome. In H. Tager-Flusberg (Ed), *Constraints on Language Acquisition: Studies of Atypical Children* (pp. 91–140). Hillsdale, NJ: Lawrence Erlbaum Associates.

Geiselman, R.E., Fisher, R.P., Firstenberg, I., Hutton, L.A., Sullivan, S.J., Avetission, I.V. & Prosk, A.L. (1984). Enhancement of eyewitness memory: An empirical evaluation of the cognitive interview. *Journal of Police Science and Administration*, **12**, 74–80.

Geiselman, R.E. & Padilla, J. (1988). Cognitive interviewing with child witnesses. *Journal of Police Science and Administration*, **16**, 236–242.

Goodman, G.S. & Aman, C. (1990). Children's use of anatomically detailed dolls to recount an event. *Child Development*, **61**, 1859–1871.

Goodman, G.S., Bottoms, B.L., Schwartz-Kenney, B.M. & Rudy, L. (1991). Children's testimony about a stressful event: Improving children's reports. *Journal of Narrative and Life History*, **1**, 69–99.

Goodman, G.S. & Bottoms, B.L. (Eds) (1993). *Child Victims: Child Witnesses: Understanding and Improving Testimony*. New York: Guilford Press.

Goodman, G.S. & Bottoms, B.L. (1996). *International Perspectives on Child Abuse and Children's Testimony: Psychological Research and Law*. Thousand Oaks, CA: Sage.

Goodman, G.S. & Helgeson, V. (1988). Children as witnesses: What do they remember? In L. Walker (Ed), *Handbook on Sexual Abuse of Children*. New York: Springer Verlag.

Gullo, D.F. (1981). Social class differences in preschool children's comprehension of wh-questions. *Journal of Child Development*, **52**, 736–740.

Gupta, A. (1997). Black children and the Memorandum. In H. Westcott & J. Jones (Eds), *Perspectives on the Memorandum Policy, Practice and Research in Investigative Interviews*. Aldershot, Hants: Arena.

Hamond, N.R. & Fivush, R. (1991). Memories of Mickey Mouse: Young children recount their trip to Disneyworld. *Cognitive Development*, **6**, 433–448.

Harter, S. & Whitesell, N.R. (1989). Developmental changes in children's understanding of single, multiple and blended emotion concepts. In C. Saarni & P.L. Harris (Eds), *Children's Understanding of Emotion* (pp. 81–117). Cambridge, UK: Cambridge University Press.

Hendry, E. & Jones, J. (1997). Dilemmas and opportunities in training around the Memorandum. In H. Westcott & J. Jones (Eds), *Perspectives on the Memorandum Policy, Practice and Research in Investigative Interviews* (pp. 141–153). Aldershot, Hants: Arena.

Holton, J. & Bonnerjea, L. (1994). *The Child, the Court and the Video: A Study of the Implementation of the Memorandum of Good Practice on Video Interviewing of Child Witnesses*. London: Department of Health.

Home Office (1989). *Report of the Advisory Group on Video Evidence, Chairman Judge Thomas Pigot QC*. London: Home Office.

Home Office and The Department of Health (1992). *Memorandum of Good Practice on Video-recorded Interviews with Child Witnesses for Criminal Proceedings*. London: HMSO.

Horgan, D. (1978). How to answer questions when you've got nothing to say. *Journal of Child Language*, **5**, 159–165.

Hughes, M. & Grieve, R. (1980). On asking children bizarre questions. *First Language*, **1**, 149–160.

Hughes, B., Parker, H. & Gallagher, B. (1996). *Policing Child Sexual Abuse: The View from Police Practitioners*. London: Home Office.

Kennedy, M. (1992). Not the only way to communicate: A challenge to voice in child protection work. *Child Abuse Review*, **1**, 169–177.

Kennedy, M. & Kelly, L. (1992). Inclusion not exclusion. *Child Abuse Review*, **1**, 147–149.

King, P. & Young, I. (1992). *The Child as Client: A Handbook for Solicitors who Represent Children*. Bristol: Jordan & Sons.

King, M.A. & Yuille, J.C. (1987). Suggestibility and the child witness. In S. Ceci, M.P. Togia & D.F. Ross (Eds), *Children's Eyewitness Memory* (pp. 24–35). New York: Springer Verlag.

Kyle, J.G. & Woll, B. (1984). *Sign Language: The Study of Deaf People and their Language*. Cambridge, UK: Cambridge University Press.

Lamb, M.E., Strenberg, K. & Esplin, P. (1996). Making children into competent witnesses: Reactions to the amicus brief in re: Michaels. *Psychology, Public Policy and Law*, **1**, 438–449.

Leichtman, M. & Ceci, S.J. (1995). Effects of stereotypes and suggestions on preschoolers' reports. *Developmental Psychology*, **31**, 568–578.

Liles, B.Z. (1987). Episode organisation and cohesive conjunctives in narratives in children with and without language disorder. *Journal of Speech and Hearing Research*, **30**, 185–196.

MacWhinney, K., Cermak, S. & Fisher, A. (1987). Body part identification in one to four-year-old children. *American Journal of Occupational Therapy*, **41**, 454–459.

Marcell, M.M. & Weeks, S.L. (1988). Short-term memory difficulties and Down's syndrome. *Journal of Mental Deficiency Research*, **32**, 153–162.

Marchant, R. & Page, M. (1993). *Bridging the Gap: Child Protection Work with Children with Multiple Disabilities*. London: NSPCC.

Marchant, R. & Page, M. (1997). The Memorandum and disabled children. In H. Westcott & J. Jones (Eds), *Perspectives on the Memorandum Policy, Practice and Research in Investigative Interviews* (pp. 67–80). Aldershot, Hants: Arena.

McGough, L.S. & Warren, A.R. (1994). The all-important investigative interview. *Juvenile and Family Court Journal*, **45**, 13–29.

McGowan, B. (1996). Little dollies that may trap cornfield hammer killer. *The Express* Newspaper, 4 November.

Middleton, L. (1992). *Children First: Working with Children and Disability*. Birmingham: Venture Press.

Murray, N. (1993). Children on film. *Community Care*, 17 June.

NSPCC and Tower Hamlets ACPC (1996). *Protecting our Children*. London: NSPCC and London Borough of Tower Hamlets.

Open University, Department of Health and Social Welfare (1993). Investigative interviewing with children: Trainers' pack KS01, Dorset: Blackmore.

Ornstein, P.A., Gordon, B.N. & Larus, D.M. (1992). Children's memory for a personally experienced event: Implications for testimony. *Applied Developmental Psychology*, **6**, 49–60.

Ornstein, P.A., Larus, D.M. & Clubb, P.A. (1991). Understanding children's testimony: Implications of research on the development of memory. *Annals of Child Development*, **8**, 145–176.

Parnell. M.M. & Amerman, J.D. (1983). Answers to wh-questions: Research and application. In T. Gallaghar & C. Prutting (Eds), *Pragmatic Assessment and Intervention Issues in Language* (pp. 129–151). San Diego: College Hill Press.

Parnell, M.M., Patterson, S.S. & Harding, M.A. (1984). Answers to wh-questions: A developmental study. *Journal of Speech and Hearing Research*, **27**, 297–305.

Perry, N.W. & Teply, L.L. (1984). Interviewing, counselling and in court examination of children: Practical approaches for attorneys. *Creighton Law Review*, **18**, 5. Creighton University School of Law.

Phillips, M. (1993). Investigative interviewing: Issues of race and culture. In Open University Investigative interviewing with children: Trainers' pack. Open University, Milton Keynes.

Pipe, M.E. & Wilson, J.C. (1994). Cues and secrets: Influences on children's event reports. *Developmental Psychology*, **30**, 515–525.

Poole, D. (1992). Eliciting information from children with non-suggestive visual and auditory feedback. Paper presented at the Advanced Studies Institute on the Child Witness in Context, Italy.

Poole, D. & White, L. (1991). Effects of question repetition on the eyewitness testimony of children and adults. *Developmental Psychology*, **27**, 975–986.

Powell, M.B. & Thomson, D.M. (1994). Children's eyewitness memory research: Implications for practice. *Families in Society: The Journal of Contemporary Human Services*, **75**, 204–216.

Preece, A. (1987). The range of narrative forms conversationally produced by young children. *Journal of Child Language*, **14**, 353–373.

Rappley, M. & Speare, K.H. (1993). Initial evaluation and interview techniques for child sexual abuse. *Primary Care*, **20**, 329–342.

Renvoize, J. (1993). *Innocence Destroyed: A Study of Child Sexual Abuse*. London: Routledge.

Richardson, G.C. (1993). The child witness: A linguistic analysis of child sexual abuse testimony. Unpublished doctoral dissertation.

Rose, D.E., Vernon, M. & Pool, A.F. (1996). Cochlear implants in prelingually deaf children. *American Annals of the Deaf*, **141**, 258–262.

Saarni, C. & Harris, P.L. (Eds) (1989). *Children's Understanding of Emotion*. Cambridge, UK: Cambridge University Press.

Sattar, G. & Bull, R. (1994). The effects of the feltboard and auditory feedback on young children's recall of a live event. Paper presented at the Annual Conference of the British Psychological Society's Division of Criminological and Legal Psychology, Rugby.

Savic, S. (1978). Strategies children use to answer questions posed by adults. In N. Waterson & C. Snow (Eds), *The Development of Communication* (pp. 217–225). New York: Wiley.

Saywitz, K.J., Geiselman, R.E. & Bornstien, G.K. (1992). Effects of cognitive interviewing and practice on children's recall performance. *Journal of Applied Psychology*, **77**, 744–756.

Saywitz, K. & Jaenicke, C. (1987). Children's understanding of legal terms: A preliminary report of grade-related trends. Paper presented at the Biennial meeting of the Society for Research on Child Development, Baltimore, MD.

Saywitz, K.J., Nathanson, R. & Snyder, L. (1993). Credibility of child witnesses: The role of communicative competence. *Topics in Language Disorders*, **13**, 59–78.

Sharland, E., Jones, D., Algate, J., Seal, H. & Croucher, M. (1995). Professional intervention in child sexual abuse. In Department of Health, *Child Protection: Messages from Research*. London: HMSO.

Shuy, R.W. (1986). Language and the law. *Annual Review of Applied Linguistics*, **7**, 50–63.

Shuy, R.W. (1993). *Language Crimes: The Use and Abuse of Language Evidence in the Courtroom*. Oxford: Blackwell.

Siegal, M., Waters, L. & Dinwiddy, L. (1988). Misleading children: Causal attributions for inconsistency under repeated questioning. *Journal of Experimental Child Psychology*, **45**, 438–456.

Social Services Inspectorate (1994). *The Child, the Court and the Video*. London: HMSO.

Spencer, J.R. (1992). The complexities of the legal process for children with disabilities. *Child Abuse Review*, **1**, 200–203.

Spencer, J.R. & Flin, R.H. (1990). *The Evidence of Children: The Law and the Psychology*. London: Blackstone.

Spencer, J.H. & Flin, R.H. (1993). *The Evidence of Children*. London: Blackstone.

Steller, M. & Boychuck, R. (1992). Children as witnesses in sexual abuse cases. In H. Dent & R. Flin (Eds), *Children as Witnesses*. Chichester: Wiley.

Tissier, G. (1995). A clouded lens. *Community Care*, February.

Toglia, M.P., Hembrooke, H., Ceci, S.J. & Ross, D.F. (1994). Children's resistance to misleading post-event information, when does it occur? *Current Psychology*, **13**, 21–26.

Toglia, M., Ross, D. & Ceci, S. (1992). The suggestibility of children's memory. In M. Howe, C. Brainerd & V. Reyna (Eds), *The Development of Long-term Retention*. New York: Springer Verlag.

Tomasello, M. (1987). Learning to use prepositions: A case study. *Journal of Child Language*, **14**, 79–98.

Turk, V. & Brown, H. (1992). Sexual abuse and adults with learning disabilities: Preliminary communication of survey results. *Mental Handicap*, **20**, 55–58.

Tyack, D. & Ingram, D. (1977). Children's production and comprehension of questions. *Journal of Child Language*, **4**, 211–224.

Vizard, E. (1987). Child sexual abuse. *Lancet*, **2**, 8572: 1397–1398.

Wade, A. & Westcott, H. (1997). No easy answers: Children's perspectives on investigative interviews. In H. Westcott & J. Jones (Eds), *Perspectives on the Memorandum Policy, Practice and Research in Investigative Interviews* (pp. 51–65). Aldershot, Hants: Arena.

Walker, A.G. (1993). Questioning young children in court: A linguistic case study. *Law and Human Behaviour*, **17**, 59–81.

Walker, A.G. (1994). *Handbook on Questioning Children: A Linguistic Perspective*. Washington: ABA Center on Children and the Law.

Walker, A.G. & Warren, A.R. (1995). The language of the child abuse interview. Asking the questions, understanding the answers. In T. Ney (Ed), *True and False Allegations of Child Sex Abuse: Assessment and Case Management* (pp. 153–162). New York: Bruner-Mazel.

Warren, A., Hulse-Trotter, K. & Tubbs, E. (1991). Inducing resistance to suggestibility in children. *Law and Human Behaviour*, **15**, 273–285.

Warren-Leubecker, A., Tate, C., Hinton, I. & Ozbek, N. (1988). What do children know about the legal system and when do they know it? In S. Ceci, D. Ross & M. Toglia (Eds), *Perspectives on Children's Testimony* (pp. 131–157). New York: Springer Verlag.

Waterson, N. & Snow, C. (Eds) (1978). *The Development of Communication*. New York: Wiley.

West, R. (1997). A fair hearing. *Community Care*, **14–20 August**, 23.

Westcott, H.L. (1991). The abuse of disabled children: A review of the literature. *Child Care, Health and Development*, **17**, 243–358.

Westcott, H.L. (1992a). Memorandum of Good Practice (Commentary on Davies, Protecting the child witness in the courtroom). *Child Abuse Review*, **1**, 77–79.

Westcott, H.L. (1992b). The disabled child witness. Paper presented at the Nato Advanced Studies Institute on the Child Witness in Context, Italy.

Westcott, H.L. (1993). *Abuse of Children and Adults with Disabilities*. London: NSPCC.

Westcott, H.L. & Cross, M. (1996). *This Far and No Further: Towards Ending the Abuse of Disabled Children*. Birmingham: Venture Press.

Westcott, H.L. & Davies, G. (1996). Sexually abused children's and young people's perspectives on investigative interviews. *British Journal of Social Work*, **26**, 451–474.

Westcott, H.L. & Jones, J. (1997). *Perspectives on the Memorandum Policy, Practice and Research in Investigative Interviews*. Aldershot, Hants: Arena.

White, S. (1990). The investigatory interview with suspected victims of child sexual abuse. In A. La Greca (Ed), *Through the Eyes of the Child: Obtaining Self-reports from Children and Adolescents*. Boston: Allyn & Bacon.

*Working Together* (1988). London: HMSO.

# INDEX

Note: Page references in **bold** refer to tables

ABCD training and resource pack 198
anatomically correct dolls 101
anger, understanding of 174
arithmetical ability, assessment of 46–52
ataxia 200
attached adult presence 28–32
augmentative communication systems 191, 202–3

bilingual children 212–16
Bishop Auckland ritual abuse case 11
Blissymbolics 203
body part terminology 87, 157–63
sexual 163–72, **164**
Bowis, John 11
Bracewell, Mrs Justice 10
British Sign Language (BSL) 201
Bulger, James 1
Butler, Tony 12
Butler-Sloss, Lord Justice 4

camera equipment
disabled children and 209–10
explanation of 55–8
centring 84
cerebral palsy 191, 195
linguistic skills 198, 199–200
chaining 84
choice questions 135
Cleveland Inquiry (1987) 3, 4, 11
closed questions 115, 124–5, 136–8
closure phase 5
cochlear implant 202
coercion, understanding of 175
Cognitive Interview protocol 90, 101

colour naming, assessment of 46–52
communication board, use of 195
*Community Care* 11
competency test 3
confidentiality 216
conjunctions 84–5
contradiction 112–14
corroboration requirement 3
Criminal Justice Act
(1988) 4, 6
(1991) 4, 7
cultural influences on language development 188, 216

descriptive information 85–6
detached adult presence 32
development, assessing 46–52
in disabled children 208–9
diplegia 200
disabled children 189–212
interviewing 203–12
conducting 195–6, 207–12
planning 203–7
special facilities 204–5
linguistic skills 198–203
MOGP and 194–8
professionals' experience of interviewing 192–4
vulnerability to abuse and access to justice 189–92
disclosure, fear of 73–6
dolls 100, 120
anatomically correct 101
"don't know", children's use of 125–6, 139, 210
double negatives 115
Down's syndrome 191, 205
linguistic skills 198, 200–1

embarrassment  74, 75, 76, 161,
    163
emotion descriptive vocabulary
    172–6
"empty sandwich" accounts  78
evaluative information  85–6

"fair hearing campaign"  190–1
fear  175
felt boards  102
follow-up questions  83
forensic value of interview  142–3
free narrative phase  4, 5, 70–106
    children's reticence  73–6
    children's unfamiliarity with free
        narrative exchanges  73
    disabled children and  210–12
    dos and don'ts  103–5
    helping to support children's
        narratives  94–103
    cognitive interview with practice
        session  101
    directing towards salient types of
        information  96–101
    felt boards  102
    framework  95–101
    narrative elaboration  102
    playing back the child's initial
        account  102–3
    presenting information in a logical
        order  96
    how to proceed  71–2
    importance  71
    language skills  81–8
    memory skills  81
    over-hasty entry into a specific
        questioning phase  88–90
    providing opportunities for free
        narrative  90–4
    quality of accounts  78–81
    quantity of accounts  76–8

Guardian, The  10–11, 11–12

hearing impairment
    in Down's syndrome  200
    linguistic skills  201–2

inappropriate questioning  108–9
inappropriate responses  111–14
inattention  59

incoherence  79
Independent on Sunday  11
induction loop facilities  195, 206
information
    evaluating  85–6
    linking  84–5
    specific  86–8
    type of  82–3
informational units  82
interpreters, use of  191, 197,
    206–7

language and development, child
    146–86
    body part and sexual terminology
        157–63
    dos and don'ts  184–6
    emotion descriptive vocabulary
        172–6
    evaluation of information on
        19–21
    legal terms  149–57
    police-officer and social worker
        149–55
    prepositions  181–3
    pronouns  176–81
    questioning phase and  122–7
    same word with different
        meanings  147–8
    sexual body parts, terms for
        163–72, 164
        condoms  171–2
        ejaculation  169–70
        erection  170–1
        penetration  167–8
        stimulation/masturbation
            168–9
    using a word the child doesn't know
        or understand  146–7
    vocabulary  148–9
    see also language skills
language game  77–8, 83, 166
language problems  16–19
    academics' reflections on adult
        interviewers  18
    child witness' reflections on adult
        interviewers  18–19
    professionals' attitudes to child
        witnesses  16–17
    professionals' reflections on their
        own performance  17–18

language skills 81–8
  in disabled children 198–203
  evaluating 85–6
  linking 84–5
  specific information 86–8
  type of information 82–3
leading questions 116, 125, 138–9
learning disabilities, children with,
  linguistic skills of 198, 199
legal terms, understanding of
  149–57
Levy, Allan 12
lighting 206
lip reading 201, 206
location of the interview 26–8, 83,
  204

Makaton sign language system 200,
  201, 203
Mayer-Johnson Communication
  system 203
media coverage of child witnesses
  cases 10–12
Memorandum of Good Practice (MOGP)
  2, 4
  advantages of 6–9
  aims 5–9
  disabled children and 194–8
  disadvantages to video
    interviewing 15–16
  media coverage of child witnesses
    cases 10–12
  operational problems 14–16
  problems 9–14
  professionals' opinions 12–14
  statistics 9–10
  summary 5–6
memory skills 81
  in Down's syndrome 201
minority language speakers 212–16
mirroring 214
multiple sclerosis 191, 195

non-responsive children 109–11
non-verbal communication 191, 195

open questions 108, 114–15, 122
Orkney child abuse cases 3, 11

Paget Gorman sign language system
  200, 201

perseveration 123
personalized comments, interviewer
  41
phased interview 5
Pictures Please! 203
police-officer, understanding of role
  of 149–54
pre-interview screening 14
prepositions 82, 181–3
pronouns 176–81
props, use of 100–1, 195–7
  disabled children and 196, 211

quadriplegia 200
quality of accounts 78–81
quantity of accounts 76–8
questioning phase 4–5
  advice for professionals 126–7
  children's understanding of
    questions 118–22
  difficulties with 107–14
  disabled children and 212
  guidelines 144
  purpose of questioning phase
    114–17
  repeating questions 140–2
  specific questions 123–7
  specific yet non-leading questions
    115
  transcript data 127–39
  types of question 116–17
  use of published advice 139–44

racial influences on language
  development 188
rapport phase 4, 5, 25–69, **53–4**
  assessing development 46–52
  building effective rapport 36–46
  with disabled children 208
  discussion topics 36–43
    friends 38
    holidays and Christmas 40–1
    pets 40
    school 36–8
    television, videos and films
      39–40
    toys and hobbies 38–9
    with younger children 42–3
  dos and don'ts **66–9**
  emphasis of need to speak the truth
    58–64, 210

rapport phase (*cont.*)
  explanation of camera equipment
    55–8, 209–10
  explanation of reason for interview
    52–3
  fact vs fantasy  64–6
  minimalizing  41–2
  reassurance that child has done
    nothing wrong  54–5, 209
  use of toys  43–6
reason for interview, explaining  52–3,
  209
reassurance that child has done
  nothing wrong  54–5, 209
Rebus symbols  203
religious influences on language
  development  188
research
  children's understanding of
    questions  118–22
reticence, children's  73–6
Rochdale child abuse cases  3, 11
Russell, Josie  1, 196

second chance free narrative
  opportunity  91–4
sensory impairment, children with,
  linguistic skills  198, 201–2
sex, different attitudes to  188
sex education, different attitudes to
  188
shyness  74, 76

signer  197
sign language  200, 206
sign supported English (SSE)  201
social worker, understanding of role
  of  154–5
spastic hemiplegia  200
speech impairments  205
starting interview  32–5
stereotypical answers  134

tag-questions  121, 124, 135–6
time, comprehension of  51, 143
timing the interview  26, 204
training, need for  22–3, 108, 114
toys, use of  43–6, 101, 120
truth telling, need for  58–64, 210
twins, language development in  188

visually impaired children, linguistic
  ability of  202
vocabulary  148–9

Waller, Brian  11
wh-questions  118–19, 124, 130–2
  strategies used when answering
    120–1
wheelchair access  195, 204
*Working Together*  4
Working Together Act (1987)  5

yes/no questions  118, 123, 128–30

*Related titles of interest from Wiley...*

## From Hearing to Healing
Working with the Aftermath of Child Sexual Abuse, 2nd Edition
Anne Bannister
Published in association with the NSPCC
0-471-98298-9    216pp    1998    Paperback

## Making Sense of the Children Act
Third Edition
Nicholas Allen
0-471-97831-0    304pp    1998    Paperback

## Women Who Sexually Abuse Children
From Research to Clinical Practice
Jacqui Saradjian in association with Helga Hanks
Wiley Series in Child Care & Protection
0-471-96072-1    336pp    1996    Paperback

## The Emotionally Abused and Neglected Child
Identification, Assessment and Intervention
Dorota Iwaniec
Wiley Series in Child Care & Protection
0-471-95579-5    222pp    1995    Paperback

## Cycles of Child Maltreatment
Facts, Fallacies and Interventions
Ann Buchanan
Wiley Series in Child Care & Protection
0-471-95889-1    328pp    1996    Paperback

 ## Child Abuse Review
ISSN: 0952-9136

 ## Children & Society
Published in association with the National Children's Bureau
ISSN: 0951-0605